THE STAR WARS POSTER BOOK

BY
STEPHEN J. SANSWEET
AND
PETER VILMUR

CHRONICLE BOOKS
SAN FRANCISCO

Copyright © 2005 and trademark™ by Lucasfilm Ltd.
All rights reserved. Used under authorization.
No part of this book may be reproduced in any form
without written permission from the publisher.
Page 320 constitutes a continuation of the copyright page.

Library of Congress Cataloging-in-Publication Data :
Sansweet, Stephen J., 1945–
   The Star Wars poster book / by Stephen J. Sansweet and Peter Vilmur.
   p. cm.
   ISBN 0-8118-4883-3
   1. Star Wars films. 2. Film posters—Catalogs. I. Vilmur, Peter. II. Title.
   PN1995.9.S695S243 2005
   791.43'75—dc22
                                2004028139

Manufactured in Hong Kong
Designed by Benjamin Shaykin

Distributed in Canada by Raincoast Books
9050 Shaughnessy Street
Vancouver, British Columbia V6P 6E5

10 9 8 7 6 5 4 3 2 1

Chronicle Books LLC
85 Second Street
San Francisco, California 94105
www.chroniclebooks.com

NOTE: *All poster dimensions are given in inches.*

CONTENTS

Introduction / 6

Star Wars / 9

The Empire Strikes Back / 71

Return of the Jedi / 121

The Interregnum / 165

The Prequels / 219

Appendix / 289

    BOOTLEGS AND REPRINTS / 289

    STAR WARS POSTER LIST / 289

    THEATRICAL POSTERS / 290

    EVENTS POSTERS / 300

    ADVERTISING & PROMOTIONAL POSTERS / 302

    COMMERCIAL POSTERS / 311

Index / 317

Acknowledgments / 320

Credits / 320

INTRODUCTION

It was just meant to be.

I still clearly remember the day that I bought my first *Star Wars* poster. It was about a month after the movie had opened and knocked the socks off critics, science fiction and fantasy fans, and just about all of America—myself included. I was instantly hooked for life! I had decided to alter my usual Saturday rounds of browsing the standard comic book shops and nearby toy stores by venturing into Los Angeles' San Fernando Valley to visit a comic book/collectibles shop where I had found a few interesting things once before. It was the kind of neighborhood place—hidden away up a narrow stairway above a clothing store—that you needed to know about in order to find it.

I found a couple of magazines—nothing too exciting—and was just working my way to the cash register when a man entered. In my mind's eye he was wearing a London Fog raincoat and a snappy fedora with the brim down, covering his face. He was talking to the guy behind the counter, and as I got closer I heard the words "*Star Wars*." I looked down, and there on the counter was a strange poster I had never seen before. But, boy, was it hot: Luke Skywalker looked mean enough to take on the entire Empire, Han looked super cool, and Leia—well, she had her eyes closed for some reason. There was a mean-looking Darth Vader, and the Death Star was erupting into a yellow-orange nova.

The man had a roll of them, and they were for sale.

I'm usually shy about these kinds of things, but *Star Wars* emboldens me. "I wonder if you could tell me what these are," I asked.

"The people who made *Star Wars* printed these last year and had a bunch left over," said the fedora. "It's done by the guy who does the art for the *Star Wars* comics, Howie Chaykin."

It looked a little odd to me, bearing the inscription "*Star Wars* Corp." and "Poster 1," but I asked the guy behind the counter if he minded if I bought one directly. He didn't, so I forked over a ten-dollar bill and went happily on my way. It wasn't until years later that I discovered that this was the *first* poster for *Star Wars* ever printed and that a thousand were made to sell for $1.75 each at two summer fan conventions the year before the movie opened. These days, the going collectible price is $400 and skyward.

Today, some two thousand posters later, I'm still collecting. What is it about a movie poster that makes kids want to tape them to their walls, young adults tack them up in dorm rooms, and grown men and women hunt down their favorite titles or actors even if they don't have the room to display all the posters they own? When a poster works, when it is the perfect confluence of art and marketing, the result is a unique image that becomes shorthand for a film. In the case of *Star Wars*, the theatrical posters—often called "key art"—hit their mark. They distill the essence of the films and entice millions of people worldwide to see the movies. Then people can bring posters home and relive the emotional high that the movies gave them.

My favorite *Star Wars* poster is . . . well, it's impossible to say. There's the one that looks like a wild-posting on a fence, with Luke and Leia swinging on a rope; there's the one that has the Happy Birthday cake and all the little action figures; there's the one that has young Anakin Skywalker casting Darth Vader's shadow; there are the surreal Polish and Russian posters, some of which are just being discovered by the collecting community. And besides theatrical posters, there have been hundreds of promotional, event, and commercial posters over a nearly thirty-year span since the creation of "Poster 1" in 1976. It is an extraordinary output and collection.

Of course, nothing about *Star Wars* has been small or ordinary. From the start in 1977, the six-film saga has swept up tens of millions of fans across the globe, minting indelible pop culture icons like Darth Vader and popularizing catch phrases such as "I've got a bad feeling about this."

While thousands of stories and books have been written about the films, less has been written about the marketing behind the *Star Wars* phenomenon. The success of the films didn't just happen; people had to be drawn to them. And from the time the movie industry began more than a hundred years ago, the tried-and-true way to attract people to the theater has been advertising, particularly the theatrical posters that are usually the basis for newspaper or magazine ad campaigns.

The first *Star Wars* movie, now known as Episode IV: *A New Hope,* came out near the end of the Silver Age of movie posters. The Golden Era started with some of the amazing artistry on posters for silent films and thrived through the beginning of World War II, with incredible U.S. and international key art for even many lesser-known titles. Great illustration continued for several decades after the war, but photography and then computer graphics eventually took over. The Hollywood studios moved away from painted images to more photo-realistic posters, partly out of cost considerations and partly because photos and graphics looked more "current."

Artist and designer Tom Jung, the only illustrator to have painted posters for all three of the original *Star Wars* films, says that as far as movie posters go, the day of the illustrator has passed. "Sometimes they can be a real pain in the butt," he laughs. "Anyway, computers have taken over, and they're doing a wonderful job." But something has definitely been lost. As Jung explains, it's "the little fantasy, the little piece of 'not quite real but real,' like a small light that comes from some unexplained source that makes a poster magical. We're losing something that makes posters more than reality, because movies are more than reality. Why do we go to movies except for the fun and the escape?"

George Lucas, for one, has stuck to his guns. Proud to be out of lockstep with Hollywood in so many ways, the writer-director has turned his personal interest in art, illustration, and movie posters into a large and magnificent collection that hangs on the walls and in the corridors of his company's offices. He is one of the last remaining filmmakers who still insists on using art on his movies' main release posters.

But even for Lucasfilm, the old ways have changed; international distribution practices and the worldwide immediacy of information and images over the Internet have required it. Where marketing for the original trilogy had included totally different campaigns in the countries with the largest movie-going populations, today, for the new trilogy, a single image usually prevails everywhere. Also, despite the fact that one artist may end up with his or her signature at the bottom of a theatrical poster, the end result is usually a true collaborative effort among the filmmaker, the studio, one or more advertising agencies, a designer, and perhaps several poster concept artists.

Star Wars posters are part of what has made *Star Wars* one of the best-known movie series in history. There are well over two thousand posters worldwide that co-author Pete Vilmur and I own or have seen and are able to document. (My friendship with Pete started with a few poster trades many years ago, showing a side benefit of poster collecting: expanding your circle of friends!) There could easily be hundreds more that have so far escaped us, although persistent collectors are making new "old" finds every day. Who knew Romanians even saw *Star Wars*, much less had posters for it during the Cold War? The more than three hundred examples in this book are among the best in each category and are a whole new way to look at—and collect—the amazing artistry of *Star Wars*.

—STEVE SANSWEET

STAR WARS

Poster 1 — 1st Edition Artist: Howard Chaykin — **Luke Skywalker** — © The Star Wars Corporation 1976

George Lucas just knew that he had a disaster on his hands.

So did the august directors of 20th Century Fox, who thought that studio head Alan Ladd Jr. had been crazy in the first place to have "greenlighted" this weird movie with bizarre aliens, strange names, and what read like a hokey plot. Signing up licensees to help promote and advertise the movie proved daunting, and the very first *Star Wars* poster was sort of an afterthought.

In early 1976 Charles Lippincott, head of marketing, advertising, and promotion for the still small Lucasfilm Ltd., went to New York to try to get a deal with Marvel Comics. He hoped to get several issues of a *Star Wars* comic published before the movie opened in order to get some positive buzz. It was a hard sell. Then chief honcho Stan Lee said no, but Lippincott found an ally in writer Roy Thomas, who helped to convince Lee. All agreed that Howard Chaykin should do the artwork. Both Lippincott and Lucas were familiar with Chaykin's work. "He had done an independent science fiction comic called *Cody Starbuck,* and that's the reason we wanted him," says Lippincott. Cody was a swashbuckling space adventurer, a Han Solo type.

With the comics deal sealed, Lippincott and producer Gary Kurtz decided to take a new, grassroots approach to promoting their film. "The time came for fan conventions in the summer of 1976," recalls Kurtz. "After we finished shooting we presented Fox with a plan to do a poster to take to the conventions, and sell it there for a minimal amount to help promote the movie." Who better to illustrate it than Chaykin?

That summer, Chaykin's "*Star Wars* Corp. Poster 1" was sold for a paltry $1.75 at Comic-Con in San Diego and WorldCon in Kansas City. With no film yet available, Chaykin worked from a handful of stills and the paintings of concept artist Ralph McQuarrie for inspiration. "I was doing something that wasn't going to be advertising so much as selling the material and cross-marketing to science fiction fans," Chaykin recalls. To drum up interest in the comic series and the film, the artist and writer joined Lippincott in San Diego, while Kurtz and actor Mark Hamill followed him to WorldCon. With about a thousand of the posters printed, sales were slow. "It didn't sell as well as I thought, but it did help to impress a lot of people," Lippincott says.

The poster and presentations were important, agrees Johnny Friedkin, a Fox publicist at the time. "I credit Charlie and Gary because we didn't have a lot to spend on advertising," he says. "Word of mouth is the best friend you can ever have."

For Christmas 1976, Fox released the first theatrical trailer for *Star Wars,* accompanied by the first "teaser" poster for theaters. It was printed on a shiny Mylar stock, a type of polyethylene film bonded to a heavy cardstock surface. The phrase "Coming to Your Galaxy This Summer" boldly heralded the film. Fox's New York ad agency, Doyle Dane Bernbach, did the design work on the posters. With many potential slogans being tossed around, there was disagreement on the direction the campaign should take. "We kept trying to tell them that most of the taglines they came up with seemed to imply that the audience wasn't up to whatever we were going to show them," says Kurtz. "I've always felt posters should underplay a movie, never overplay it. This is one of the reasons why we didn't have any graphics early on."

Though the poster contained no painted imagery, it did introduce a new logo to the campaign, one that had been designed originally for the cover of a Fox brochure sent to theater owners. The job went to an agency owned by Tony Seiniger, now known as Seiniger Advertising. Since the mid-1970s the agency has been known for its design of Hollywood film posters. Suzy Rice, who had just been hired as an art director, remembers the job well. She recalls that the design directive given by Lucas was that the logo should look "very fascist."

"I'd been reading a book the night before the meeting with George Lucas," she says, "a book about German type design and the historical origins of some of the popular typefaces used today—how they developed into what we see and use in the present." After Lucas described the kind of visual element he was seeking, "I returned to the office

STAR WARS **CORP. POSTER 1**

United States / 1976 / 20 × 29
As the "Poster 1" title suggests, this early poster painted by comic artist Howard Chaykin was to be the first in a series done to promote the film. The early logo was designed by *Star Wars* concept artist Ralph McQuarrie. Perhaps because of slow sales of the initial one thousand printed (they were sold for $1.75 each), no more in the series were produced. Still, it was helpful to get the word out to core fans a year before the movie's release. Today the poster fetches at least $400.

and used what I reckoned to be the most 'fascist' typeface I could think of: Helvetica Black."

Inspired by the typeface, Rice developed a hand-drawn logo that translated well to the poster campaign, and ultimately to the movie itself. "I did have the screen in mind when I drew the logo originally," explains Rice, who "stacked and squared" the words to better fit the brochure cover. It was an aesthetic choice that has lasted nearly three decades.

The now-familiar "S" ligature extensions that Rice drew were modified a bit after Lucas "remarked that it read like 'Tar Wars,'" says Rice. "He asked me to make some revisions on the leading and concluding 'S.'" With the new logo in place, the posters were sent out to theaters showing Fox films that Christmas. The print run had been extremely limited due to the expense and to the fact that barely thirty theaters had expressed interest in *Star Wars*.

The *Star Wars* Mylar Advance remains a celebrated milestone in the *Star Wars* poster campaign. "The idea of going with the Mylar was absolutely brilliant," says ex–Fox Marketing executive Marc Pevers. "The whole mystique about *Star Wars* was in that poster."

A short time later, a second version of the Advance teaser was issued, only this time it was printed with silver ink on regular paper. Rice's logo would see a slight modification as well. Instead of a very pointed "W," Rice explains, "they had the bottom of the 'W' flattened out so it would read more easily in the quick pan they were planning for the opening credits." The logo that appeared on the so-called Style "A" Advance has remained with the saga to this day.

In the spring of 1977, with the film's premiere closing in, Fox executives scrambled to release a second teaser poster for wide distribution. With an artwork campaign still not agreed upon, they tried coming up with a slogan or phrase that conveyed the spirit of the film. David Weitzner, who'd come to Fox in February as the new head of marketing, came up with the Style "B" teaser. "I created a poster . . . to get something up in theaters as soon as we could to announce the film," he remembers. "We were trying to be highly creative, but true to the film and to the filmmaker."

Producer Gary Kurtz recalls some bickering over what text to use for the poster. "They

left

STAR WARS TEASER THEATRICAL ADVANCE
United States / 1976 / 27 × 41
The second version of the Advance poster on regular paper features the standardized "W" used today. The modification was made by ILM conceptual artist Joe Johnston after it was decided that the original didn't work well in the pan shot that was initially planned for the opening credits. This poster seems to be at least as scarce as the Mylar and was likely sent to circuit theaters not showing Fox films in early 1977.

above

STAR WARS MYLAR THEATRICAL ADVANCE United States / 1976 / 27 × 41
There were two initial theatrical posters accompanying trailers that began running in theaters during the 1976 Christmas season. They were issued by 20th Century Fox to promote its upcoming "adventure as big as the cosmos itself." Fox marketers, desperate to come up with a hook audiences could relate to, played on George Lucas' reputation as director of the youth hit *American Graffiti*. Not content with one tagline, they tried several, including the "cosmos" one and "The story of a boy, a girl, and a universe." The design came from one of Fox's main agencies at the time, Doyle Dane Bernbach. The so-called Mylar was printed first on plasticized foil backed with a heavy coated-paper stock, using the early pointy "W" in "Wars." Likely printed for those select theaters exhibiting a Fox film that December, a less-expensive, plain-paper version with a redesigned "W" was sent to remaining venues. Only a few hundred of the foil posters were printed, since few theater owners and chains had expressed much interest in booking an unknown space fantasy. Some of the Mylars were distributed at fan conventions.

***STAR WARS* WILD-POST HANDBILL** United States / 1977 / 7.5 × 9.5
This handbill reveals an early, and quickly changed, tagline for the film. "What I was trying to do with that piece of copy was to really be true to the fantasy," explains then–Fox Marketing executive David Weitzner.

wanted something they could put on billboards and elsewhere," says Kurtz. "They came up with a whole group of taglines that were terrible because they were typical for Hollywood movies, like 'An Adventure to the End of Your Imagination . . . and Beyond.'" Actually, a similar phrase was used on small handbills.

Weitzner recalls the dilemma. "Every piece of copy that I had written for this film did not meet with George's approval. It dawned on me one day that the best way to solve that was to use words that were not written by anyone *but* George. 'A long time ago in a galaxy far, far away' was very simple, and I felt that George wouldn't be negative toward his own words."

The new tagline was used on wild-post street flyers (like concert posters that are slapped up on construction-site fences), one-sheets, and billboards. The large seven-sheet billboard version even incorporated the film's release date, May 25. Kurtz had been reluctant about putting out a release date too soon. "We didn't actually have the [test] screening at the Northpoint Theater in San Francisco until April, . . . so we were slightly nervous about them targeting the May 25th date before that. We weren't sure whether [Fox] would like the movie or would want minor adjustments that might delay it."

It was becoming clear that Fox and Lucasfilm would have to reach an agreement on the artwork if a poster was to be released in time for the premiere. Early on, Lucasfilm had gone out on its own to solicit concepts. "We commissioned a lot of art separate from what Fox did," explains Kurtz. "We thought that several artists who were used to doing science fiction book covers would be ideal to consider for the posters."

Among those approached were *Star Wars* concept artist Ralph McQuarrie, Frank Frazetta, Jeff Jones, and John Berkey. "George loved John Berkey's work," Lippincott recalls. Still basking in the glow of his success with the 1976 poster for the new King Kong movie, Berkey was asked to submit several concepts for *Star Wars*. "George Lucas had

***STAR WARS* TEASER "B" SEVEN-SHEET**
United States / 1977 / 84 × 91
The large seven-sheet Advance is formally called an "out-of-home" poster, since most were printed for small billboards and transit stations. These were probably distributed to just Los Angeles, New York, and San Francisco, which had the only theaters to open *Star Wars* in 70mm, a fact called out on the poster. The poster is unique because it is the only one that has the May 25 release date, a date immortalized by *Star Wars* fans.

***STAR WARS* TEASER "B" THEATRICAL ADVANCE**
United States / 1977 / 27 × 41
Arriving in the spring of 1977, with the film just about complete, the second Advance "teaser" poster had the benefit of using the now-famous words "A long time ago in a galaxy far, far away. . . ." David Weitzner of Fox Marketing wrestled with many potential taglines for this poster, finally settling on the simple but eloquent phrase that opens the film.

opposite
***STAR WARS* STYLE "A" THEATRICAL ONE-SHEET**
United States / 1977 / 27 × 41
Although Tom Jung's Style "A" artwork met high praise at Fox, the image was not widely circulated at first. Instead, the public was given the Hildebrandt version for various media exposure, including newspapers, T-shirts, and retail posters. As a result, when Jung's one-sheet was finally given wide exposure, the "Hildebrandt" title was still used by many to refer to this poster. As was typical for the time, the poster was released in a variety of sizes besides this one-sheet and the Jung half-sheet (22 × 28). It was also available as an insert (14 × 36), a 30 × 40, a 40 × 60 (often joined to a cardboard backing and called a standee), a three-sheet (41 × 77), a six-sheet (77 × 79), a seven-sheet (84 × 91), and a twenty-four-sheet billboard (105 × 235). The *Star Wars* trilogy films were among the last to be represented by so many poster format variations.

bought six paintings [of mine], and they used those during preproduction on the film," says Berkey. "He said that when it came time to wrap the movie, he'd like to have me do the poster."

The studio had other plans. "Fox thought that a Berkey one-sheet would be too 'modern art looking,'" Kurtz says. "They wanted a more literal piece." Although Berkey's art wasn't used on theatrical posters, one of his concepts ended up as an insert for the soundtrack album, and he also did a book cover for the second printing of the movie's novelization.

By late spring, Weitzner was still trying to get an artwork poster released. Research was telling him that the use of "Wars" in the title would alienate women, and that any overt reference to science fiction on the poster would turn off the general population. Weitzner says, "*Star Wars* baffled me in the sense that my head of research was telling me women aren't going to come, so how can we mitigate that to a degree? Then how can we try to position this so that we don't oversell it one way and fail to reach out to a broader audience?"

In a meeting with Lucas, Weitzner expressed his concerns. It was a watershed moment for Weitzner: "George said to me, 'David, what are we going to tell them the film is the day after we open?' And the light bulb went on, and I realized exactly what he was saying, which is, simply put, that an elephant is an elephant, a giraffe is a giraffe. This is what this film is—now let's get around to selling it."

Weitzner continues, "And that led me to develop the first piece of art, which was the piece done by Tommy Jung. It had to be illustration, because that's what was needed for the spirit of the film. Its vitality, its fantasy, its story—all this was best served with illustration."

Tom Jung was brought in by the agency of Smolen, Smith, and Connolly, which Weitzner had contracted for the poster. A designer by trade, Jung had composed but not illustrated many well-known posters, including ones for *Dr. Zhivago* and the 1967

STAR WARS STYLE "A" THEATRICAL HALF-SHEET
United States / 1977 / 22 × 28
The first main images to launch *Star Wars* in poster form came on the Style "A" theatrical one-sheet and half-sheet by artist Tom Jung. The one-sheet artwork, which later was reinterpreted by fantasy artists Tim and Greg Hildebrandt for a commercially licensed poster, has become one of the most recognized images in movie poster history. While the faces resemble stars Mark Hamill and Carrie Fisher, the bodies come straight from pulp magazine covers. The half-sheet design, which was designed before the one-sheet but printed later, is considered by many to be the more attractive of the pair. Its horizontal format gave Jung more of a canvas to work with, allowing more scenes from the movie to be added and greater detail on the X-wing fighters. In both instances the droids were added later by different artists to save time.

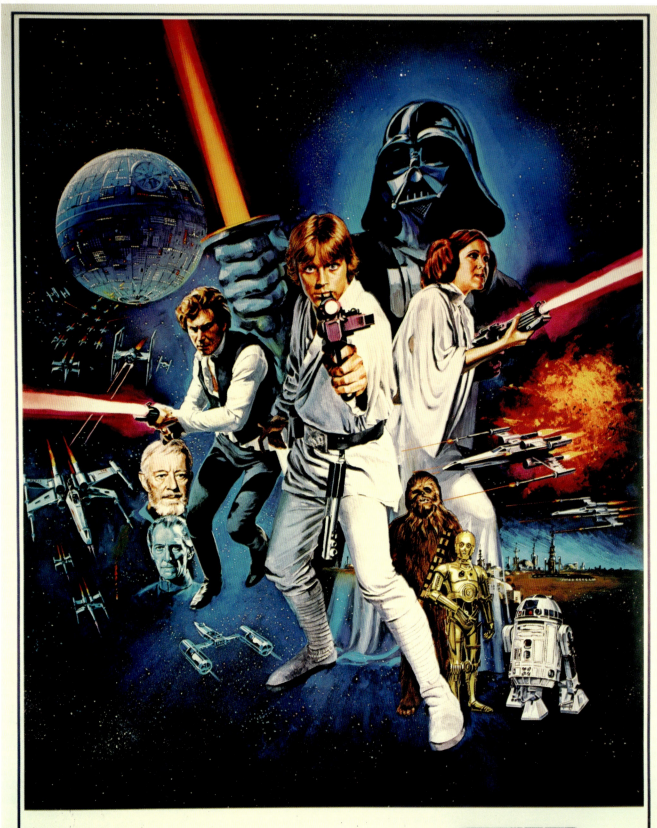

previous spread, left
***STAR WARS* STYLE "C" INTERNATIONAL THEATRICAL ONE-SHEET** United States / 1977 / 27 × 41
This striking artwork by British artist Tom Chantrell became an instant hit with fans when it made the scene in late 1977. Because of its action-oriented tone, this image was also popular with foreign distributors. Han Solo, who had been mysteriously absent from most of the print campaign, was finally given a place at the center of the action. This poster also established the color blue as a predominant feature of *Star Wars* poster campaigns to come. But since this poster was never intended for U.S. distribution, it lacks the "PG" rating in the credit block. A small number were printed with the "PG" block, either for use at U.S. military bases or because of an error.

previous spread, right
***STAR WARS* STYLE "D" (CIRCUS) THEATRICAL ONE-SHEET** United States / 1978 / 27 × 41
The Style "D," also known as the "Circus poster," is widely regarded as one of the most inspired *Star Wars* posters ever produced. When *Star Wars* was rereleased during the summer of 1978, Lucasfilm sought a new look for the poster campaign. Nearly a year earlier, Charles White III had been asked to produce a poster image that would capitalize on the swashbuckling appeal of the film. While White airbrushed the droids, Vader, landspeeder, and other images, he brought in his colleague Drew Struzan to render the portraits of Luke and Leia, Han Solo, and Ben Kenobi. The "wild-posting" effect became a necessary modification when it was discovered there wasn't enough room at the bottom for the credit block.

rerelease of *Gone with the Wind*. Although an accomplished artist himself, Jung thought it would be the same routine for the *Star Wars* Style "A" poster.

"When I first came up with that version, I intended not to execute it myself," says Jung. "Being an art director, I usually have a person in mind. I was thinking Frazetta might do it." So Jung loosely based the figures on Frazetta's style: heroic, well-muscled men and sparsely clad, buxom women. "When I first designed the poster, I had Princess Leia more scantily clad in a costume that wasn't in the film." For the finished painting, Jung was asked to hit the actors' likenesses and make Leia's costume more closely resemble the one in the movie.

One of the more bold graphic elements in the painting is the use of a white streak across the top of the lightsaber beam, forming a cross. "I think the cross is such a super graphic," explains Jung. "It didn't make any real graphic sense, but I put it in because it was strong, and it was good over evil." Jung's horizontal version of the Style "A" artwork, which also uses the Luke/Leia graphic, was actually designed before the one-sheet, but printed later. "They liked the lightsaber 'cross' and wanted to incorporate that icon into the [one-sheet] poster," says Jung.

Jung's finished paintings were well-received at Fox, with the staff christening the one-sheet "the Buck Rogers poster." Some at Lucasfilm, however, felt it might not work for an unknown film. "Too dark" was Lippincott's first reaction to the imagery. "The image was dark, the tone was dark, the title didn't pop, and it didn't tell you what the film was about. It didn't grab you."

Because Fox liked the "Buck Rogers" poster, and because Lucasfilm wanted to explore other possibilities, Weitzner went back to Smolen, Smith, and Connolly for ideas. They hired twins Tim and Greg Hildebrandt, who were well-known fantasy artists at the time, to paint their own take on the Jung design. "The reason they called us is because Tim and I had just done the *Lord of the Rings* calendar, and we had a fan following," says Greg Hildebrandt. "We had come through literally overnight for them on a poster for *Young Frankenstein*. It wasn't used, but we did it overnight, so they called us and said we need a poster fast."

With the deadline to compose newspaper ads just nine days away, the agency needed the artwork done in two. Gathering some stills and a photo of Jung's concept from the agency in New York, the brothers raced back to their studio in New Jersey to start the painting. The only direction they were given was to make the image look "comic bookish."

Greg Hildebrandt remembers the tag-team approach they used to complete the piece. "I grabbed my then-wife, threw a nightgown on her, and tore it in a few places to get that 'Frazetta' look," Hildebrandt says. "I had a friend throw on a bathrobe for Luke, then I took Polaroid photos, and Tim and I started to draw. By then it was around 8 p.m. We drew together until about midnight, then I went to sleep and Tim transferred what we had drawn to art board, painted for three or four hours, woke me up, and then I painted for a while. We worked like that for thirty-six hours before we finished."

Shortly after the painting was completed and photographed, the Hildebrandts were called in to do some touch up. The brothers had a suggestion. "We thought there should be more characters, especially in the space to the right of Luke," Greg Hildebrandt says. They asked if they could paint in C-3PO and R2-D2, and the studio approved. With a handful of acrylics, the brothers added the droids to the painting right there on the spot.

Public response to the artwork was overwhelmingly positive. But because the brothers were told not to worry about the actors' likenesses, Fox opted to keep Jung's original for the release poster. When the studio decided to merchandise the Hildebrandt image as a retail poster, printer Factors Etc. reported that it outpaced their bestselling Farrah Fawcett swimsuit pin-up poster five to one a few weeks after the film's release.

Going against the advice of research, Fox decided to add the droids to Jung's artwork as well. However, with painting and artist on opposite

Star Wars Happy Birthday One Sheet

STAR WARS "HAPPY BIRTHDAY" THEATRICAL ONE-SHEET United States / 1978 / 27 × 41
For the first anniversary of *Star Wars*, a special poster was created that depicts most of the first series of *Star Wars* action figures (excluding the height-challenged Jawa) around a cake. It is highly sought after by *Star Wars* poster and toy collectors alike. The poster was distributed to theaters still showing the film a year after its opening. Movie release patterns have changed dramatically since 1978. Distributors are lucky to have their movies in theaters two months after opening, much less a year. Detail-obsessed collectors have long wondered why the descriptive "*Star Wars* Happy Birthday One Sheet" text in the lower left corner was printed in an unconventional font with a bit of a slant. According to Ronald Kalter, who worked as traffic manager for printer Gore Graphics in 1978, the text was slapped on at the last minute using the font off of his secretary's IBM Selectric typewriter. The stripped-in plate started to slip in the press, resulting in the signature slant of the text on every poster printed.

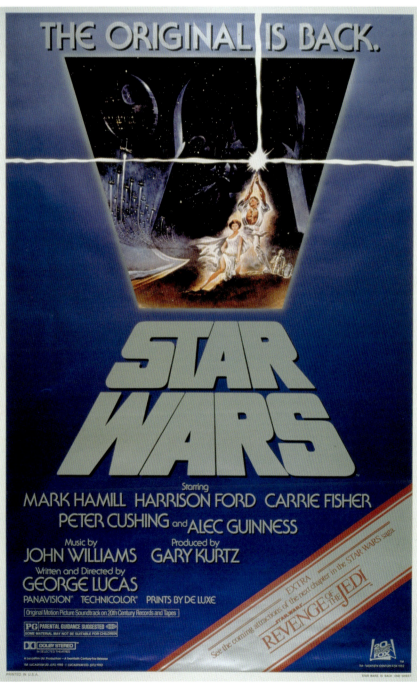

far left
STAR WARS "IT'S BACK!"
THEATRICAL RE-RELEASE ONE-SHEET
United States / 1979 / 27 × 41

left
STAR WARS "TWO WEEKS ONLY"
THEATRICAL ONE-SHEET
United States / 1981 / 27 × 41

below
STAR WARS "REVENGE" STRIPE
THEATRICAL ONE-SHEET
United States / 1982 / 27 × 41

For the three rerelease posters for 1979, 1981, and 1982, the *Star Wars* "space-crawl" logo was used effectively in conjunction with Tom Jung's classic Luke and Leia pose. The blue-and-red 1979 poster is noteworthy for its lack of border and Kenner toy snipe, while the 1982 version touts a trailer preview for the saga's third installment, *Revenge of the Jedi*. The silver title and credits lend an added class to these posters, which seem to employ the "less is more" philosophy of design.

coasts, and with no time to spare, Fox contracted illustrator Nick Cardy, a highly regarded comic artist, to add the droids and adjust a few details on Luke and Leia's clothing. Fox finally had its first artwork poster in the campaign. But would it be ready in time?

According to published reports and eyewitness accounts, the Jung Style "A" poster was nowhere to be seen opening day, or even weeks after *Star Wars*' release. None of the people involved at the time have a clear recollection one way or the other, so it's possible the campaign's key art wasn't seen until later in the summer as the movie spread to more and more theaters.

In November 1977, England was introduced to *Star Wars* with the Hildebrandt art on a "quad," the British horizontal equivalent of the American one-sheet. By New Year's, however, a new artwork poster was distributed. Thomas Chantrell, a well-known poster artist and record-jacket illustrator in England, was hired by producer Kurtz through the London office of Doyle Dane. Free to explore possibilities outside the U.S. campaign, Kurtz was able to shape the image he wanted. And he wanted action.

"We called it the '*Dirty Dozen* poster,'" says Kurtz, "because it was similar in style to what they had done with that film's poster in terms of a group of people pointing out at the audience." Chantrell's artwork was painted to fit the horizontal format of the quad, with the illustration reaching far into the title field on the right. "That's why the vertical versions of that poster look a bit strange," notes Kurtz. Chantrell's art was used extensively internationally, but always reformatted for vertical posters. In the United States, the striking artwork was used only for black-and-white print ads; a one-sheet was produced, but it was earmarked for foreign theaters.

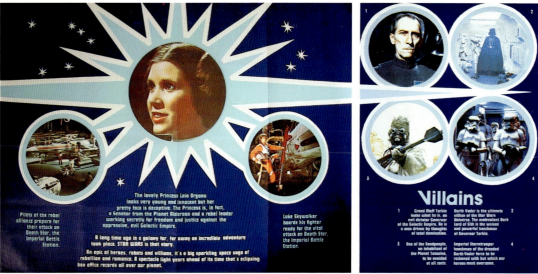

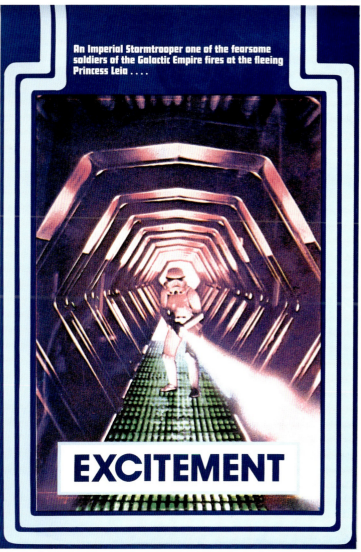

clockwise from top left

***STAR WARS* THEATRICAL DOUBLE CROWN: "HEROES"** United Kingdom / 1977 / 20 × 30
***STAR WARS* LEIA THEATRICAL QUAD CENTERPIECE** United Kingdom / 1977 / 30 × 40
***STAR WARS* THEATRICAL DOUBLE CROWN: "VILLAINS"** United Kingdom / 1977 / 20 × 30
***STAR WARS* THEATRICAL DOUBLE CROWN: "EXCITEMENT"** United Kingdom / 1977 / 20 × 30
***STAR WARS* THEATRICAL DOUBLE CROWN: "ADVENTURE"** United Kingdom / 1977 / 20 × 30

This British poster set saw limited use in large theaters opening *Star Wars* in November 1977. By then, promoters were savvy to the retro appeal of its storytelling, which included "Heroes," "Villains," "Excitement," and "Adventure." These are part of a "Marler Haley" ensemble of six posters that included the Hildebrandt theatrical quad pictured on page 24.

STAR WARS HILDEBRANDT THEATRICAL QUAD United Kingdom / 1977 / 30 × 40
Apparently only used in London and for a very short time, the Hildebrandt quad features added imagery to accommodate the horizontal shape of the poster. The extended landscape may appear original to the artwork, but was actually added by another artist.

Unlike movie-release patterns today, where major films usually open huge and then play out in four or five weeks before dropping off the radar, *Star Wars* was still playing at some theaters a year later. So a special poster was planned to commemorate the film's first anniversary. Early concepts included a portrait of the droids presenting a birthday cake, photographed by Bob Seidemann, whose portfolio includes the likes of Janis Joplin, Blind Faith, and Jerry Garcia.

Opting for a simpler composition and gently plugging the new line of action figures just released by Kenner Products, a new poster was conceived that would have a birthday cake surrounded by eleven of the twelve new figures in the line. Weitzner remembers calling ad agency head Tony Seiniger with the idea. "I said, 'Tony, I want you to go out and get a cake baked, in blue and white, and on the icing on the top we'll say *"Star Wars."* Instead of candles I want to surround it with the Kenner toys, the characters, and the copy—which was mine—was 'One year old today.'"

Arranging for the custom cake through West Hollywood's Cake & Art bakery, Seiniger brought in photographer Weldon Anderson to shoot the setup. Of the first twelve action figures produced by Kenner, only the Jawa was left out of the photo. Apparently, his vertically challenged stature didn't work with the composition. (The vinyl-caped Jawa that was omitted from the photo has become one of the most sought-after figures from the *Star Wars* line. But that's another story. . . .)

Distribution of the poster was very limited. "We didn't put them everywhere," remembers Weitzner. "We wanted them in the best theaters we had." Some were also sent to selected media. At Mann's Chinese Theatre in Hollywood, an identical cake was provided to give Mayor Tom Bradley the perfect photo-op to celebrate the film's anniversary. The platter the cake arrived on survives today as a bedside table owned by an ex-employee of the theatre.

In July 1978, the film was rereleased in theaters across the country, and a new poster was released

STAR WARS STYLE "C" THEATRICAL QUAD WITH ACADEMY AWARDS United Kingdom / 1978 / 30 × 40
Just after New Year's 1978, British artist Tom Chantrell's artwork started being displayed in front of British cinemas. After the Academy Awards were held that March, this second version of the poster touting the film's seven Oscars replaced the original version.

that sent the campaign in a different direction. Turning from the timeless but quiet image designed by Jung, the new poster was all action, with a decidedly "old-time" flavor. "George really wanted us to develop different posters" to keep the campaign fresh, Weitzner says. "In particular he wanted one where Luke and Leia were swinging on a rope."

What has come to be called the "Circus Poster," the *Star Wars* Style "D" one-sheet, was actually created before the film's initial release over a year earlier. Charles White III of the Charles White III and Friends studio in southern California was contacted by Weitzner to come up with an image reminiscent of the old Hollywood adventure films. White quickly composed a black-and-white sketch and took the image to Lucas, who was running sound checks on his soon-to-be-released film. The director loved it. "He bought off on that sketch with no color comp," says White. "To be able to do one sketch and then go to a finish was pretty amazing in those days."

The final painting needed to be completed within a matter of days. White remembers the deadline was so tight because the image was being considered to open the campaign. "They were going to try and make this the first poster, but they had so much already in place that they decided against it," he says.

Because White worked with airbrush, and this was to be a 1940s-style poster, he needed someone who could paint accurate portraits in the classic style using oils. He decided to call on friend and former classmate Drew Struzan. Until that point, Struzan had been involved primarily with album covers and B-movie poster artwork. "I kind of fell into doing movies because of my portrait work, since portraits are considered the hardest things among artists," Struzan says.

To get the bodies of Luke and Leia into a position that fit the design, Drew looked through production stills provided by Fox. Nothing worked. "We had a concept that didn't jibe with the stills, so I had some friends pose as Luke and Leia, and I

KRIEG DER STERNE

STAR WARS

Es war einmal in ferner Zukunft

Gewitzte Roboter, starke Männer, schlaue Monster im Kampf gegen den Todesstern

Luke Skywalker: „Wenn Prinzessin Leia in Gefahr ist, dann pfeife ich auf ein ruhiges Leben. Mir ist kein Plan zu verwegen und kein Risiko zu groß, um diesen verdammten Todesstern in die Knie zu zwingen."

Prinzessin Leia: „Es muß mir gelingen, alle Kräfte gegen die Tyrannei des galaktischen Imperiums zu sammeln, und wenn es tausendmal gefährlich ist."

A

B

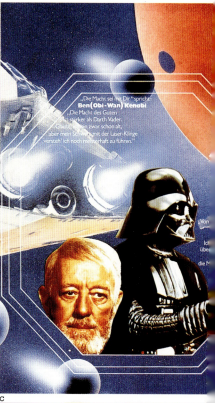

„Die Macht sei mit Dir" spricht **Ben (Obi-Wan) Kenobi** „Die Macht des Guten ist stärker als Darth Vader. Zwar ist er schon alt, aber mein Schwert mit der Laser-Klinge versteht ich noch meisterhaft zu führen."

C

Fabelwesen, Menschen und Sterne, Vergangenheit und Zukunft erleben einen gemeinsamen Krieg

F

Ce-Dreipeo: „Ohne meine vorzüglichen Kenntnisse aller galaktischen und elektronischen Sprachen hätten die Menschen und Roboter ausgesprochen unangenehme Verständigungsprobleme. Bei Gott, was würden sie ohne mich tun!"

Rzwo-Dezwo: „Raatsch, piep, piep, boing, blubber blubber, hui, hui, piep, mrrr, mrrr."

G

Die menschliche Phantasie kann verrückt, grausam, spannend und lustig sein

H

top left and right

STAR WARS THEATRICAL DEKO DISPLAY BANNER: KRIEG DER STERNE
Germany / 1977 / 19.5 × 46.5

top center

STAR WARS THEATRICAL DEKO DISPLAY PIECE: ES WAR EINMAL IN FERNER ZUKUNFT. . .
Germany / 1977 / 19.5 × 23

STAR WARS THEATRICAL DEKO DISPLAY A–J
Germany / 1977 / 23 × 33 each
German movie theaters have traditionally used large lobby displays to trumpet the *Star Wars* films, beginning with this rare twelve-piece Deko mural. Theater owners had the option of using all or part of the display in various arrangements, including an odd text portion that translates to "It was once in the distant future." The regular release posters used the U.S. Tom Jung artwork, followed by the International Tom Chantrell art, both with silver borders.

Das Display—Material für Ihre Theaterdekoration.

Das Dekorationsmaterial vermittelt in seiner Gesamtheit eine überzeugende Werbebotschaft. Die Formate sind im Baukasten-System aufeinander abgestimmt, so daß bei allen Größen von Foyerwänden, Schaukästen, Staffeleien etc. ein einheitliches Bild erzielt werden kann. Verwenden Sie die Buttons und Endlos-Klebestreifen für innen und außen. Letztere vor allem auch zu einer wirkungsvollen Treppenstufen-Werbung. Führen Sie die Werbung von außen in das Theater und wie den berühmten roten Faden durch das ganze Haus. Um Ihnen die Auswahl zu erleichtern, finden Sie auf diesem Musterbogen die Abbildungen und Größen aller Werbemittel. Schnell können Sie sich so entscheiden, was Sie benötigen, welche Größen, welche Anzahl etc. Bedienen Sie sich also der beigefügten Bestellkarte und sie erhalten **kostenlos** das von Ihnen gewünschte Material.

Anwendungsbeispiele

Das hier abgebildete 4-farbige Großplakat, das es in 2 Größen gibt, ist die Basis für alle Anwendungsbeispiele. Es besteht aus 10 Einzelplakaten DIN A1 (Grösse 1) bzw. DIN A2 (Grösse 2) und den dazugehörenden Titel- und Schlagzeilen-Plakaten. Alle Einzelelemente sind bei der Dekoration entsprechend aneinanderzufügen. Wenn Sie dieses Großplakat wie hier abgebildet dekorieren, benötigen Sie folgende Dekorationsflächen:
Grösse 1: Breite 297 cm
Höhe 218 cm
Bestell-Nr. 1
Grösse 2: Breite 210 cm
Höhe 154 cm
Bestell-Nr. 2

Je Abbildung 5 Einzelplakate, 2 Titelplakate, 1 Schlagzeilenplakat. Grösse 1: Breite 297 cm/Höhe 134 cm   Grösse 2: Breite 210 cm/Höhe 94 cm

Diese Beispiele bestehen aus jeweils 8 Einzelplakaten und 2 Titelplakaten. Beide Möglichkeiten ergeben, wie auch in allen anderen Fällen, eine in sich geschlossene bildhafte Form.
Grösse 1:
Breite 238 cm
Höhe 218 cm
Grösse 2:
Breite 168 cm
Höhe 154 cm

Je Abbildung 4 Einzelplakate und 1 Titelplakat.
Grösse 1: Breite 119 cm/Höhe 218 cm   Grösse 2: Breite 84 cm/Höhe 154 cm

Jede Abbildung besteht aus 6 Einzelplakaten, 2 Titelplakaten, 1 Schlagzeilenplakat.
Grösse 1: Breite 178 cm/Höhe 201 cm   Grösse 2: Breite 126 cm/Höhe 144 cm

Diese Dekorations-Form eignet sich besonders für kleinere Wandflächen, für Wände an Treppenaufgängen, an freistehenden Bausäulen im Foyer etc. Jede dieser Abbildungen besteht aus 2 Plakaten.
Grösse 1: Breite 59,4 cm/Höhe 201 cm
Grösse 2: Breite 42 cm /Höhe 144 cm

Hinweis

Bei der Begutachtung der hier abgebildeten Werbemittel wollen Sie bitte berücksichtigen, daß alle Einzelplakate die zu dem Großplakat gehören, sowie die Buttons, von uns mit Schlagzeilentexten und ergänzenden Werbetexten versehen werden. Dadurch ist gewährleistet, daß auch bei Einzelverwendung jedes Plakat und jeder Button eine eigenständige Bild- und Textaussage hat.

Je Abbildung 2 Einzelplakate und 1 Titelplakat. Grösse 1: Breite 119 cm/Höhe 134 cm   Grösse 2: Breite 84 cm/Höhe 94 cm

Je Abbildung 3 Einzelplakate und 3 Titelplakate. Grösse 1: Breite 178 cm/Höhe 117 cm   Grösse 2: Breite 126 cm/Höhe 84 cm

Je Abbildung 4 Einzelplakate und 2 Titelplakate. Grösse 1: Breite 238 cm/Höhe 134 cm   Grösse 2: Breite 168 cm/Höhe 94 cm

ENDLOS-PLAKATE zur Dekoration an Wänden, um Säulen herum und als Hintergrund für Ihre Schaukasten-Dekoration. Die Plakate werden von links nach rechts aneinander gereiht.
Format 70 x 40 cm
Bestell-Nr. 5

Je Abbildung 1 Einzelplakat und 1 Titelplakat. Grösse 1: Breite 59,4 cm/Höhe 117 cm Grösse 2: Breite 42 cm /Höhe 84 cm

BUTTONS, selbstklebend
Ø 21 cm (mit wieder ablösbarem Klebstoff)
5 verschiedene Motive = 1 Satz
Bestell-Nr. 3
Bitte bestellen Sie komplette Sätze und nicht einzelne Motive

ENDLOS-STREIFEN, selbstklebend für Treppenstufen usw.
(mit wieder ablösbarem Klebstoff)
Format 95 x 9 cm Bestell-Nr. 4

Hinweis

Bitte berücksichtigen Sie bei der Planung Ihrer Dekoration, daß das Großplakat nur **komplett** bestellt und geliefert werden kann, d.h. jeweils 10 Einzelplakate mit der dazugehörenden Anzahl von Titel- und Schlagzeilenplakaten.

STAR WARS BILLBOARD France / 1977 / 59 × 78
The French created an airy poster using mainly the Tom Jung image of Luke and Leia for *panneaux*, or billboards.

opposite

STAR WARS THEATRICAL DEKO DISPLAY INSTRUCTION SHEET
Germany / 1977 / 25 × 35
This rare instruction sheet showed German theater managers the various ways they could assemble the Deko display, depending on available space.

just stuck the [actors'] heads on. That's why you'll never find a photo that looks like that."

Struzan worked hard to capture the right tone. "We weren't looking to take a frame from the film," he explains. "We wanted to emphasize the spirit, the feeling of the film. So you've got to invent something." It was decided that Struzan would paint Luke and Leia with oils first, then White would follow with the landspeeder, droids, Vader, and background in airbrush. Because oils don't mix with water-based dyes, getting the two to work together on the same board called for some creativity.

"I gessoed the art board just in the places where I was going to work, so that the oil wouldn't bleed," says Struzan. "I painted very carefully on the gessoed part, and when my part was done and dried, [Charlie] did his part on the raw board." At last the painting appeared finished, or so they thought. "I had forgotten that there's a certain scale of type to the credits," says White. In other words, there wasn't enough room for the type, but they came up with a brilliant solution. "The original design

was of a poster with torn edges," recalls Struzan. "So we decided, let's make it look wild-posted. Charlie painted the wood fence texture, and I did the portrait of Obi-Wan on the side." A pasted-on inset of Han Solo made the poster complete.

White describes the additions in artistic terms. "There were several stories involved. Obi-Wan Kenobi's life was a prior story. So he was a worn piece of another poster from the same 'series.' So there's a reason to it." Completed in April 1977, the poster wouldn't be printed until the following year. As successful as the image was in the United States, Spain was the only other country to pick it up, which it did for a 1979 rerelease of *Star Wars*. It remains one of the most highly regarded movie posters by *Star Wars* fans and poster collectors alike.

Star Wars inspired many different theatrical posters throughout the world; the movie was released toward the end of the era when regional studio offices were allowed to hire local artists to come up with their own campaign imagery. Italy's

30 **STAR WARS THEATRICAL "PRETTY IN PINK"** Italy / 1978 / 26.5 × 37.5
Among a flurry of posters created for Italy's *Star Wars* campaign, this one seems to make a point to show, with color tints, that Luke is a boy and Leia is a girl. Perhaps it was thought that Luke's 1970s hairdo made his appearance gender-neutral?

opposite

STAR WARS THEATRICAL FANTASY ART BY PAPUZZA Italy / 1978 / 39 × 55
Papuzza did several pieces of concept artwork for the Italian *Star Wars* campaign. This submission—which was actually used on an oversized poster—took the greatest creative license with the characters' likenesses.

STAR WARS THEATRICAL: MAY THE FORCE BE WITH YOU
Japan / 1978 / 20 × 29
Elements of Tom Jung's half-sheet artwork and the Hildebrandt version are featured among photos of the cast in this 1978 release poster.

opposite

STAR WARS THEATRICAL ADVANCE
Japan / 1977 / 20 × 29
The spare composition of the Japanese Advance poster for *Star Wars* seems to beckon the imagination to fill in the star-filled void.

fanciful cartoon artwork by Papuzza captured the comic book spirit of the film to a degree, while Poland's Jakub Erol offered a stark depiction of C-3PO in a hailstorm of stars, cashing in on the otherworldliness of the protocol droid's appearance. Straight text posters were also designed, including a Japanese teaser that uses an unusual amount of negative space around the film's logo. Space would be inserted into the logo itself for a striking two-sheet "panneaux" from France, with layout design by René Ferracci.

The most unusual *Star Wars* posters to see print came from the belated Russian release in 1990–91. Aside from two unusual images that took some rather extreme poetic license with the *Star Wars* denizens, one larger poster incorporates circuit boards and gizmos in a cut-and-paste photocollage resembling a space cowboy. The image harks back to the early days when reviewers were hailing *Star Wars* as a "space western." ✦

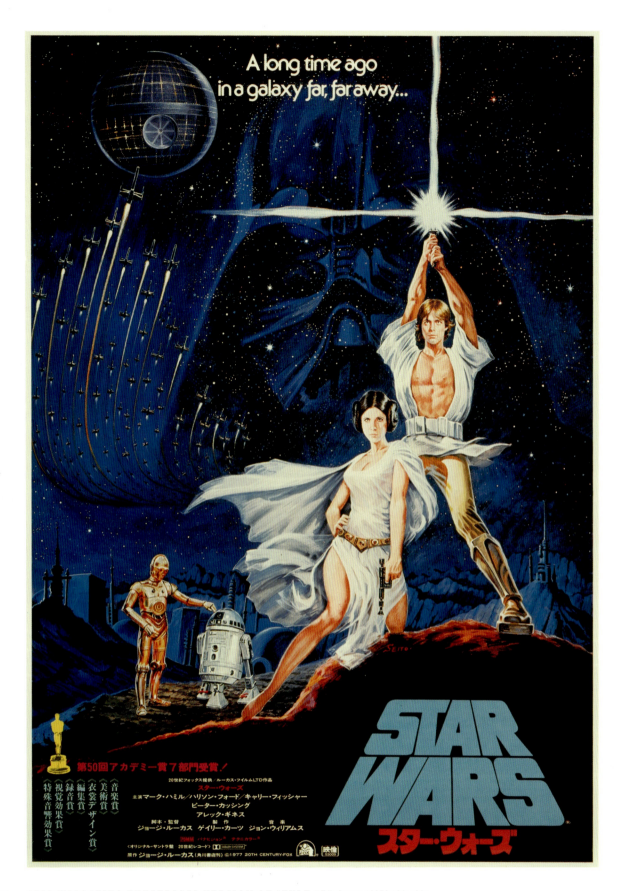

34 ***STAR WARS* SEITO THEATRICAL VERSION OF STYLE "A"** Japan / 1978 / 20 × 29
For the main Japanese *Star Wars* release poster, artist Seito redesigned some of the physical features of the characters and drew the droids further into the composition.

opposite

***STAR WARS* COMMEMORATIVE DUBBED VERSION** Japan / 1982 / 20 × 29
In 1982, Japan premiered the first version of *Star Wars* to use Japanese voice-over actors rather than subtitles. In a statement from George Lucas regarding the dubbed version, the director said that voices closely resembling those of the original actors were chosen to maintain the integrity of the presentation. This special commemorative poster by Noriyoshi Ohrai gives center stage to the *Millennium Falcon,* whose "peculiar dialect" required no voice over.

35

opposite
STAR WARS THEATRICAL STYLE "C" IN CHINESE
Hong Kong / 1978 / 21.5 × 31
The Hong Kong version of the Style "C" poster serves as a rare example of text enhancing the effect of the artwork.

STAR WARS THEATRICAL STYLE "A" IN HEBREW
Israel / 1977 / 25 × 37.5
The *Star Wars* poster from Israel presents a hybrid of the Tom Jung and Hildebrandt versions of the Style "A" artwork.

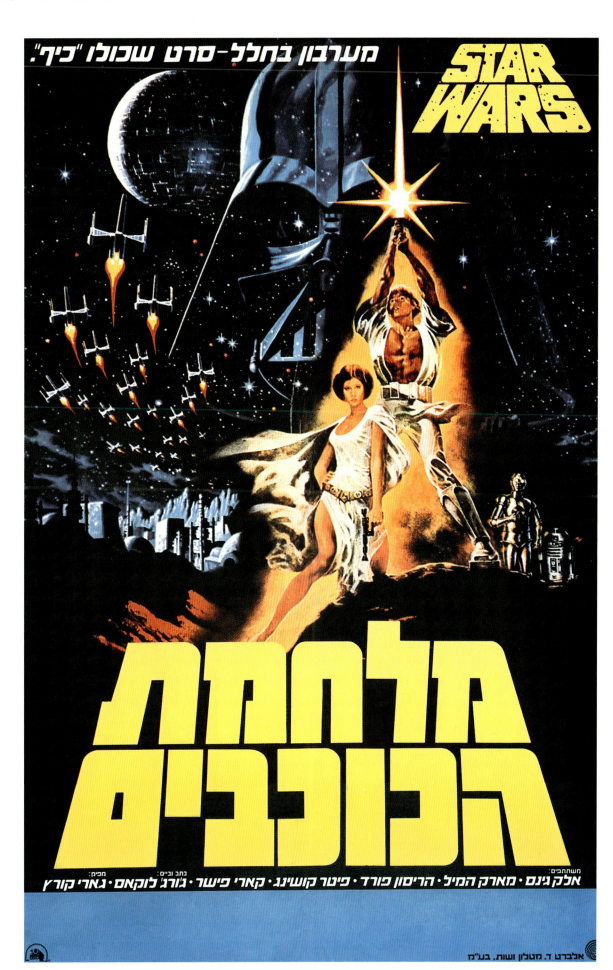

STAR WARS THEATRICAL "BIG ORANGE"

Romania / 1978 / 19 × 26
Probably one of the most crudely printed *Star Wars* posters ever produced, the black-and-white image includes the glare of the poster photographer's flash as he copied a full-color poster.

STAR WARS THEATRICAL *THE WAR OF THE WORLD*

Thailand / 1977 / 22 × 31
Besides looking to Western eyes like nearly every other letter is printed backwards, this initial release poster from Thailand is also notable for its only words in English: The War of the World. Was that supposed to be the name of the film? What were they thinking?

opposite

STAR WARS THEATRICAL YELLOW C-3PO Poland / 1979 / 26 × 38

In addition to illustrating the unusual Polish release poster for *Star Wars,* Jakub Erol also created posters for *The Empire Strikes Back* and *Raiders of the Lost Ark.* With only C-3PO represented, one wonders if the artist had any notion of what the film was about.

40 **STAR WARS THEATRICAL WITH TIME QUOTE**
Spain / 1978 / 27.5 × 39
Like the French poster, Spain opted for a stylized logo in the native language to open *Star Wars*. The quote is from *Time* magazine, which called *Star Wars* the year's best movie.

STAR WARS THEATRICAL STYLE "A" WITH PHOTOS
Sweden / 1978 / 27.5 × 39
Sweden produced one of the few posters to incorporate Tom Jung's artwork along with photos of Han Solo and Chewbacca, who were nowhere to be seen on early release posters.

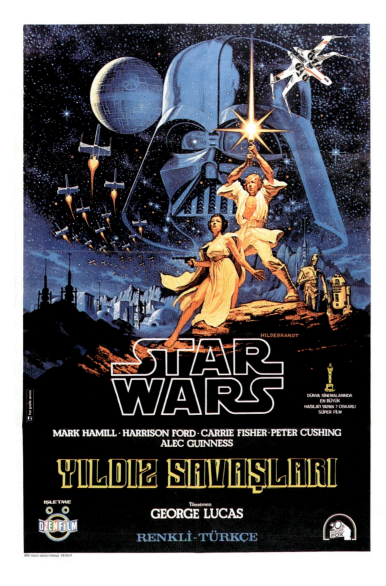

***STAR WARS* THEATRICAL HILDEBRANDT ART**

Turkey / 1978 / 27 × 39

The Turkish designer who arranged this poster included the Hildebrandt artwork as well as an X-wing fighter illustration used on the MPC model kit boxes.

STAR WARS* THEATRICAL *LA GUERRA DE LAS GALAXIAS

Spanish Language / 1977 / 27 × 41

Though the Hildebrandt artwork was not formally used in the domestic *Star Wars* poster campaign, it did see use for advertising in Mexico and in Spanish-speaking regions of the United States. The posters were printed in the United States.

42

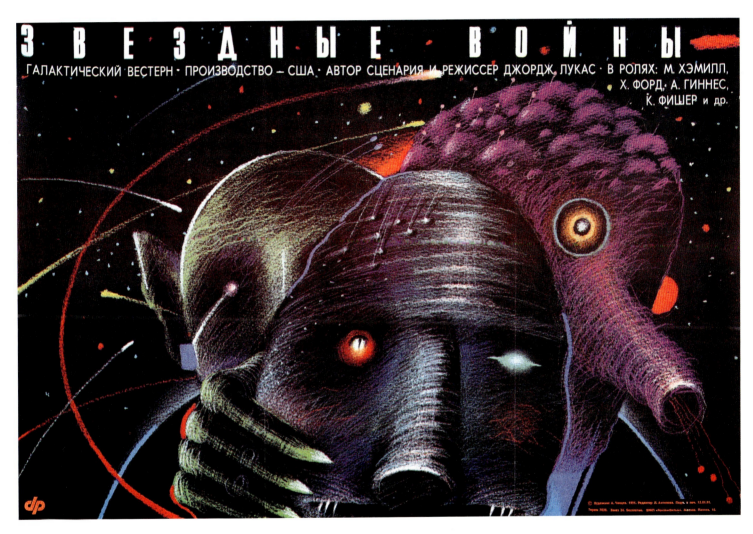

STAR WARS ALIENS THEATRICAL Russia / 1991 / 17 × 25
The Russian posters for *Star Wars*, which wasn't released in the former Soviet Union until the Cold War had come to an end, match and probably top the Polish posters for their utter strangeness. This poster, like *Star Wars*, features aliens and outer space—but you'd never run into these three in the Mos Eisley cantina. The art is attributed to Aleksandr Chantsev.

opposite

STAR WARS "VADER" ADVANCE Russia / 1990 / 21.5 × 33.5
The first Russian poster for the saga has a Darth Vader–like creature—it looks a bit like a cougar or puma—in the center with little lightsabers shooting out of its helmet. There are lots of strange drawings in the small boxes on the edge. Some have a mystical bent, while others bear a resemblance to characters from the film. Judging by the avant-garde feel of the poster as a whole, any such resemblance is purely coincidental. The art is attributed to Igor Majstrovsky.

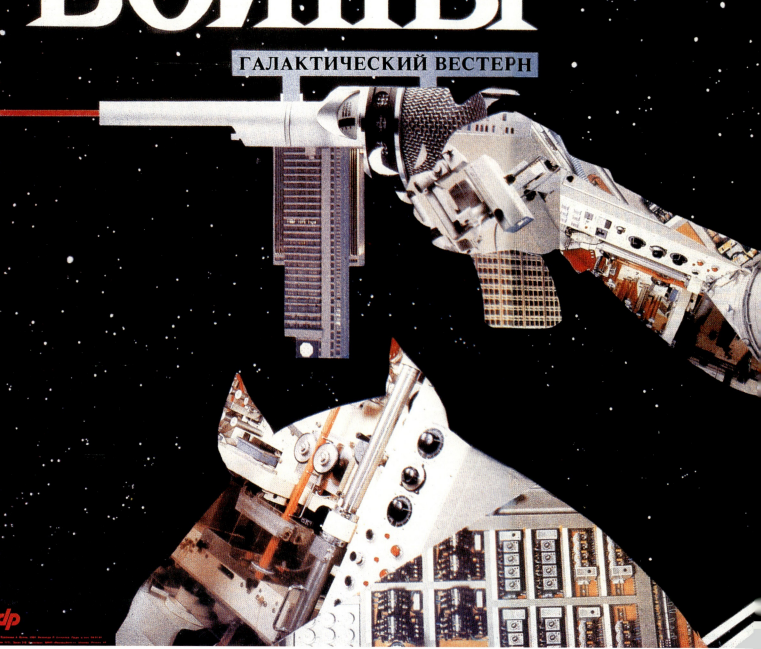

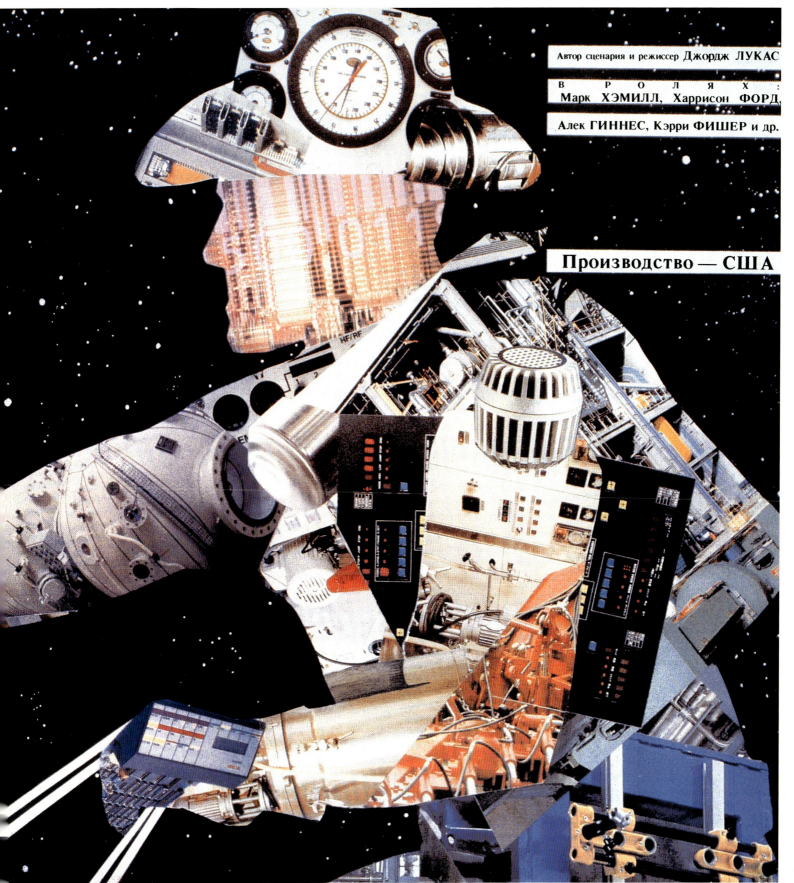

STAR WARS THEATRICAL SPACE WESTERN THREE-SHEET Russia / 1991 / 33 × 62
This unique three-sheet from Russia has a design made out of electronic parts and circuit boards, and shaped like a cowboy riding a horse and aiming a pistol. The reason? The poster calls it "*Star Wars:* A Galactic Western." Since the movie has been called a "space opera" and George Lucas has said that one of the reasons he made it was that youngsters no longer had heroes like movie cowboys to root for, the poster seems quite fitting. The art is attributed to Aleksandr Kulov.

AMERICAN MARKETING CONVENTION United States / 1977 / 18 × 23
Artist Bob Watts illustrated this very rare poster given to attendees of the American Marketing Association's San Diego convention in September 1977. Somewhat similar to the concept artwork that was developed for the release posters, Fox Marketing executive Marc Pevers requested that the event poster "coordinate with the overall campaign."

opposite

STAR WARS CONCERT POSTER United States / 1978 / 24 × 37
The notorious *Star Wars* Concert poster has been laden with misconceptions and mystery ever since it was produced in 1978. Common lore has it that this poster was available to purchase for one night only at the Hollywood Bowl premiere of a *Star Wars* concert series. However, that concert, where Zubin Mehta conducted the Los Angeles Philharmonic Orchestra, took place on November 20, 1977, almost a full year before the poster was printed in October 1978. During the run of the tour, a handful of various posters were commissioned to advertise each specific venue. However, when the management of the series changed hands in the spring of 1978, it was deemed appropriate to unify the series under a single key illustration, which was the impetus for this classic artwork art directed by Suzy Rice and illustrated by John Alvin. But it isn't clear that these posters were ever available to the public. Therefore, they are rare and highly desirable.

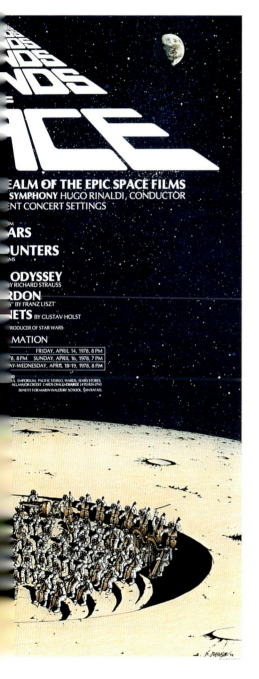

SOUNDS OF SPACE 1, 2, 3 United States / 1978 / 16 × 20 each
Ralph McQuarrie created two of the three posters printed for the Sounds of Space concert held in April 1978. Though Hugo Rinaldi was the headline conductor, John Williams actually led the symphony for the *Star Wars* suite on at least one night of the five-performance engagement. McQuarrie remembers that the French horn was the initial poster that he painted for the event, and when asked to include more science fiction elements, he started a new painting. Ultimately, both designs were used. The center artwork was done by Bob Johnson. This version is an uncut printer's proof.

STAR WARS ON FUJI FILM Japan / 1978 / 8 × 23
Fuji Film used this simple but striking poster to promote its edited *Star Wars* clips on 8mm film.

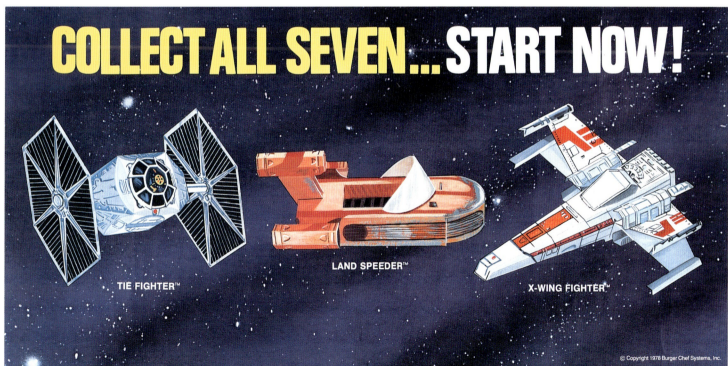

BURGER CHEF FUNMEAL TRANSLITE United States / 1978 / 13.5 × 28 each
Burger Chef promoted its seven different *Star Wars* FunMeals with this two-part translite, a poster printed on thin plastic meant to be illuminated from behind. Kids could get a board game and even make funky cardboard models of *Star Wars* ships and C-3PO and R2-D2.

52 **BURGER CHEF FUNMEAL**
United States / 1978 / 23 × 35
This early poster for Burger Chef's *Star Wars* FunMeals appears to have used the Kenner Products toy vehicles to model the spaceship illustrations.

WONDER BREAD CARDS
United States / 1977 / 12 × 16
A set of sixteen *Star Wars* cards could be amassed by purchasing countless loaves of bread. That's a lot of dough for a small set of cards. The small section of artwork shown on this poster was actually part of a larger composition illustrated by Los Angeles artist John Van Hamersveld for a *Star Wars* Toyota sweepstakes promotion in September 1977. Van Hamersveld is well-known for his design work on concert posters and album jackets, which included art for the likes of Jimi Hendrix, The Rolling Stones, and The Beatles, to name a few.

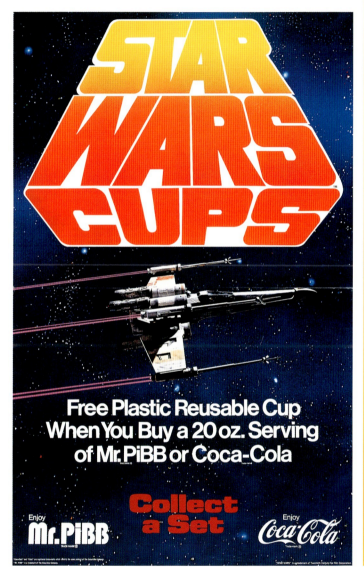
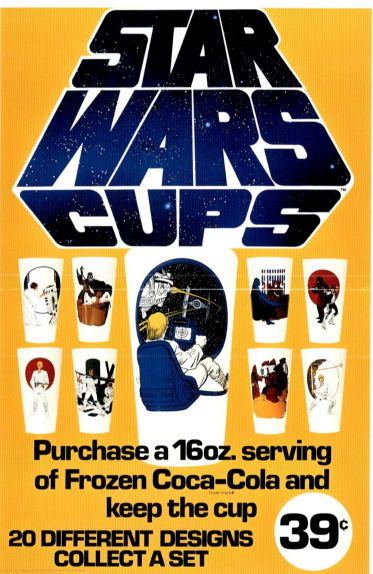

STAR WARS COKE CUPS

United States / 1977 / 23 × 35

This unusual vertical poster for Coca-Cola and Mr. Pibb uses the style of the *Star Wars* logo to get big impact.

STAR WARS FROZEN COKE CUPS

United States / 1977 / 23 × 36

This frozen Coke offer involves cups with twenty different designs.

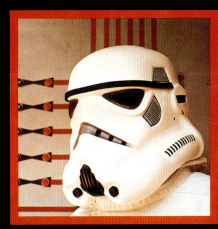

opposite

DON POST MASKS United States / 1977 / 18 × 25
Don Post Studios was one of the first licensees to come on board for *Star Wars,* and it had four masks available shortly after the film's release.

STORY OF *STAR WARS* SOUNDTRACK United States / 1977 / 22 × 33
One of the few U.S. promotional posters to display horizontally, this in-store poster for the Story of *Star Wars* soundtrack took its imagery straight from the album's cover.

overleaf, left

STAR WARS JAPANESE SOUNDTRACK Japan / 1978 / 20 × 29
Japan's King Records promoted the Star Wars original soundtrack album with an in-store poster using a shot that wasn't in the movie itself. Not a single X-wing fighter from the rag-tag Rebel Alliance was able to get a shot off at Darth Vader's TIE fighter during the dogfight sequence near the end of the film. But all fans can agree that the "posed" graphic certainly looks great.

overleaf, right

STAR WARS SOUNDTRACK PROMOTION United States / 1977 / 22 × 33
Tom Jung's portrait of Darth Vader, which graced the back cover of the soundtrack album, got some additional exposure on this rather formal foil poster printed as a promotional item.

opposite

ESTES MODEL ROCKETS United States / 1978 / 15 × 24
An example of life imitating art emerged with the Estes line of *Star Wars* rockets, even if their boosters couldn't reach galactic heights. But at least one of the toy rockets—the TIE fighter—was used by ILM as the basis for background spacecraft in the last two films of the original trilogy.

SPHERE *STAR WARS* NOVELIZATION
United Kingdom / 1978 / 20 × 30
The British paperback version of the *Star Wars* novelization uses John Berkey concept art for the cover, along with the quickly discarded pointed "W" in the logo.

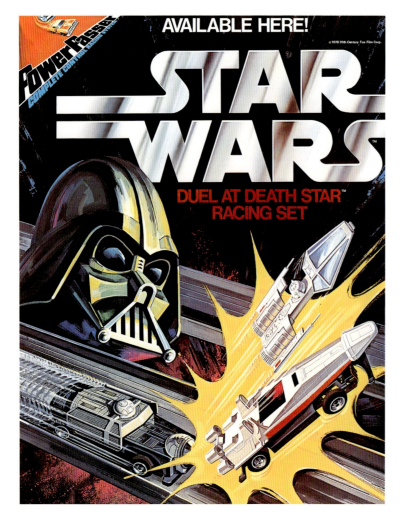

above left
DUEL AT DEATH STAR RACING SET United States / 1978 / 17 × 22
One of the more unusual toys to emerge from the merchandising blitzkrieg of the first film, the Duel at Death Star Racing Set featured break-apart X-wing and TIE slotless racers. It was made by train-maker Lionel for Kenner Products, the main toy licensee.

above right
MORINAGA CANDY Japan / 1978 / 20 × 28.5
This bold Vader and X-wing fighter were used by Morinaga, a long-established Japanese confectioner, to promote its line of *Star Wars* candies and snacks—all with small *Star Wars* premiums inside.

opposite
COCA-COLA BATTLE SCENE Japan / 1978 / 29 × 40
A premium poster from Coca-Cola in Japan was high on action and sparing in company logos. Like the King Records poster, this is not a scene from the movie.

IMMUNIZATION United States / 1979 / 14 × 22
The U.S. Department of Health issued two variations of the *Star Wars* immunization poster with some modifications made to the lower text. At around the same time, C-3PO made an antismoking public service spot, aimed at children, for television.

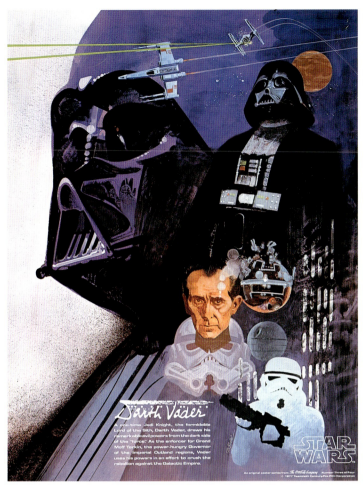

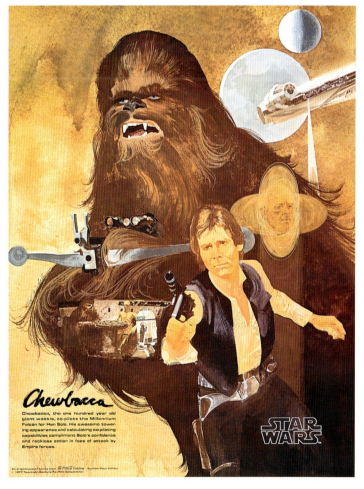

COKE/BURGER KING/BURGER CHEF: VADER, LUKE, DROIDS, HAN/CHEWIE United States / 1977 / 18 × 24
This attractive quartet was a premium with the purchase of four large Cokes at your local Burger King or Burger Chef in 1977. According to artist Del Nichols, the posters were painted in acrylics and all completed in a single weekend. There are three varieties of each: Burger King, Burger Chef, and simply Coca-Cola.

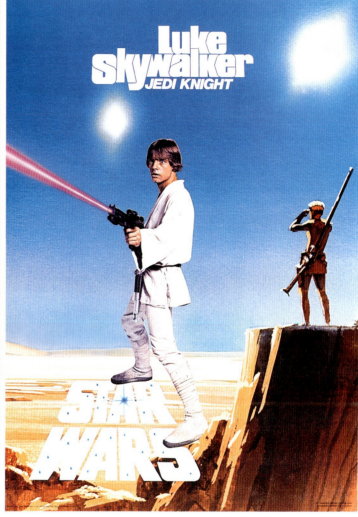

LEIA BY FACTORS ETC.

United States / 1977 / 20 × 28

Princess Leia, Luke Skywalker, and Darth Vader would all enjoy the status of the pop-culture pin-up, each shot by rock-and-roll photographer Bob Seidemann.

LUKE "JEDI KNIGHT" BY FACTORS ETC.

United States / 1977 / 20 × 28

Two versions of the Factors Etc. Luke Skywalker poster were printed, this one likely being the first. It was either unreleased or withdrawn shortly thereafter, due to its somewhat slapped-together appearance or its presumption that Luke was a Jedi Knight. As we learn from Yoda in *Return of the Jedi,* Luke must face Darth Vader before achieving knighthood.

opposite

HILDEBRANDT ART BY FACTORS ETC.   United States / 1977 / 20 × 28

Painted by the famous twin brothers and fantasy artists in just thirty-six hours due to a tight deadline, this poster is based on Tom Jung's theatrical one-sheet design. It was released as the main theatrical poster in a number of countries, and in the United States it became one of the first commercial *Star Wars* posters. "The momentum of the film had become so strong that I got a request from merchandising that they wanted to sell the poster," says David Weitzner, head of advertising for Fox in 1977. "I never thought of it as a profit center. I thought of it as a way to promote the film."

opposite

SOUNDTRACK ALBUM INSERT United States / 1977 / 22 × 33
Artist John Berkey hadn't seen *Star Wars* before painting this frenzied dogfight over the Death Star, which could explain the numerous *Millennium Falcon* images on the poster. Though not printed for the release poster, it did end up as an insert premium for the soundtrack album. Ironically, Berkey says he has never seen *Star Wars* to this day.

SWEDISH *STAR WARS* PIN-UP
Sweden / 1977 / 27 × 39
Scandecor of Sweden was able to capture the quintessential *Star Wars* pin-up with this classic image of the cast, starfighters, and logo.

MCQUARRIE FAN CLUB POSTER United States / 1978 / 20 × 28
Charter members of the Official *Star Wars* Fan Club were sent this striking poster of a climactic moment in the film, painted by concept artist Ralph McQuarrie in 1978.

opposite
CANTINA DENIZENS BY SELBY United States / 1978 / 20 × 28
According to artist Bill Selby, several of the aliens seen in this 1978 commercial poster by Factors Etc. were changed or added at the request of George Lucas. Lucas was not happy with some of the creatures he'd been forced to hurriedly shoot for the scene and didn't want them represented in the poster. This artwork originally was considered for an exclusive *Star Wars* Fan Club poster, but eventually became a limited Factors Etc. retail poster instead.

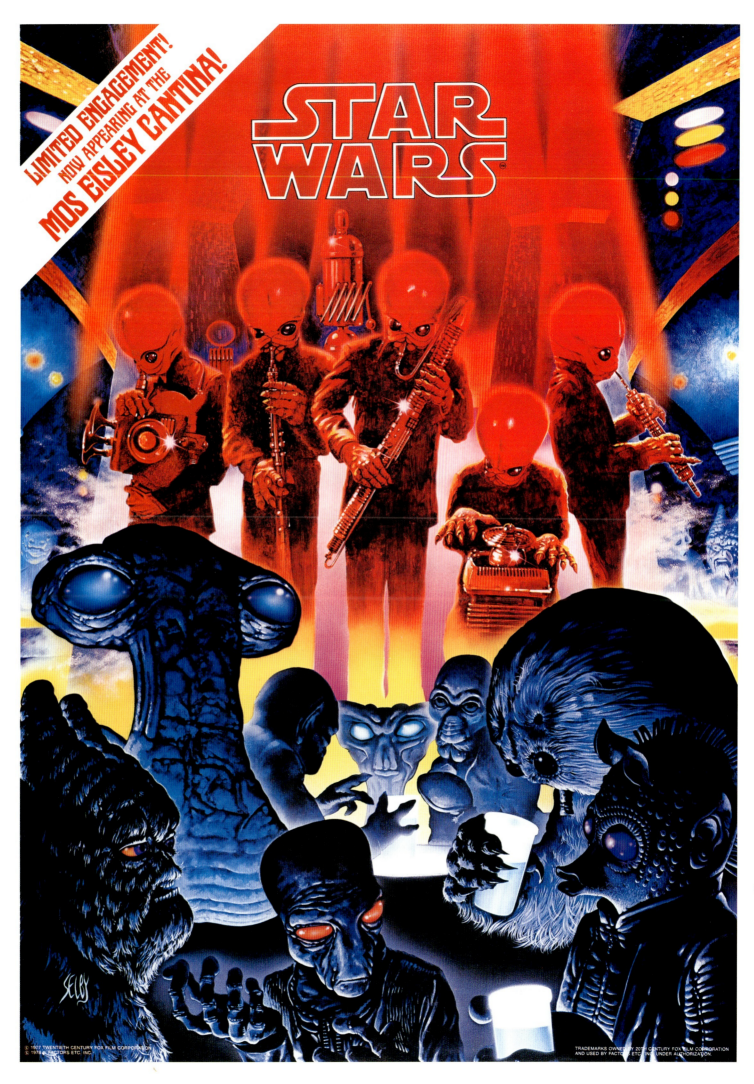

THE EMPIRE STRIKES BACK

Since *Star Wars* was such a breakout success, an outsider today might think that everything related to the next movie would have been a piece of cake.

Not so. The planned budget more than doubled, and when actual production costs went higher still, Bank of America pulled Lucasfilm's $10 million loan; the location shooting was twice as tough, since frigid, snow-covered Norway presented problems even more difficult than the Tunisian desert storms encountered in the first production; and the difficulty of the special effects shots tripled. Add to that the fact that, at the time, sequels were not common in the movie business, and those that were made were rarely successful. What seems like such a sure thing in hindsight was difficult to pull off.

Things were a little clearer to the movie's marketers. For one thing, they had established a track record and a way of doing things. For another, the second film's title practically begged for the use of one clear icon. "We felt we had gotten into the right groove," says producer Gary Kurtz. "So it was clear that we wanted to have a teaser poster, an opening poster, and then some kind of back-up poster. And the teaser poster was obviously Darth Vader." This was obvious because practically overnight Vader had become the top movie-screen villain of all time. A Vader poster would let audiences know that the man in black was back.

Lucasfilm turned again to Tony Seiniger. In recent years, Seiniger's agency has spent up to six months and $500,000 to develop just the right poster for a client. But Lucasfilm had neither the time, money, nor inclination to dawdle in 1979. It needed an Advance one-sheet for theaters to display around the holidays late that year.

The basic design of the teaser poster was done by Seiniger himself and David Reneric, then lead art director for the agency. Reneric developed the tilting *Empire* logo, boxed in by a version of the *Star Wars* logo similar to that employed on early toys. To photograph the Vader helmet, which was set against a sea of stars, they used Bob Peak Jr., son of the famous illustrator. The image worked on everything from posters smaller than the traditional one-sheet to special New York subway wall posters to large billboards. It was also used in Japan, Italy, and Australia, among other countries.

The most beautiful poster for *Empire*—maybe for all of the films—wasn't in theaters for long. It is known as the "kissing poster" or, more properly, the *"Gone with the Wind"* poster, and for good reason. It shows Princess Leia in a swoon, about to be kissed by a very romantic-looking Han Solo—a Scarlett O'Hara and Rhett Butler in space. In fact,

***THE EMPIRE STRIKES BACK* THEATRICAL ADVANCE ONE-SHEET**
United States / 1979 / 27 × 41
The image of Darth Vader was used to assure the public that their favorite man in black was back for the sequel. The successful "Coming to your galaxy this Summer" copy from the previous campaign was reused at the bottom of the *Empire* Advance one-sheet.

***THE EMPIRE STRIKES BACK* ADVANCE NEW YORK SUBWAY**

United States / 1980 / 45 × 58
Special posters printed for New York Subway advertising included line-art drawings of some of the characters in the venue boxes.

***THE EMPIRE STRIKES BACK* STYLE "A" NEW YORK SUBWAY**

United States / 1980 / 45 × 58
The two New York Subway posters for *The Empire Strikes Back* are the only such posters ever printed for the *Star Wars* saga.

opposite

***THE EMPIRE STRIKES BACK* STYLE "A" ("*GONE WITH THE WIND*") THEATRICAL ONE-SHEET** United States / 1980 / 27 × 41
Roger Kastel's "*Gone with the Wind*" poster for *Empire* can trace some of its heritage back to *Star Wars* poster artist Tom Jung, who designed the 1967 rerelease poster for the epic Civil War romance.

left

THE EMPIRE STRIKES BACK CHARITY PREMIERE, PHOENIX, ARIZONA
United States / 1980 / 17.5 × 23
Occasionally, regional posters such as this one for *Empire* were printed for special charity premieres of the films.

opposite

THE EMPIRE STRIKES BACK STYLE "B" THEATRICAL ONE-SHEET
United States / 1980 / 27 × 41
The tonality of the blue background in Tom Jung's Style "B" poster for *Empire* changed slightly between printings for the studio and for the National Screen Service—which distributed most posters to movie theaters for nearly forty years. The poster is notable for both more action and the addition of the Lando Calrissian character.

that image in the poster paid explicit homage to the 1967 rerelease poster for *Gone with the Wind*, designed by Tom Jung and painted by Howard Terpning. The artist for the Style "A" *Empire* poster was painter Roger Kastel.

Once again, the direction had come from the top. "What I remember most vividly is George Lucas saying to me, 'What I want is *Gone with the Wind*, since this movie is also about the relationship between Han Solo and the Princess,'" says Sid Ganis, then Lucasfilm's head of marketing. "George never strayed from that, and although we worked on other concepts, he always came back to that look. So we worked on it, refined it, and that became the opening art for the movie."

Painter Kastel recalls that six freelance artists were hired to work on concepts. "The art director wanted a lot of color and the aurora borealis in it," he says. "And Lucasfilm kept adding things while I was working on it. The account exec would fly the paintings out to California and come back, and it seemed like there always would be something more that they wanted." Added to the basic composition were the floating Cloud City, Lando Calrissian, the bounty hunter Boba Fett, and an ion cannon from the ice planet Hoth. The last thing Kastel remembers

EMPIRE STRIKES BACK

ONE SHEET B

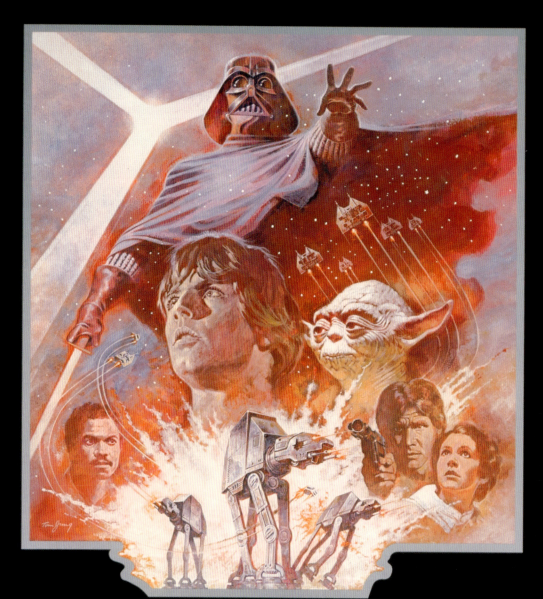

ONE SHEET–EMPIRE STRIKES BACK–RERELEASE SUMMER 81

previous spread, left
THE EMPIRE STRIKES BACK 1981 RERELEASE THEATRICAL ONE-SHEET
United States / 1981 / 27 × 41
Yoda is shown for the first time on an official U.S. theatrical poster for the 1981 rerelease of *The Empire Strikes Back*.

previous spread, right
THE EMPIRE STRIKES BACK 1982 RERELEASE THEATRICAL ONE-SHEET
United States / 1982 / 27 × 41
Tom Jung reconfigured the elements of his 1981 rerelease poster for this second version printed the following year. Neither of his rerelease artworks were printed outside the United States. Notice the increased prominence of Han Solo in this version.

adding were three X-wing fighters in the upper right-hand corner.

The poster also was clearly influenced by Jung's original *Star Wars* poster, with the large Vader helmet looming above everything. While it was Lucasfilm that asked Kastel for all the additions, the consensus after it was done was that the poster was "a bit too busy," Kurtz recalls. "It seemed a little too cluttered with those secondary characters," adds Ganis, "so the decision was to go with the money shot, which was the three main heroes." Out went Cloud City, Boba Fett, the cannon—and the swashbuckling Lando Calrissian. Not long after the poster was printed, it became clear that eliminating Lando had been a mistake.

"As soon as the poster came out, everybody realized that it was a bit of a slight, since Billy Dee Williams was the only main character who wasn't on the poster," Kurtz recalls. "I'm not sure why we didn't pick that up before the poster went out. In the mock-up stage there was a lot of analysis of where everything was placed and what it looked like and all that. But that was just an oversight." Billy Dee's agent raised the issue, and there was a concerted effort to make sure that Lando was in the follow-up poster, which arrived more quickly as well.

THE EMPIRE STRIKES BACK STYLE "A" THEATRICAL QUAD United Kingdom / 1980 / 30 × 40
This extremely rare British quad for *The Empire Strikes Back* apparently was used only for London-area transit stations and theaters. It was quickly replaced by a quad with the U.S. "B" Style art by Tom Jung.

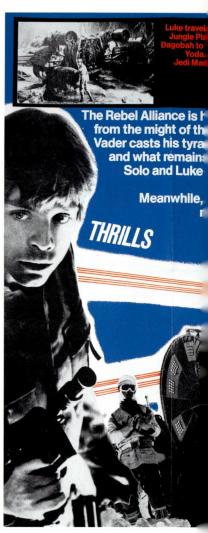

clockwise from top left
THE EMPIRE STRIKES BACK RETRO THEATRICAL DOUBLE CROWN (HEROES) United Kingdom / 1980 / 20 × 30
THE EMPIRE STRIKES BACK RETRO THEATRICAL QUAD United Kingdom / 1980 / 30 × 40
THE EMPIRE STRIKES BACK RETRO THEATRICAL DOUBLE CROWN (VILLAINS) United Kingdom / 1980 / 20 × 30
THE EMPIRE STRIKES BACK RETRO THEATRICAL DOUBLE CROWN (ROMANCE) United Kingdom / 1980 / 20 × 30
THE EMPIRE STRIKES BACK RETRO THEATRICAL DOUBLE CROWN (ADVENTURE) United Kingdom / 1980 / 20 × 30
Romance! Adventure! What more could a movie fan want? This retro-looking set of five posters featuring various characters and scenes was exhibited in British theater lobbies for *The Empire Strikes Back,* usually along with the release quad as part of a six-piece "Marler Haley" set.

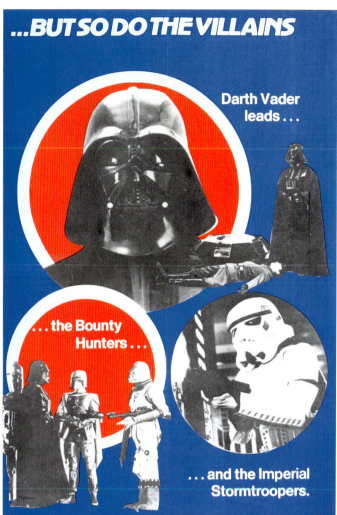

THE EMPIRE STRIKES BACK "BEWARE" QUAD
United Kingdom / 1980 / 30 × 40
Although England officially did not have an Advance poster for *The Empire Strikes Back*, this quad used by a theater chain fulfilled the role with a rather B-movie flair.

opposite

THE EMPIRE STRIKES BACK THEATRICAL WITH YODA

Germany / 1980 / 23 × 33
Yoda makes a rare appearance on the German poster for *The Empire Strikes Back*, which incorporated elements of several posters into its design. Yoda's image was withheld from most first-run posters because of secrecy surrounding his appearance. This poster is actually for the video release but is nearly identical to the theatrical version.

In 1980, the only places in the United States where Kastel's unaltered painting appeared were as the book cover for the novelization of *Empire* and the back cover of the soundtrack album. In a few countries, such as Spain and France, another artist added back in Lando and Fett. Another major figure was omitted on both the first and second release posters, but as far as anyone knows, it didn't bother him. Of course, puppets rarely get upset. To preserve secrecy, Yoda didn't appear on an *Empire* poster until the movie's 1981 rerelease. And in 1984, when the complete Kastel artwork was used for the first video release of *Empire*, the image of the Jedi Master was discreetly added to the composition.

Another reason for the hasty exit of the Style "A" poster from theaters, says Kurtz, was that distributor 20th Century Fox thought there wasn't enough action in it. "They wanted something else that they could use as an alternate that had more Vader, more spaceships, more stormtroopers . . . and less romance," the producer adds. Says Ganis: "Fox was a little chagrined about the look; they would have liked a full-out action campaign, as you would expect."

Ganis says the new poster wasn't done to "pacify" Williams, but "definitely to accommodate Billy" and also to freshen the campaign. "It was the right thing to do," he adds. "You open with the emotional drama, the heroic strength of the film. But the plan all along was to switch to a campaign that had more physical strength to it."

So Tom Jung was called upon once again, this time to do the Style "B" poster, which hit theaters within a month of the opening. Jung remembers

Der Krieg der Sterne geht weiter

C-3PO R2-D2

Die beiden liebenswerten Roboter, die einfach alles können. Millionen Menschen haben sie schon ins Herz geschlossen.

Ein mutiger junger Mann, der schon bei der Befreiung der Prinzessin gezeigt hat, was er kann. Jetzt nennt ihn seine kampferprobte Mannschaft respektvoll »Commander«.

Luke Skywalker

Darth Vader

Der Herr des Imperiums, der den großen Feldzug gegen die jungen Rebellen anführt – eine unheimliche, finstere Erscheinung, ein harter, herzloser Krieger.

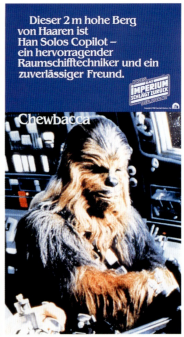

Dieser 2 m hohe Berg von Haaren ist Han Solos Copilot – ein hervorragender Raumschifftechniker und ein zuverlässiger Freund.

Chewbacca

Yoda

Ein 800 Jahre alter Zwerg. Er lebt auf dem Sumpfplaneten und bildet die Jedi-Ritter aus – Männer, die sich für Frieden und Gerechtigkeit einsetzen.

Ihre Befreiung ist das stärkste Motiv für die Rache des Imperiums. Aber sie ist nicht nur eine schöne, sondern auch eine hochintelligente Frau – und sie hat gute Freunde.

Prinzessin Leia

Kampfläufer

Sie stampfen auf ihren Gelenkbeinen vorwärts wie riesige, gepanzerte Dickhäuter. Gelbrote Flammenwolken fauchen aus ihren Waffen. Kanonen ragen wie Hörner aus den Köpfen der Vernichtungsmaschinen.

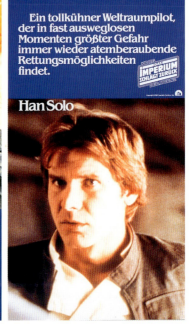

Ein tollkühner Weltraumpilot, der in fast ausweglosen Momenten größter Gefahr immer wieder atemberaubende Rettungsmöglichkeiten findet.

Han Solo

THE EMPIRE STRIKES BACK **THEATRICAL DEKO BANNER** Germany / 1980 / 7 × 94
THE EMPIRE STRIKES BACK **THEATRICAL DEKO DISPLAY (EIGHT PIECES)** Germany / 1980 / 18 × 33 each
THE EMPIRE STRIKES BACK **THEATRICAL DEKO CENTERPIECE** Germany / 1980 / 47 × 67
The large German Deko lobby display for *The Empire Strikes Back* concentrates on the characters for the most part, with a bit of hardware thrown in for good measure. The large Luke on Tauntaun poster would have likely been the centerpiece to this sizeable ensemble.

THE EMPIRE STRIKES BACK ADVANCE BANNER France / 1980 / 27 × 108
Because television stations were not permitted to advertise film releases in France, posters were one of the primary means of promotion. This large advance banner for *The Empire Strikes Back* includes artwork used on no other poster.

getting direction from Ganis on *what* to include in the poster, but not how to place the various elements. "I really don't consider this art," Jung says. "I consider it a craft. The most important thing is the concept; the execution can be done by a lot of good artists." Jung says he doesn't consider himself a stylist. "What I do is create posters that kids on the street would do if they could paint."

Jung doesn't mind being handed a concept by a studio or other client. "I tell them that it's a relief that they've given me something to develop. But when they don't give me anything, I usually come up with a half a dozen of my own ideas, hoping that one will be wonderful, two will be good, and the rest will be solid." In Jung's book, the artist, mar-

keters, advertisers, and merchandisers all have the same goal: to sell the movie. "I'm really a propagandist," he adds.

The poster the "propagandist" came up with uses a full-figure Vader with lightsaber ablaze and one hand reaching out, eight stormtroopers running and blasting away, Lando Calrissian firing his blaster, a squadron of TIE bombers, and a grouping of X-wing fighters. It cries out "Action!" Jung also did the posters for *Empire*'s rereleases in 1981 and 1982. For the 1981 poster, Vader, Luke, and Yoda loom large in the composition, focusing the central theme of the story on these three characters. The 1982 poster changed the focus to Han Solo by painting the space mercenary much larger and firing a blaster. By then, of course, Harrison Ford had become a hot box-office draw in his own right after starring in *Raiders of the Lost Ark*.

As with *Star Wars*, there were many differences in the international posters for *Empire*. Famed Japanese fantasy artist Noriyoshi Ohrai created a montage that didn't just include Lando Calrissian, it prominently featured him. Spain used the Kastel design, but painted by a different artist. German theaters sported a set of nine related posters. And in Poland, the semi-abstract poster may, or may not, represent Luke Skywalker on Hoth. ☼

THE EMPIRE STRIKES BACK THEATRICAL ADVANCE France / 1980 / 23 × 31.5
This unusual French Advance poster for *Empire* features several magazine articles touting the sequel's success in other countries.

opposite

THE EMPIRE STRIKES BACK THEATRICAL ADVANCE Japan / 1979 / 29 × 41
By 1979, Darth Vader had become so recognized the world over that no words were necessary to herald the dark lord's return in the sequel.

THE EMPIRE STRIKES BACK ADVANCE DAYBILL

Australia / 1980 / 13 × 27
This Australian Advance "daybill"—a poster size similar to the U.S. insert but on paper rather than cardstock—features the film's Force-wielding trio.

THE EMPIRE STRIKES BACK THEATRICAL ONE-SHEET

Australia / 1980 / 26.5 × 40

Enigmatic artist Noriyoshi Ohrai created a wealth of artwork for the *Star Wars* films in Japan, including the release poster for *The Empire Strikes Back*. Australia's use of the art for its one-sheet has made it one of the most sought-after posters from the international campaign.

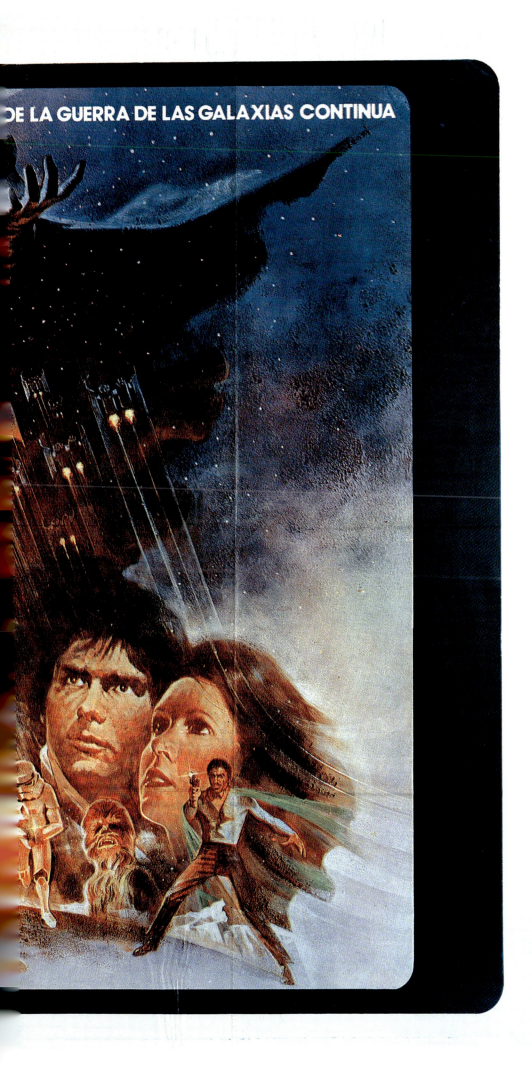

THE EMPIRE STRIKES BACK THEATRICAL TWO-SHEET

Argentina / 1980 / 42 × 58

Tom Jung's Style "B" artwork for *The Empire Strikes Back* is given a grand presence with this large two-sheet from Argentina.

THE EMPIRE STRIKES BACK THEATRICAL STYLE "B" IN CHINESE
Hong Kong / 1980 / 21.5 × 31
The bright logo and copy seem to punch up the action in this one-sheet poster from Hong Kong.

opposite
THE EMPIRE STRIKES BACK THEATRICAL STYLE "A" IN CHINESE Hong Kong / 1980 / 21.5 × 31
This busy looking but exciting version of the "Gone with the Wind" poster includes the photographic addition of Imperial Walkers, or AT-ATs.

THE EMPIRE STRIKES BACK PHOTOBUSTA Italy / 1980 / 18.5 × 26.5
The photobusta is the Italian equivalent of a U.S. lobby card. The set for *Empire* was given added class by being "framed" in silver.

opposite

THE EMPIRE STRIKES BACK THEATRICAL ONE-SHEET WITH PHOTOS
India / 1980 / 27 × 40
Noriyoshi Ohrai's lavish *Empire* artwork was used for the film's release in India, with character photos added to the composition.

***THE EMPIRE STRIKES BACK* THEATRICAL STYLE "A" WITH LANDO**
Spain / 1980 / 27.5 × 39
Empire's "romance" posters from Spain and other European countries used artwork crudely copied from Roger Kastel's elegant composition. Note the inclusion of the extra characters and hardware, which were also part of Kastel's original version.

opposite

***THE EMPIRE STRIKES BACK* THEATRICAL WITH RED CREDIT BLOCK**   Romania / 1980 / 18 × 26
Tom Jung's artwork seems to play second fiddle to the red credit block that highlights this poster from Romania, cheaply printed on newspaper stock.

THE EMPIRE STRIKES BACK THEATRICAL "IMPARATOR" Turkey / 1980 / 27 × 39
This Turkish one-sheet is notable for several reasons. The main Tom Jung art has had several additions, including an Imperial Walker and a photograph of Yoda stuck on a bit haphazardly, replacing Lando Calrissian. The Turkish title treatment is a bold one, with C-3PO and R2-D2 placed on either side.

opposite

THE EMPIRE STRIKES BACK THEATRICAL "IMPERIUM" Poland / 1982 / 26 × 38
Artist Jakub Erol produced a rather ambiguous image for Poland's release of *The Empire Strikes Back*. It's most likely a stylized Rebel Hoth trooper, . . . or an X-wing pilot, . . . or Luke Skywalker, . . . or . . . .

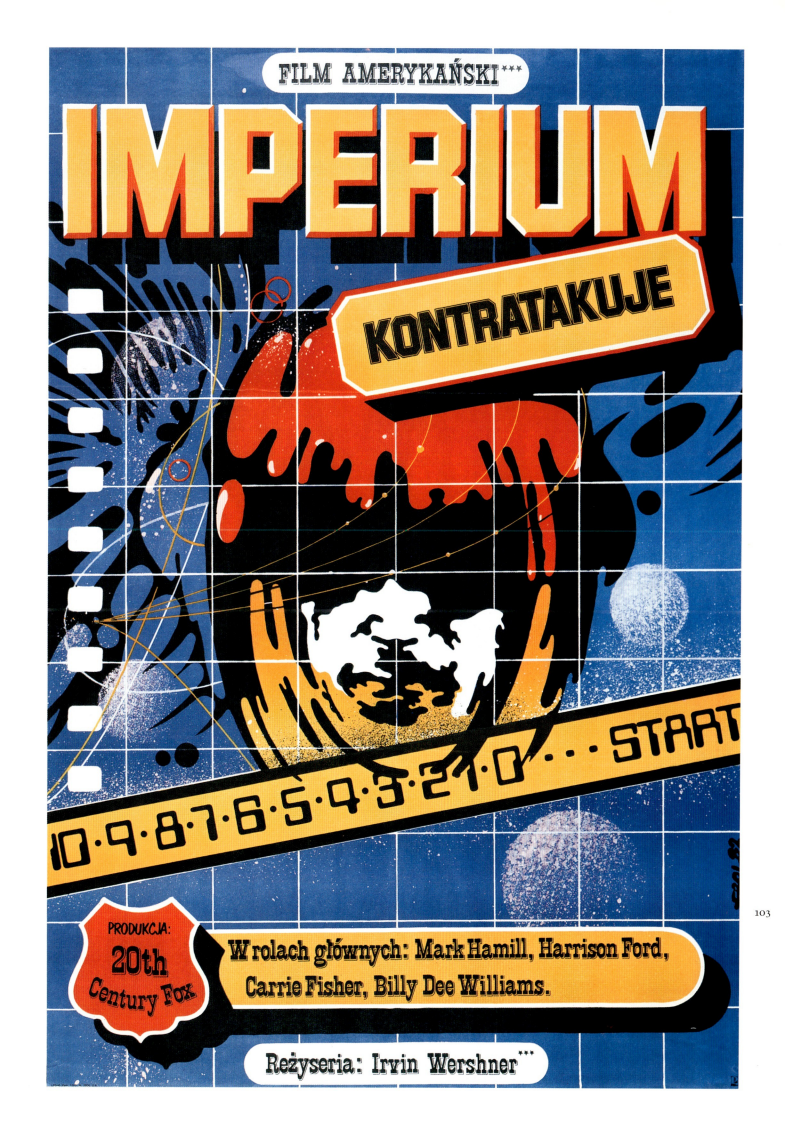

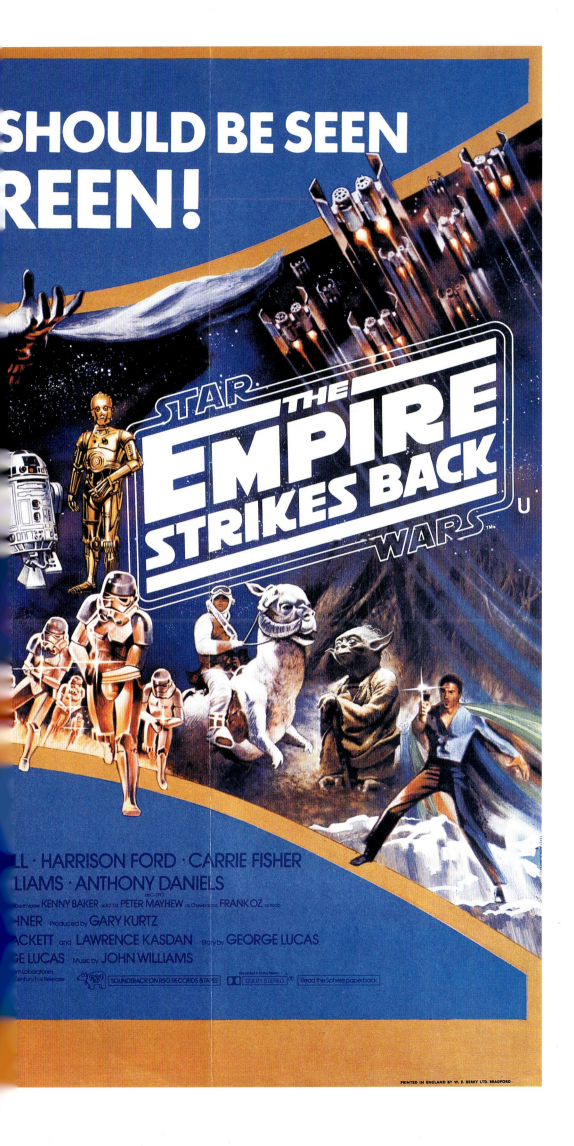

STAR WARS/EMPIRE THEATRICAL DOUBLE-BILL QUAD

United Kingdom / 1982 / 30 × 40
In May 1982, British theaters featured *Star Wars* and *The Empire Strikes Back* as a double-bill. The horizontal format of the quad lends itself well to the Cinerama-like graphic used to frame the action.

opposite

***STAR WARS/EMPIRE* THEATRICAL DOUBLE-BILL DOUBLE CROWN**
United Kingdom / 1982 / 20 × 30
This British double crown for the 1982 double-bill calls for a photo to be attached to the poster. It is part of a six-piece "Marler Haley" display used at larger British theaters.

B. DALTON DARTH VADER United States / 1980 / 22 × 28
This interesting variation on the Vader theme was a retailer's in-store promotion for books issued along with the release of *The Empire Strikes Back*.

DIXIE CUPS PROMOTIONAL
United States / 1980 / 15 × 21
American Can Company used this cartoonish art to promote Dixie Cups' tie-in with Lucasfilm. In all, the small paper cups had scores of different *Star Wars* designs.

opposite

CHRISTMAS IN THE STARS ALBUM United States / 1980 / 24 × 36
RSO promoted the *Star Wars* Christmas album with fanciful cover art by Ralph McQuarrie. The album featured that all-time favorite ditty, "What Can You Get a Wookiee for Christmas (When He Already Owns a Comb)?" as well as the tuneful stylings of Anthony Daniels (C-3PO) and the first recording of a very young Jon Bon Jovi.

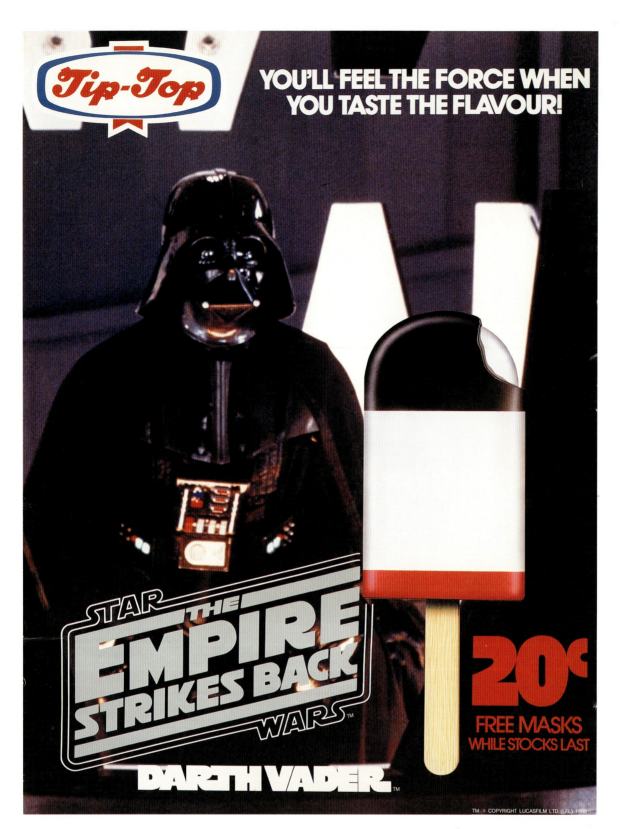

TIP-TOP VADER POPS New Zealand / 1980 / 14 × 19
Tip-Top came up with the perfect color combination for its iced treats: basic Darth black, white, and red. It's tagline was to the point, too.

opposite

BOY'S PHOTO NEWS TRANSIT AD Japan / 1980 / 21 × 30
This transit ad for Boy's Photo News touted the magazine's coverage of *The Empire Strikes Back*.

少年写真新聞 ★BOY'S PHOTO NEWS★
少年写真ニュース No.853 1980年7月8日号
株式会社 少年写真新聞社

映像が描きだした未知の世界

宇宙にうかぶ未知の惑星を「スター・ウォーズ/帝国の逆襲」で見てみましょう

日本十進分類法(NDC) 芸術 映画 778

広い宇宙の中には、わたしたちの想像をはるかにこえる科学文明をもった惑星があると、考えられています。

宇宙には、何億もの星が、地球の誕生以前からあり、科学の進んだ惑星もあると思われます。
「スター・ウォーズ/帝国の逆襲」には未知の惑星のようすや、宇宙の生物の活躍するさまを、想像力ゆたかにえがいています。

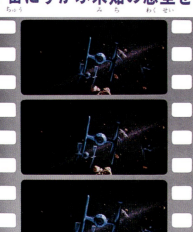

宇宙船といん石の特撮シーン。

全体を、一つの宇宙船のように作り変えられた惑星。

超能力をそなえた生物のいる惑星。

地球では考えられないような、さまざまな科学メカも生みだされているでしょう。

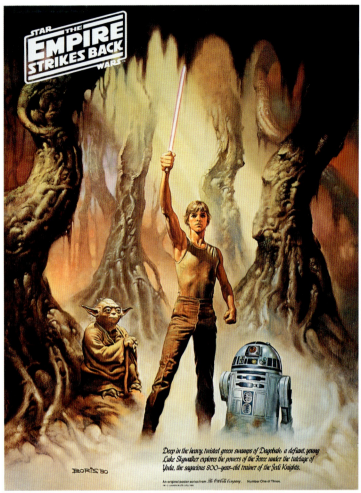
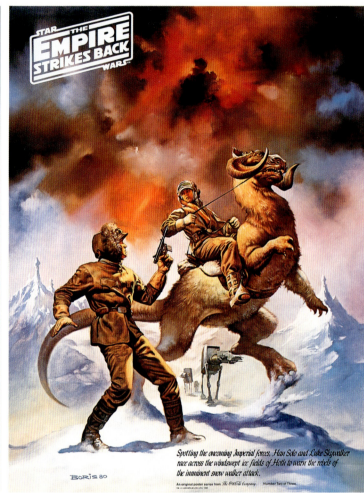
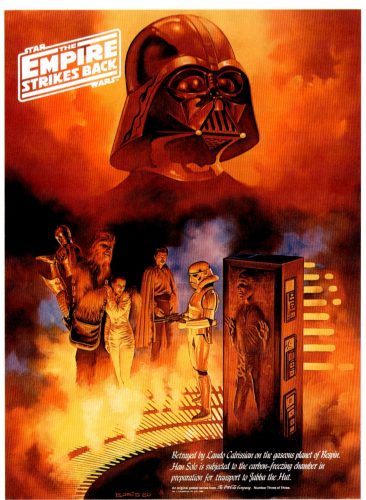

above left

COCA-COLA: LUKE AND YODA
United States / 1980 / 18 × 24

above right

COCA-COLA: LUKE ON TAUNTAUN
United States / 1980 / 18 × 24

left

COCA-COLA: HAN IN CARBON FREEZE
United States / 1980 / 18 × 24
This threesome by famous fantasy artist Boris Vallejo was available with purchase at Burger King restaurants in 1980.

opposite

BORIS VALLEJO PROMOTIONAL IN-THEATER
United States / 1980 / 24 × 33
Long before Anakin Skywalker (who would become Darth Vader) dueled with two lightsabers in *Attack of the Clones*, Boris Vallejo gave Vader a pair of light swords to cross over the heroes in this theater-sales Coca-Cola exclusive from 1980.

NATIONAL PUBLIC RADIO *STAR WARS* PROMOTIONAL

United States / 1981 / 17 × 29

Sharp-eyed fans might notice that both of the TIE fighters in this illustration by Celia Strain appear to be flying backwards. The poster was sent to National Public Radio stations across the country for customizing with their call letters and spot on the dial. The NPR broadcast of thirteen episodes of an expanded *Star Wars* radio drama was a huge success.

NATIONAL PUBLIC RADIO *THE EMPIRE STRIKES BACK*

United States / 1982 / 17 × 28

NPR was tight with the number of posters per station to promote its *The Empire Strikes Back* radio series, although more were made available to the public through donation drives. Ralph McQuarrie says that his pensive Yoda portrait originally was commissioned for a book cover but also became the basis of this poster.

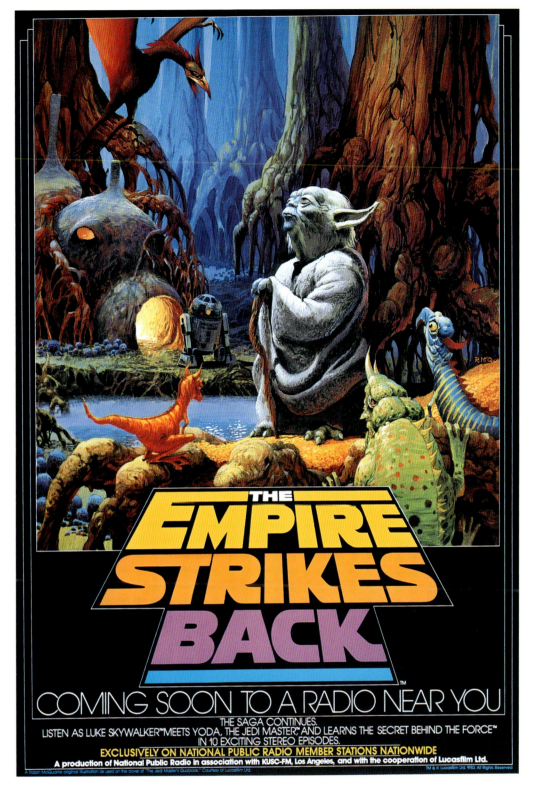

NATIONAL PUBLIC RADIO *EMPIRE ADVANCE*

United States / 1982 / 10 × 22

Although Ralph McQuarrie provided the artwork for the regular NPR *Empire* poster, Celia Strain's black-and-white Yoda illustration also found limited distribution as an Advance poster.

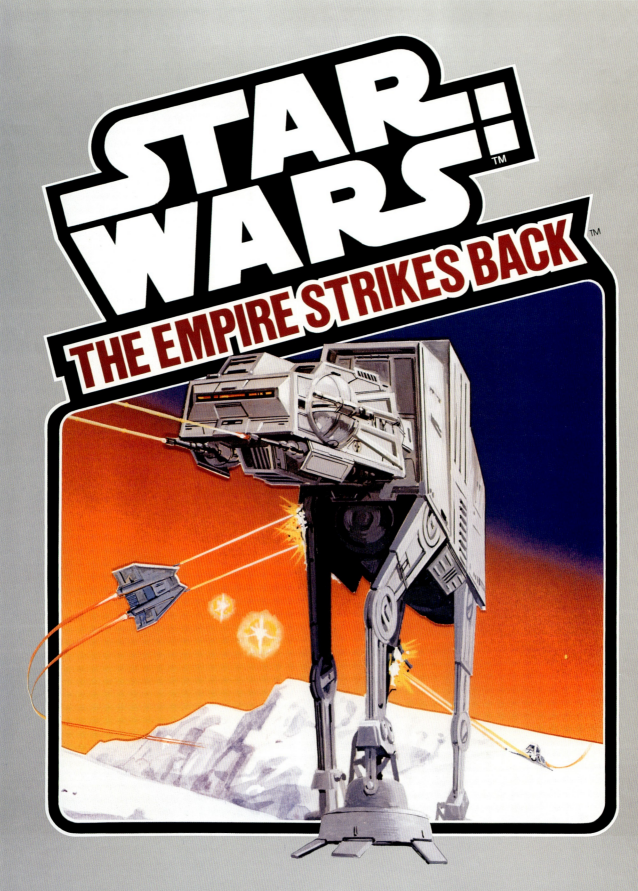

STAR WARS ON CED FROM RCA United States / 1982 / 28 × 40
RCA used a free *Star Wars* video disc to promote its patented CED video disc player, a challenge to the laser disc system. The CED system didn't last long.

opposite

THE EMPIRE STRIKES BACK VIDEO GAME United States / 1982 / 23 × 36
This 1982 poster to promote *The Empire Strikes Back* video game cartridge was the first in a long line to use the AT-ATs and snowspeeders to attract gamers.

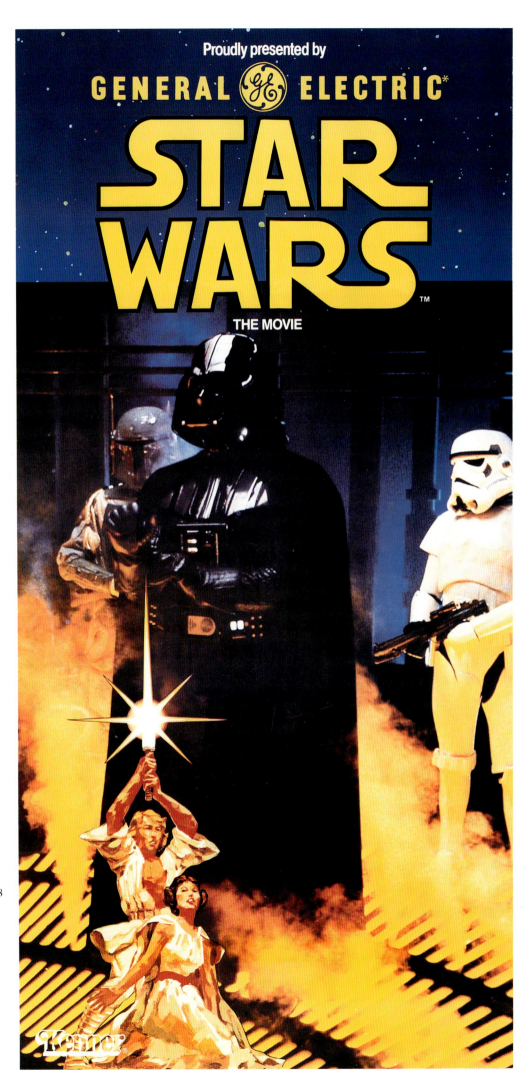

left
GE PRESENTS *STAR WARS* ON TELEVISION
Australia / 1982 / 18 × 36
General Electric of Australia promoted its sponsorship of the first television showing of the original *Star Wars* in 1982 (although it used a photo from *The Empire Strikes Back*). One lucky family of four could win a trip to the United States to see the world premiere of Episode VI, then titled *Revenge of the Jedi*.

opposite
CINCINNATI POPS CONCERT
United States / 1982 / 18 × 28
A 1982 *Star Wars* concert seemed a natural for Cincinnati, since major *Star Wars* licensee Kenner Products was then based there. "Juggling, bullwhip demonstrations, mime performances and star shows" could all be witnessed at this one-night concert conducted by Erich Kunzel. Even the Dark Lord of the Sith himself was scheduled to make a cameo appearance.

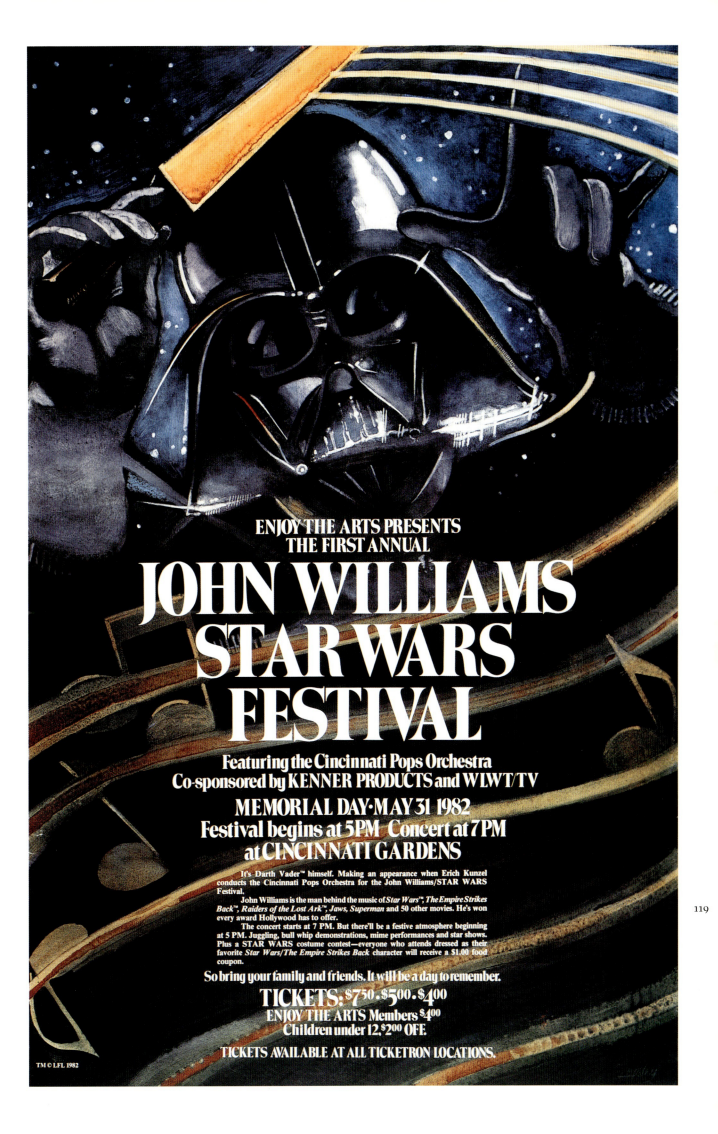

RETURN OF THE JEDI

REVENGE OF THE JEDI **THEATRICAL ADVANCE ONE-SHEET WITH DATE**
United States / 1982 / 27 × 41
The *Revenge of the Jedi* Advance poster has attracted more notoriety than perhaps any other modern-day film poster. There was huge media attention paid to the movie's change of title—from *Revenge* to *Return*—and to the fact that a sheet of paper for an upcoming film could shoot up in price overnight from $10 to $200, which seemed like a revival of the Gold Rush.

For all its attributes, the third *Star Wars* film was destined to be known to fans as the movie of many names.

While *The Empire Stikes Back* was a very successful film both at the box office and with many reviewers and fans, it didn't sell nearly as many tickets as the original *Star Wars*, which had added the tags of "Episode IV" and *"A New Hope"* for its April 1981 rerelease. Since both *Empire* and the upcoming third movie were financed totally by George Lucas and his wholly owned Lucasfilm Ltd., the clear goal of the company's marketers was to surpass the total brought in by *Empire*.

Legally, the company making the film was incorporated as Chapter III Productions Ltd. Then, when filming moved to the United States from England, the production adopted an alias. To put fans off the scent—and to make sure suppliers didn't jack up prices because it was a *Star Wars* movie—it assumed the cover name of "Blue Harvest," which had the tagline: Horror Beyond Imagination. The real name of the film underwent significant changes, too.

"George first told me the movie's name, and that title was *Return of the Jedi*," remembers *Jedi* producer Howard Kazanjian. "I said, 'George, I think it's a weak title.' He came back within a week or less, and said, 'OK, make it *Revenge of the Jedi*.'"

In the autumn of 1982, happy with what he too felt was a stronger title, head of Lucasfilm marketing Sid Ganis approached artist Drew Struzan, who was then at Pencil Pushers Inc., to design a teaser poster for *Revenge of the Jedi*. Opting for a spare but bold composition, Struzan designed what would become one of the most recognizable *Star Wars* poster images ever created. There was an elegant simplicity to it, and "part of the reason was that I didn't have a lot of materials to work with," Struzan confesses. " I didn't know what the story was, I hadn't seen the film, and I hadn't read the script. I probably had only a couple of stills, and I used what I had to come up with something strong."

Selecting photographic references that actually were from *Empire,* Struzan began with Darth Vader's helmet as the primary compositional element. "I just had a big solarized Photostat [an overexposed black-and-white copy] made up poster-size, and painted on top of that," he says. "I added the color, more texture, and painted the two figures [Luke and Vader engaged in a lightsaber battle] at the bottom."

The bold use of red was an unexpected change for a *Star Wars* poster, setting it apart from the cool hues that had predominated in all previous theatrical posters. "It suggested that you were going to see something new and fresh and different," says Ganis. For a third movie, "That's what we were after."

Once the artwork left Struzan's studio for the printer, the poster's history becomes a bit hazy. A transparency of the artwork was said to have been delivered to the printer locked to the wrist of a courier, and batches of fifty at a time were rolled in long boxes marked "Blue Harvest" to discourage pilfering.

THE REVENGE OF THE JEDI TEASER ONE SHEET

left
REVENGE OF THE JEDI THEATRICAL ADVANCE ONE-SHEET WITHOUT DATE
United States / 1982 / 27 × 41
When posters were prematurely distributed exhibiting the *Revenge* logo, two versions emerged from the print house—most dated for a May 25 premiere, and others without a date. Establishing concrete facts regarding the so-called dateless *Revenge* poster has been elusive at best. According to Bill Moss, a pressman for printer Gore Graphics at the time, the dateless version was actually printed concurrently with the dated one, separated only by the amount of time it took to "reverse out" the copy to create new plates. Far fewer of the undated versions were ordered, resulting in the variation's heightened status among poster collectors.

opposite
RETURN OF THE JEDI STYLE "A" THEATRICAL ONE-SHEET
United States / 1983 / 27 × 41
Tim Reamer's iconic lightsaber image for the *Return of the Jedi* Style "A" poster was used extensively both at home and abroad in 1983 and was resurrected in a new guise for 1995's international video campaign.

Ultimately deciding that "revenge" did not befit a Jedi, Lucas decided to reinstate his original title, *Return of the Jedi*. Toy and other licensees were quietly told of the name change at the beginning of December 1982. Fox, for some reason, was apparently unaware of the change at that time, so the studio forged ahead with its Christmas campaign and sent out hundreds of *Revenge* posters to its district offices nationwide for distribution to theaters. It apparently wasn't until weeks later that Fox, and the public, learned of the title change.

Sandy Rivkin, who was a sales representative at the time for Gore Graphics, which printed most of the *Star Wars* posters for the first trilogy, remembers the day the word came down to stop shipping the *Revenge* posters. "I read in the newspaper that

RETURN OF THE JEDI STYLE B ONE SHEET

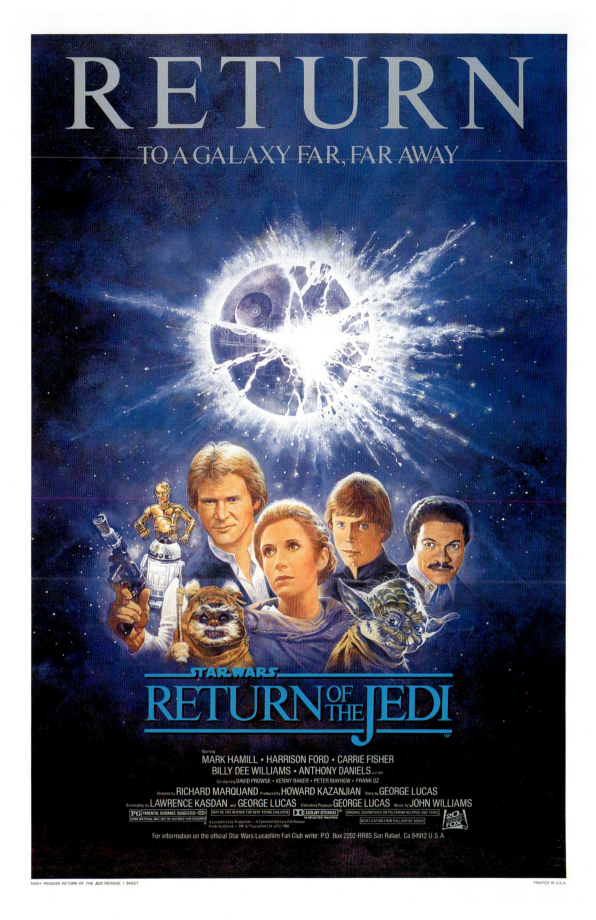

***RETURN OF THE JEDI* 1985 RERELEASE ONE-SHEET** United States / 1985 / 27 × 41
A tamer poster image was used for *Jedi*'s 1985 rerelease, quietly focusing on the characters of the saga. Apparently, based on this art, the Empire had been more successful in completing the second Death Star than we had imagined! The art is by Tom Jung.

opposite
***RETURN OF THE JEDI* STYLE "B" THEATRICAL ONE-SHEET** United States / 1983 / 27 × 41
Kazuhiko Sano's visceral portrait of Luke punched up the energy of the *Return of the Jedi* poster campaign.

they were going to change the name, and sure enough that morning I got a call that they didn't want us to ship any more of them." Published accounts at the time suggested that Lucasfilm had descended on a warehouse to personally supervise the destruction of all remaining *Revenge* posters, a scenario that turned out to be true. "They sent somebody down here to watch us destroy the balance," adds Rivkin. "We took the posters, put them in the cutter, and then knifed them."

A story in the *Los Angeles Times* reported that *Revenge* posters on the black market had soared to $200 each. For lucky members of the Official *Star Wars* Fan Club, however, 6,800 pristine examples had been reserved by Lucasfilm and went on sale to members for the bargain price of just $9.50. They sold out in three days.

To launch the actual release of *Return of the Jedi* in theaters, the design team of Melanie Paykos and Rio Phior were contracted to submit ideas for what would become the *Jedi* Style "A" poster. Having left successful careers at Lucasfilm to open their own design studio, both were intimately familiar with the saga's narrative and texture. "The story almost has a religious undertone," says Paykos of *Jedi*. "I don't think it was deliberate, but it kind of had that feeling."

Phior remembers the original direction proposed by Sid Ganis. "He said 'I'm looking for something that's basically not prose but poetry, you know, one symbol that sums up all of what the movies represent: the Force, victory over darkness, and a bit of something mystical, something kind of spiritual.'"

The Jedi lightsaber quickly emerged as the logical choice. The "cross" first introduced in Tom Jung's *Star Wars* poster was reincorporated to visually bridge the three films of the saga. "It was intentional," Phior remembers. "The original direction was to sum up all three films in one kind of poetic symbol."

Tim Reamer, then a freelance illustrator who had been contacted by Paykos, admits he wasn't satisfied with the first comps he did. "It had all the characters running around doing stuff," says Reamer. "You know, montages; I just can't do them." Focusing instead on the lightsaber, he submitted a sketch without the actors, which he unexpectedly found to his liking. "I think it was the fact that it was pristine, that it didn't have a whole army in the background.

RETURN OF THE JEDI ADVANCE QUAD
United Kingdom / 1983 / 30 × 40
Drew Struzan's *Revenge* artwork was used on the early 1983 British quad, but with the correct title attached. This particular poster was also printed with different licensee names to cross-promote the film in retailers' windows.

STAR WARS
RETURN OF THE JEDI

IN YOUR GALAXY SOON

I like it. I think it's beautiful. Even if someone else had done the illustration, it's a good concept."

With a handful of comps, the design team turned to some of the visual effects cameramen at Industrial Light & Magic to enhance their slide presentation to Lucas. "Our concepts were composited so that all the lightsabers glowed and all the stars glowed," recounts Paykos. "We wanted to incorporate into our presentation some of the aspects of how they actually made the film."

The artistry and dazzling presentation by Paykos/Phior won out. Lucas approved but insisted on one addition. A small Death Star was added "as an element of conflict," suggests Phior. "It represents darkness and the sword represents light. I thought it was a brilliant suggestion."

To get the correct position for the hands holding the lightsaber, Lucas ended up lending his own to the cause. "Sid [Ganis] came down with two or three temp posters, and George didn't like the hands," remembers Kazanjian. "We were in the editing room, which was right next door to ILM, and I said 'Come on over, we're going to take a picture of you holding the lightsaber.' So he held the lightsaber up, we took the picture, and gave

it to Sid. Those are George's hands." Reamer says that the final illustration was a composite of Lucas' hands and those of a friend.

With the film's release looming near, Reamer was required to complete the finished artwork in a week. "It was a lot of fun, it was exciting, but it was a crash program," says Reamer. "It was very difficult to do, even though it's not that complex a layout. It's all airbrush—not one brush stroke in it. It was an intense time."

Several weeks after the Style "A" poster opened *Jedi*, the campaign introduced its first montage poster. Christopher Werner, who had replaced Rio Phior as art director after she'd left Lucasfilm, sought out an old colleague from his days at the publisher Harcourt Brace. Kazuhiko (Kazu) Sano, who had done some freelance textbook illustration for Werner, had previously done a 1982 trade ad taken out by Lucas to publicly congratulate Steven Spielberg for outgrossing *Star Wars* at the box office with his *E.T. The Extra-Terrestrial*. In it, Sano depicted the *Star Wars* troupe lifting E.T. on their shoulders in a triumphant pose. Remembering the success of the ad, Werner asked Sano to produce a poster image for *Jedi*.

RETURN OF THE JEDI THEATRICAL QUAD
United Kingdom / 1983 / 27 × 40
Artist Josh Kirby painted a sweeping montage exclusively for the British release of *Return of the Jedi*. Kirby is best known to science fiction fans for his cover paintings of Terry Pratchett's *Discworld* novels. This version has been trimmed for the London Underground.

"My agent called and said there was a job offer from Lucasfilm," Sano remembers. "I thought that it was just for some kind of retail poster." Happy to oblige nonetheless, Sano set to work on the composition. "There wasn't any special art direction when I started out," says Sano. "I looked at it and something had to be really exciting—with energy and force."

After submitting several black-and-white sketches and character studies, it was decided that Sano's character montage fit what the campaign was after. One request: portray Leia as the slave girl in Jabba's palace. There wasn't any request to include the droids, which makes the Style "B" one of the few U.S. theatrical Star Wars posters to lack their likenesses.

Sano had scheduled a three-week trip to Japan just after submitting the final artwork. A few last-minute refinements were requested by Werner, which Sano was able to complete just under the wire. As soon as he left, however, Lucasfilm decided that the depiction of Lando Calrissian was too small.

To make the adjustment in Sano's absence, Werner contacted artist Bunny Carter, who would later illustrate several children's books and greeting cards for Lucasfilm. Unfortunately, the original reference photo Sano had used could not be located. "Lucasfilm couldn't find anything because I used a very small picture and even flipped it," Sano says. Upon his return, he painted a correction to enlarge Lando yet a third time, but not before Carter's version had been sent out for use internationally.

"Chris told me that he had to submit it for some country, and it had to be done very quickly," notes Sano. "They couldn't wait until I came back." Consequently, the posters released in Japan and some other Asian countries feature a reduced likeness of Lando.

For Jedi's 1985 rerelease, Sano again was asked to submit several comps, one of which would eventually be printed years later for the film's tenth anniversary. Ultimately, however, the campaign would come full circle by returning to Tom Jung.

"The last one was being done by someone else," recalls Jung. "My family asked, 'How come you're not doing this?' so I contacted Sid Ganis." The marketing chief gave Jung a chance to illustrate the final poster for the classic trilogy, making him the only artist involved with all three films. Having already settled on the poster's design, however, Fox

RETURN OF THE JEDI REVISED THEATRICAL QUAD

United Kingdom / 1983 / 30 × 40
For the second version of the *Jedi* montage quad, changes were made to add an Ewok and to relate more stylistically to the U.S. Style "B" poster by Kazu Sano.

opposite
**RETURN OF THE JEDI
HONG KONG TRANSIT**
Hong Kong / 1983 / 21.5 × 31
This rare and very busy-looking transit station poster from Hong Kong features a soft drink promotion that includes gliders, space shuttles, and *Star Wars* vehicles as prizes.

right
**RETURN OF THE JEDI
THEATRICAL ADVANCE
ONE-SHEET**
Germany / 1983 / 23 × 33
Often mistaken for a triple-bill advertisement, this German poster touts *Return of the Jedi* by noting the record-breaking attendance for its two predecessors.

and Lucasfilm only required Jung to illustrate it. "They sent a guy from Lucasfilm to stand over my shoulder as I painted . . . until I got it the way they wanted it," Jung says.

The release of *Jedi* internationally produced a number of different artwork campaigns. As in the United States, Japan began advertising early, incorporating the English *"Revenge"* logo on the first teaser poster in late 1982. Additionally, Noriyoshi Ohrai, who had produced stunning artwork for the previous two films in Japan, created a formally composed image of the droids before a hot nebula sky as a limited commercial poster.

Michel Jouin's artwork for the French release successfully employed the production color scheme of *Jedi* in his composition, from the verdant greens of Endor to the warm hues of the Tatooine desert. In Poland, where *Jedi* was released in 1984, artist Witold Dybowski provided two different images, including an unforgettable portrait of Vader's helmet exploding into fragments of . . . camera parts!

opposite
RETURN OF THE JEDI DEKO DISPLAY F (BANNER) Germany / 1983 / 16 × 47

below, left to right
RETURN OF THE JEDI THEATRICAL DEKO DISPLAY B (VADER) Germany / 1983 / 16 × 34
RETURN OF THE JEDI THEATRICAL DEKO DISPLAY C (LUKE & LEIA) Germany / 1983 / 16 × 34
RETURN OF THE JEDI THEATRICAL DEKO DISPLAY A (LOGOS) Germany / 1983 / 16 × 34
RETURN OF THE JEDI DEKO DISPLAY E (YODA & HEROES) Germany / 1983 / 16 × 34
RETURN OF THE JEDI THEATRICAL DEKO DISPLAY D (GAMORREAN GUARD) Germany / 1983 / 16 × 34
Keeping with tradition, Germany created a lavish lobby Deko display for *Return of the Jedi*, featuring the cast of characters amid columns of raised lightsabers.

STAR WARSシリーズ第3弾⇒エピソード完結篇！

STAR WARS
REVENGE OF THE JEDI

スター・ウォーズ
ジェダイの復讐

いよいよ今夏《東宝系》一斉ロードショー！　20世紀FOX映画

***RETURN OF THE JEDI* THEATRICAL PHOTOCOLLAGE** Japan / 1983 / 29 × 41
Japan occasionally turned the traditionally vertical poster format on its side to present a design more effectively.

opposite

***REVENGE OF THE JEDI* LOGO THEATRICAL ADVANCE**

Japan / 1982 / 29 × 41

Outside of the United States, one of the few countries to use the *Revenge of the Jedi* title on early Advance posters was Japan. This version is far more scarce than the American poster. Japan is also the only country where *Revenge of the Jedi* remained the movie's title, as translated into Japanese.

England ultimately produced three posters for *Jedi,* starting with a reformatted version of Struzan's *"Revenge"* art but with the *"Return"* title. Following the U.S. lead of switching to blue for the second poster, Josh Kirby produced a stylish pastiche of characters and scenes. A second version, which tightened up the array of portraits in Kirby's poster, includes the addition of an Ewok and the removal of several elements.

England was also the first country to stage a triple-bill presentation of the trilogy in 1983; the campaign's poster showed art from all three films. Italy, Australia, Germany, and the United States would follow with their own triple bills in 1985, each accompanied by a new poster.

The U.S. presentations, which were to benefit the Corporation for Public Broadcasting, were limited to just eight venues; there was a ninth in Canada. Because of the limited release, only two posters were allotted to each theater, each with venue-specific information. These were printed on photographic paper instead of the traditional coated paper stock, since printing presses would have been required to run off several hundred copies of each. So while these are probably the least attractive of all *Star Wars* theatrical posters, they are among the most rare. One example changed hands a few years ago for around $6,000.

A year after *Jedi*'s release, the first of two Ewok movies, *The Ewok Adventure,* was released as a TV movie in the United States and in movie theaters abroad. For affiliate stations of the ABC Network, an extremely limited poster featuring artwork by Sano was printed with the date and time of the broadcast. This same artwork was enlarged to one-sheet size and printed as an international release poster along with a Style "B" version illustrated by Drew Struzan. For the international release, the title was expanded to *Caravan of Courage: An Ewok Adventure.* Most of the print run for both were sold through the *Star Wars* Fan Club that year.

In some countries, such as Germany, original art was commissioned for the film, including a large horizontal two-sheet and a pair of unusual smaller posters featuring full-figure paintings of an Ewok on each. Japan, ahead of the photomontage trend, printed an unusual poster prominently featuring the villainous Gorax behind the heroes, probably to emulate the looming Vader figure of the *Star Wars* poster tradition.

In 1985, a second Ewok feature, *Battle for Endor,* aired on ABC domestically and also was released

left
RETURN OF THE JEDI THEATRICAL STYLE "B" WITH SMALL-HEAD LANDO
Japan / 1983 / 20 × 29
Japan printed Kazu Sano's *Return of the Jedi* artwork before the artist had a chance to enlarge the depiction of Lando Calrissian.

opposite
RETURN OF THE JEDI THEATRICAL: EXPLODING VADER HEAD
Poland / 1984 / 26.5 × 38
Polish artist Witold Dybowski incorporated photographs of camera parts into the composition of his explosive Darth Vader portrait. Ironically, because of the unrest in Poland at the time, the artist didn't see *Return of the Jedi* until three years after he had finished the painting.

theatrically in selected international markets. Far fewer posters were created for the second Ewok adventure, with a U.S. version missing in action until the video release five years later. Germany used original imagery the second time around too, this time created by well-known Italian illustrator Renato Casaro. Japan again opted for photomontage, focusing on the cuteness of young Cindel Towani, the young girl who was the central human character of the story. New Zealand renamed the feature *Ewoks and the Marauders of Endor* and used the same artwork by Berrett that would be chosen for the U.S. video campaign in 1990.

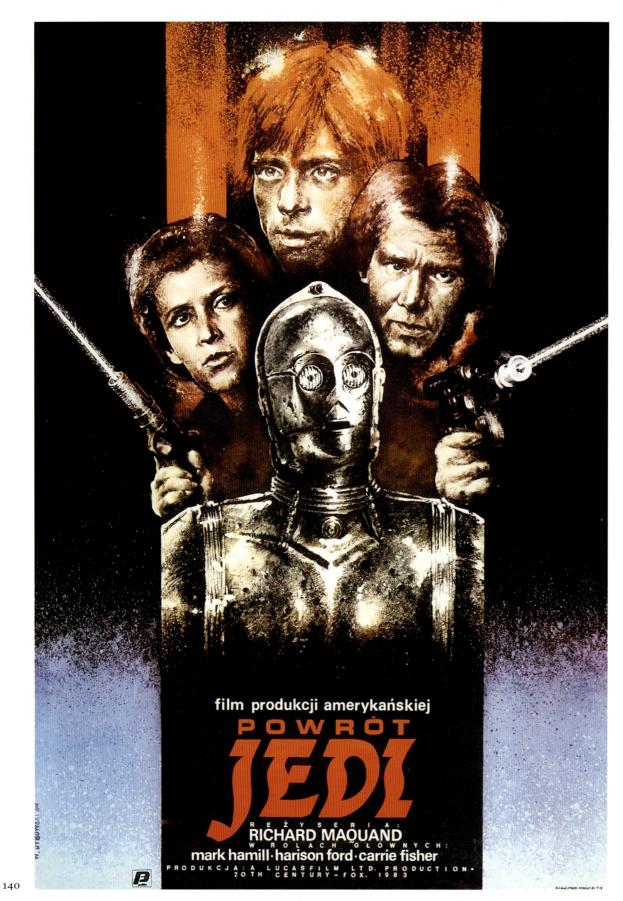

***RETURN OF THE JEDI* THEATRICAL: HEROES** Poland / 1984 / 26.5 × 38
In addition to the Darth Vader poster, Witold Dybowski also illustrated an uncharacteristically literal poster for *Jedi*'s Polish release in 1984. But what's C-3PO doing at the center of the composition?

opposite

***RETURN OF THE JEDI* THEATRICAL ONE-SHEET** Hungary / 1984 / 16 × 22
Hungary joined Russia and Poland with a set of abstract posters produced for the original trilogy. The *Return of the Jedi* poster, which includes a green alien probably light years away from the *Star Wars* galaxy, was the only full-color illustration produced for a first release. Those created for *Star Wars* and *Empire* were printed in monotone; they were colored for a rerelease. Notice the Death Star as Darth Vader's eye.

***STAR WARS/EMPIRE/JEDI* TRIPLE-BILL THEATRICAL QUAD**

United Kingdom / 1983 / 30 × 40

England's triple-bill poster actually incorporates elements from four different *Star Wars* posters, including the addition of Yoda.

***STAR WARS/EMPIRE/JEDI* TRIPLE-BILL THEATRICAL ONE-SHEET** United States / 1985 / 27 × 41
The plainest theatrical poster is also among the rarest. Since Fox needed only two posters for each of the nine theaters showing the triple-bill in a one-time charity performance, and the information had to be theater-specific, these posters are photo blow-ups and not printed. This is one of the originals that was posted at the Continental Theater in Denver. A widely sold bootleg, which *is* printed, is easily spotted. The bootlegger used as his model the newspaper ad—which had only two lines of type at the top—instead of the actual poster, which has three.

opposite
***STAR WARS/EMPIRE/JEDI* TRIPLE-BILL ONE-SHEET** Australia / 1985 / 27 × 40
Although Australia's triple-bill poster received a mostly black-and-white treatment, the silver pyramid-shaped logos lend it some compositional weight.

Protest gegen „Krieg der Sterne"
Düsseldorfer Nachrichten

Kritik an Frankreichs «Star Wars»-Relativierung
Neue Zürcher Zeitung

Kampfsterne und Killersatelliten: Wird das All zum Kriegsschauplatz der Zukunft?
Neue Presse

Ein Kriegsfilm – auch für Friedensfreunde
Welt am Sonntag

Im Kreml sieht man nur noch Sterne
Frankfurter Allgemeine

Der „Krieg der Sterne" macht Amerika in Genf nach
Stuttgarter Zeitung

„Kein Krieg der Sterne"
Sonntag Aktuell

Gewaltig: Blitze aus der Laserwaffe
Neue Presse

Reagan hält an US-Weltraumwaffen fest
Die Welt

„Der Sieg im Weltraum ist möglich"
Der Spiegel

Krieg der Sterne – nicht so weit entfernt?
Stuttgarter Zeitung

Den KRIEG DER STERNE sollte man dem Kino überlassen:

Ein Film von George Lucas

opposite
STAR WARS / EMPIRE / JEDI TRIPLE-BILL THEATRICAL
Germany / 1985 / 23 × 33
For Germany's triple-bill presentation, separate posters—all exactly the same except for the movie logos—were created for each film in the classic trilogy, each plastered with the day's headlines about President Ronald Reagan's proposed Strategic Defense Initiative, called the "Star Wars" defense system by its detractors. The German poster's sentiment: Better on the screen than in the skies.

STAR WARS / EMPIRE / JEDI TRIPLE-BILL STACKED ART
France / 1985 / 23 × 62
France advertised its triple-bill presentation by stacking the trilogy's artwork in a door poster.

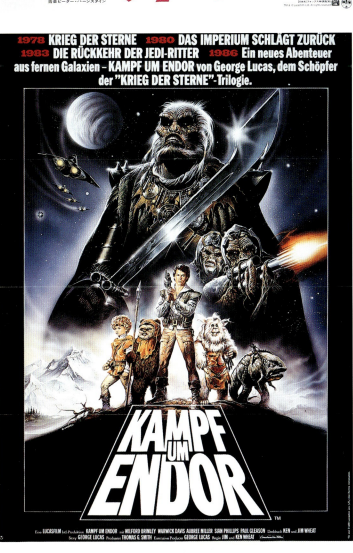

clockwise, from top left

CARAVAN OF COURAGE INTERNATIONAL STYLE "A" ONE-SHEET

United States / 1984 / 27 × 41

Taking the Ewoks from *Return of the Jedi,* Lucasfilm produced two movies that aired first on television in the United States but played on the big screen in major international markets. In Kazu Sano's *Caravan of Courage* artwork, irises were added to the Ewoks' eyes to "make them more expressive," according to the artist.

CARAVAN OF COURAGE INTERNATIONAL STYLE "B" ONE-SHEET

United States / 1984 / 27 × 41

Drew Struzan created a dynamic composition for the Style "B" version of the *Caravan of Courage* poster.

CARAVAN OF COURAGE THEATRICAL MONTAGE

Japan / 1984 / 20 × 29

Japan relied on the tried-and-true photomontage method to promote *Caravan of Courage.*

MARAUDERS OF ENDOR THEATRICAL ONE-SHEET

New Zealand / 1986 / 27 × 40

New Zealand released the second Ewok adventure under the title *Ewoks and the Marauders of Endor.*

BATTLE FOR ENDOR THEATRICAL ONE-SHEET

Germany / 1986 / 23 × 33

The evil Gorax occupies a large part of the German poster for *Battle for Endor* by Renato Casaro. Leading little lady "Cindel Towani" is tiny by comparison.

CARAVAN OF COURAGE THEATRICAL BY ROB

Germany / 1985 / 47 × 66

Germany produced numerous pieces of exclusive artwork for *Caravan of Courage,* including this large two-sheet by artist Rob.

IMMUNIZATION PROMOTIONAL Australia / 1983 / 15 × 20 and 40 × 59
Let's hope the children of earth got the message from their parents, via this unusual poster from the Australian Minister for Health. Lucasfilm has allowed *Star Wars* characters to be used in a variety of public service campaigns across the world.

YODA "READ" POSTER United States / 1983 / 22 × 34
This quietly elegant poster of Yoda with a book was first distributed by the American Library Association in April 1983 and has remained in production for more than twenty years because of its popularity.

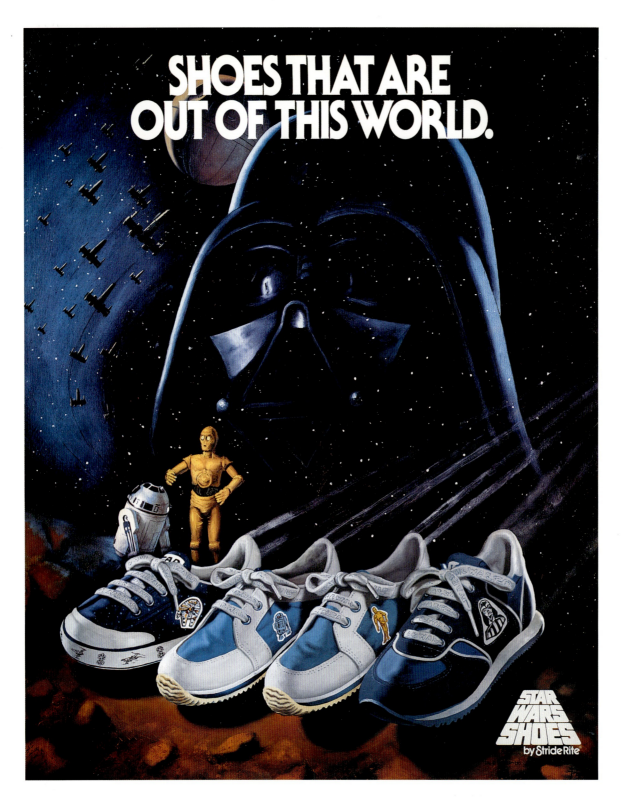

STRIDE-RITE SHOES United States / 1983 / 22 × 28
Taking a cue from Tom Jung's original *Star Wars* poster, Stride-Rite used kids' shoes instead of spacecraft. Poor R2-D2 seems to be frightened and has turned around to scoot away.

opposite
ATARI *STAR WARS* VIDEO ARCADE United States / 1983 / 20 × 30
The first *Star Wars* coin-operated arcade game pushed its then state-of-the-art vector graphics technology on this poster from Atari.

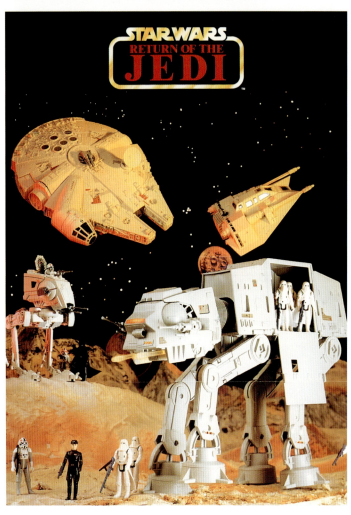

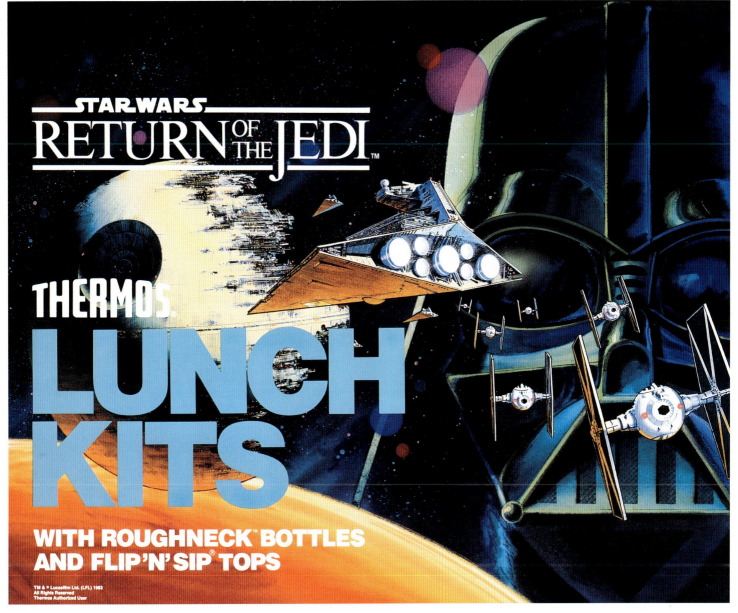

***RETURN OF THE JEDI* LUNCH KIT**
United States / 1983 / 16 × 20
Gene Lemery's artwork for the *Return of the Jedi* Thermos Lunch Kit was also used as an in-store poster.

opposite, top
PEPPERIDGE FARM COOKIES United States / 1983 / 18 × 27
Lucasfilm finally made good on the obvious "Wookiee Cookies" with these Pepperidge Farm goodies from 1983. In chocolate, vanilla, and peanut butter, they were in the shape of *Star Wars* characters.

opposite, far left
KENNER VEHICLES Germany / 1983 / 23 × 33
Many of the international toy pack-in catalogs were printed in the form of fold-out posters, such as this one from Germany.

opposite, left
KENNER/COKE THEATER CONTEST United States / 1985 / 18 × 24
To *Star Wars* memorabilia collectors, this poster has everything going for it. The contest offers the rare Power of the Force line of figures as a prize, and it also features the extremely hard to find Huffy Speeder Bike prize. There is even a Coca-Cola cross-promotion in this theater-exclusive display.

left

DARTH VADER DOOR POSTER

United States / 1983 / 11.5 × 23.5

Darth Vader became a door man for an unusually tall poster from Sales Corp. of America. This smaller promo for the poster itself measures in at just under two feet.

opposite, top

RETURN OF THE JEDI COLLECTOR CUPS

Canada / 1983 / 25 × 38

This Coca-Cola promotion for frozen soft drinks and the collectible plastic cups they came in uses an image of Darth Vader that makes him look a little like a hulking Neanderthal.

opposite, right

ATARI JEDI ARENA GAME

United States / 1983 / 23 × 36

The artwork lavished on the 1983 Jedi Arena Game poster far surpassed the clumsy graphics featured in the game itself.

opposite, far right

DRAWING BOARD GREETING CARDS

United States / 1983 / 20.5 × 30

The excitement for Drawing Board actually started in 1978 with an extensive line of *Star Wars* greeting cards, gift wrap, and party supplies.

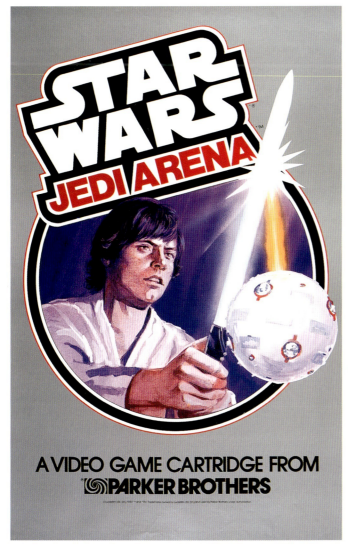

right

PETERS ICE POPS WITH JEDI JELLY

Australia / 1983 / 16.5 × 22.5

Who could possibly resist these colorful ice popsicles filled with the ubiquitous Jedi Jelly? Not Australian youngsters, who were also enticed by the chance to win *Star Wars* toys and other goodies.

opposite

TIP-TOP WITH JEDI JELLY New Zealand / 1983 / 12 × 19.5

Wow, kids! Green-yellow-red ice popsicles stuffed with Jedi Jelly! What more could you want from Tip-Top, except perhaps all four cool Ewok stickers buyers could collect.

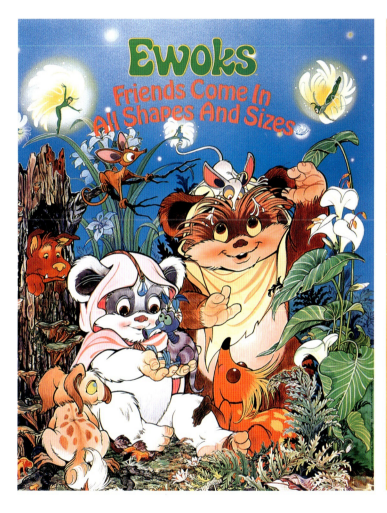

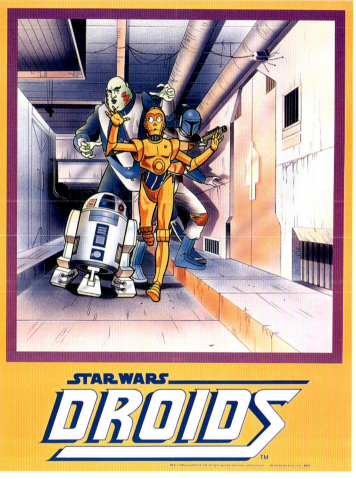

EWOKS: "FRIENDS COME IN ALL SHAPES..."
United States / 1985 / 17 × 22
This rare Ewoks poster was painted by children's book illustrator Pat Paris.

WEEKLY READER: *DROIDS*
United States / 1985 / 17 × 20
Boba Fett makes a cameo appearance in this Weekly Reader poster promoting the animated *Droids* television show. Getting *Star Wars* images and stories into the hands of eager children was a fairly easy task, and sometimes whole lesson plans revolved around the movies.

opposite

LUKE PROMOTES CASSETTES Sweden / 1983 / 18 × 25
This unusual artwork, with Luke Skywalker having almost a Japanese Manga look, advertised a set of cassettes and books for each of the three original movies.

A STARRY VADER HELMET United States / 1983 / 24 × 25
It appears that Vader's got his head in the stars on this unusual 1983 mail-in premium poster from Sales Corp. of America.

opposite
OHRAI "STARFALL" Japan / 1983 / 21 × 30.5
Noriyoshi Ohrai created a beautiful illustration for this Yamakatsu premium poster from Japan. It was produced in very small quantities and was hard to find even the year it was printed. A rough composition for the poster, known to collectors as "Starfall," was included in a portfolio of prints Ohrai did for *Return of the Jedi*.

THE INTER REGNUM

After nearly a decade of hard work getting his *Star Wars* trilogy on screen, George Lucas was exhausted.

Yes, he had more stories to tell—in particular, how it all began—and he hoped to get to them one day. But there were no promises, no commitment, not even a possible year for *Star Wars* fans to grasp hold of for encouragement. After the Ewok television/movie events faded away, there was no major media presence for the franchise except for the occasional airing of the films on television. These were, in some fans' eyes, the dark years. Lucasfilm saw them more as the quiet years and kept the hope alive by saying that when fans were again ready for *Star Wars,* then *Star Wars* would be there for them.

Things weren't completely quiet. There were events, theme park attractions, merchandise, and finally the Special Editions of the original trilogy in 1997—all a prelude to the prequels.

For the *Star Wars* tenth anniversary in 1987, there was a large convention in a hotel near the Los Angeles airport. It was the first—and last—convention that George Lucas himself attended. Artist John Alvin remembers pitching the idea for an anniversary poster to Lucasfilm. "I started describing to them a panorama of a boy about to face his destiny," says Alvin. He suggested the letters in the title itself act as windows to view the characters and scenes. "There's Vader on one side and Kenobi on the other, kind of bracketing our initial impressions of the duel between good and evil," explains Alvin. "Even though there were other lightsaber fights, I thought that was the one to suggest."

Choosing a horizontal format, Alvin hoped to evoke the spirit and scope of the big screen. A vast Tatooine landscape grounds the image, and Luke is depicted as the land-locked farm boy on the brink of adventure. "Luke, instead of looking at us, is looking away, kind of acknowledging his own fate," suggests Alvin.

Lucasfilm liked the idea but wanted Alvin to use the familiar *Star Wars* logo. "I said it wouldn't work for me on this. That's a graphic for itself, and I need a window." Incorporating the attached "S" ligatures, Alvin succeeded in creating an original, albeit similar, version of the *Star Wars* logo. In keeping with the hopeful spirit of the artwork, he added "The First Ten Years" below the title. "Wasn't it more inspirational to regard it as the first ten years, rather than the last?" the artist asks.

Drew Struzan also created a poster for the tenth anniversary, among the first in a series of commemoratives printed by Jeff Kilian of Kilian Enterprises. Kilian had published a popular *Star Wars* checklist poster in 1985, giving fans their first glimpse at the extensive artwork created for the domestic campaign. Drew welcomed the opportunity to return to the *Star Wars* universe and began contemplating possible designs for the poster. "So how do you sum up ten years of the coolest movie

***STAR WARS* TENTH ANNIVERSARY: GOLD MYLAR**

United States / 1987 / 27 × 41

This gold Mylar poster version of the silver *Star Wars* tenth anniversary poster was printed with an edition size of three hundred, available only to the publisher Kilian Enterprises' regular customers.

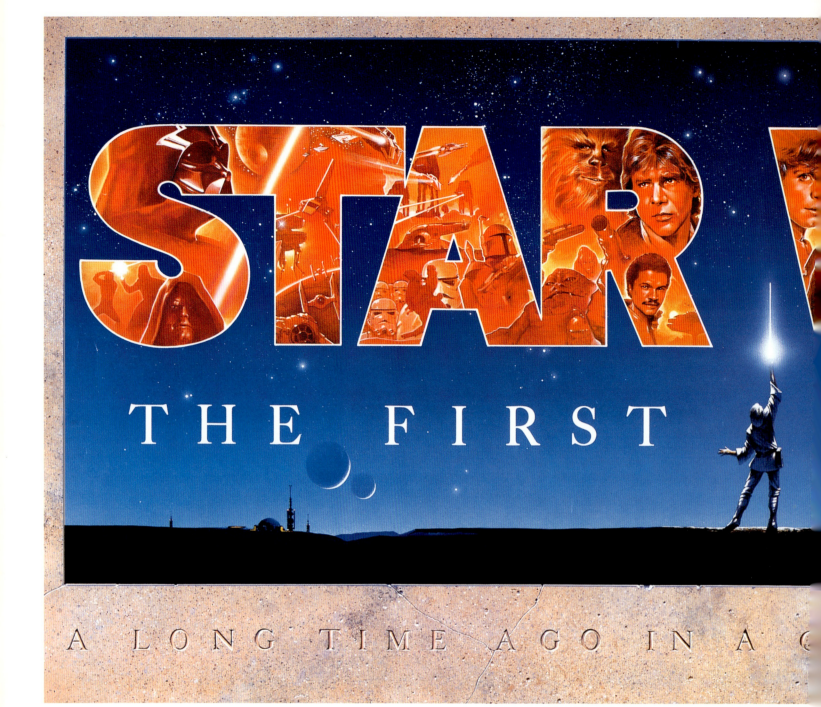

of all time?" asks Struzan. "I always viewed it as the story about Luke Skywalker, the young man growing up, facing his challenges and coming to adulthood. So I featured him and his nemesis Darth Vader."

Using color to further suggest the contrast between hero and villain, Luke was rendered in the warm tones of Tatooine, while Vader emerges behind him as if from the cold darkness of space. The logo and foreground were slanted to give the artwork an added dynamic. "Art is not storytelling for me. It's basically touching emotions," explains Struzan. The slant "gave it a little bit of power and movement, rather than making it static. When you put it on an angle like that it elicits the feeling that there's movement."

After a detailed comp was submitted, Kilian requested that Han, Leia, and Obi-Wan also be featured, and Struzan deftly added them in unobtrusively. Illustrated in actual size to maintain what Struzan has called the "vitality" of the piece, the poster was printed with an edition size of three thousand. After the convention, Disneyland was said to have taken the lion's share of the run and sold them out within a few months at $100 each.

Kilian also produced a pair of Mylar posters for the *Star Wars* tenth anniversary, including a version to commemorate the film's British debut. For *Empire*'s anniversary in 1990, two more Mylar posters were created in addition to an artwork poster. Resurrected from the original 1980 campaign, Lawrence Noble's concept for the first release poster finally made its one-sheet debut ten years after he'd created it.

"Out of nowhere, that image surfaced," remembers Noble. "At the same time that Kilian contacted me saying he'd like to use it as a tenth anniversary poster, the *Star Wars* Fan Club said they'd like to

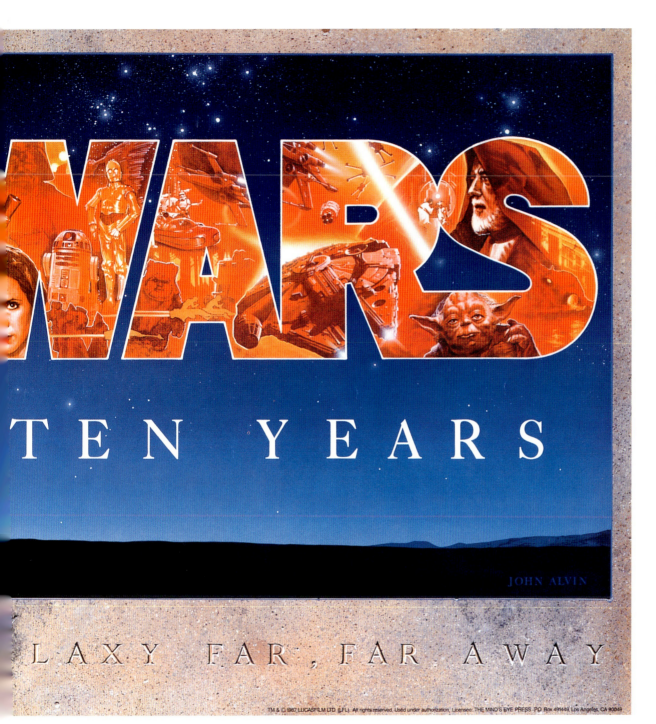

STAR WARS TENTH ANNIVERSARY: JOHN ALVIN
United States / 1987 / 17 × 36
According to artist John Alvin, seventy-seven elements were inserted into the letter forms of his tenth anniversary poster. That figure, of course, references the film's year of release. How many can you find?

use it as a poster for new subscribers." Both had come across the concept independently in the Lucasfilm archives. "To me, it just reinforced the whole reason why I did it," adds Noble.

Unlike the *Star Wars* anniversary poster commissions, which for the most part granted creative freedom to the artists, Noble was given guidelines for the original 1980 campaign. "I was working under direction from Sidney [Ganis] to think in two terms: myth and legend," explains Noble. The design "had its roots in militaristic science fiction. There was Vader who was larger than life, and Luke and Leia caught in the middle with the *Millennium Falcon* almost within the grasp of Darth Vader. The only thing that can stop him is Luke and Leia."

Though Noble's art was not used during *Empire*'s original release, it did inspire some of the design elements seen in the campaign's Style "B"

poster. "I was pleased that I had contributed to one of the final campaign posters, but I was a little disappointed that it hadn't gone through my hands," says Noble. An artist of many talents, Noble has since produced several sculptures related to the *Star Wars* universe, including a life-size bronze Yoda that adorns the entrance to Lucasfilm's offices at Big Rock Ranch, in northern California.

For *Return of the Jedi*'s tenth anniversary, Kilian again borrowed a lost concept image from the original theatrical campaign. Kazu Sano's unused comp for the 1985 rerelease of *Jedi* was an experiment of sorts for the artist. "I was trying to make something very exciting in the way of just the movement and action," explains Sano. "The basic thing that I did was compose a capital 'S' shape inside the rectangle format. I put the explosion in the middle and that was the center of the 'S.' I have never seen

Tatooine

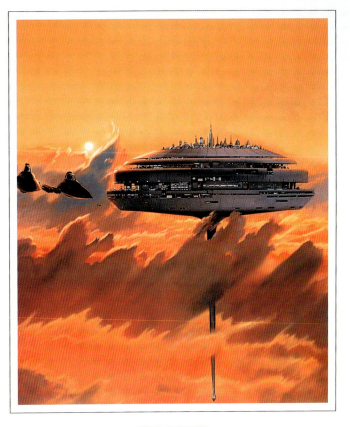

Bespin

Endor

clockwise, from top left

STAR TOURS "TRAVEL" POSTER: TATOOINE
United States / 1987 / 18 × 24

STAR TOURS "TRAVEL" POSTER: BESPIN
United States / 1987 / 18 × 24

STAR TOURS "TRAVEL" POSTER: ENDOR
United States / 1987 / 18 × 24

A set of six "travel" posters could be purchased at Disneyland's Star Tours attraction in the late 1980s, most showcasing Ralph McQuarrie's picturesque planetary vistas.

opposite

STAR WARS TENTH ANNIVERSARY: DREW STRUZAN
United States / 1987 / 27 × 41

Drew Struzan's striking tenth anniversary poster for *Star Wars* was printed by Gore Graphics, the same print house that had handled the majority of classic trilogy posters for distributor 20th Century Fox.

left

STAR TOURS OLDSMOBILE PROMOTIONAL

United States / 1988 / 20 × 30
This Star Tours poster illustrated by Richard Kriegler was produced as a park giveaway to commemorate the attraction's first anniversary as well as a brief advertising tie-in between Oldsmobile and the *Star Wars* droids.

opposite

STAR TOURS SILK-SCREENED ATTRACTION POSTER

Japan / 1989 / 33 × 47
Limited to one hundred stone lithographed prints, the U.S. Star Tours attraction poster artwork was translated for its Tokyo Disneyland opening in 1989.

anything that takes that kind of composition in the movie poster business."

In the same year that *Star Wars* celebrated its first decade, Disneyland's Star Tours attraction opened its doors to fans eager to relive the *Star Wars* experience. A set of six exclusive Star Tours "travel" posters could be bought at the gift shop strategically located at the ride's exit. Each poster featured a Ralph McQuarrie painting of a planetary location. The lithographed attraction poster printed for the park itself was a visual stunner but was not available to the public.

In the years spanning the gap between the sequels and prequels, Japan probably produced more

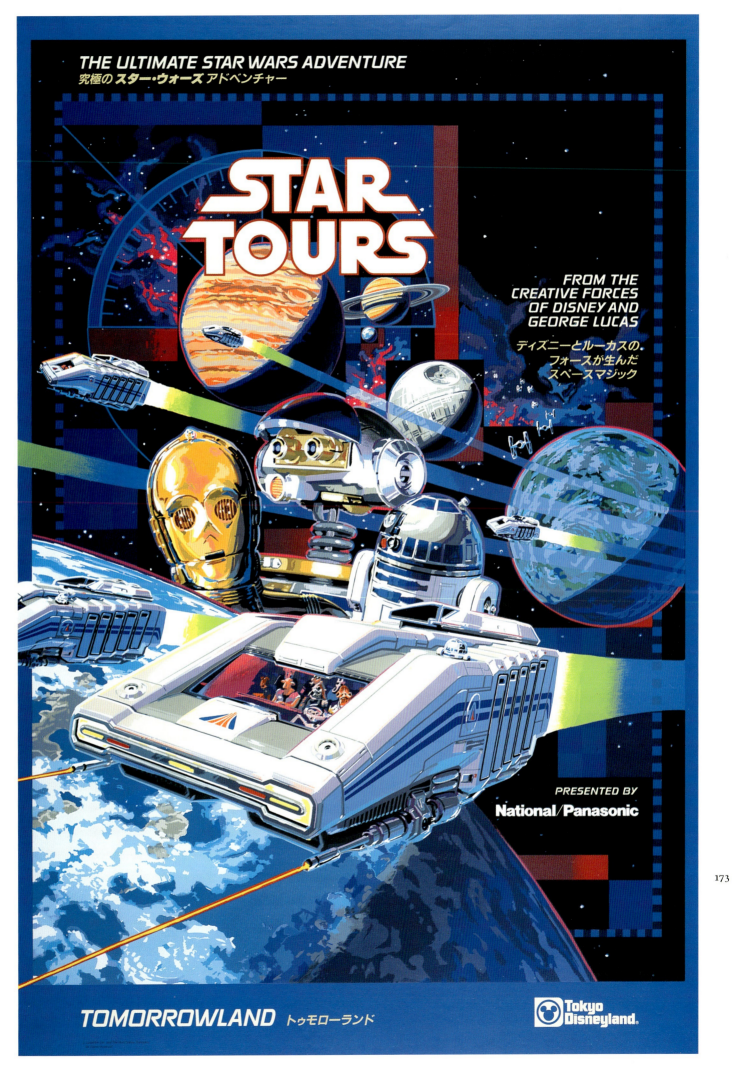

opposite, top

PANASONIC: EWOKS

Japan / 1987 / 41 × 57

These two stalwart Ewoks seem to be promoting the Panasonic brand rather than any specific product. The poster is one of scores of different images using *Star Wars* characters and even George Lucas himself in a wide-ranging multiyear marketing arrangement between Lucasfilm and Dentsu Inc., one of the world's largest advertising companies, on behalf of its client Panasonic. In Japan it is considered among the highest honors to appear in an advertising campaign.

opposite, bottom

PANASONIC: YODA

Japan / 1987 / 41 × 57

A personal stereo seems to be music to Yoda's ears in this rare Panasonic poster. Images such as these were used on billboards, at train stations, and as ads in newspapers and magazines.

above

PANASONIC: C-3PO AND R2-D2

Japan / 1987 / 41 × 57

The fastidious, umbrella-toting golden droid, C-3PO, may be carrying a Panasonic laptop computer to learn more than his normal six million forms of communication. His companion, R2-D2, isn't saying.

Star Wars posters than any other country. This included Tokyo Disneyland's debut of Star Tours in 1989, which had a version of the U.S. attraction poster artwork. Japan's Star Tours was sponsored by Panasonic, which already was featuring the *Star Wars* characters in an extensive campaign to promote its electronics line. Yoda, Ewoks, the droids, and others were seen in transit stations and billboards, promoting wares from computers to satellite dishes. George Lucas even made a few cameo appearances for the campaign, which has seldom been seen outside of Japan. More than thirty poster designs in various sizes were produced for the series between 1987 and 1991, but all are extremely hard to find, even in Japan.

In 1992, *The George Lucas Super Live Adventure* played to Japanese audiences. The arena show—which included singing, dancing, and stunts—featured characters not only from *Star Wars* and the Indiana Jones movies, but from *Tucker* and *American Graffiti*. Several posters were produced for the show, including two memorable montages by artist Hiroaki (Hiro) Shioya. Because the *Star Wars* and

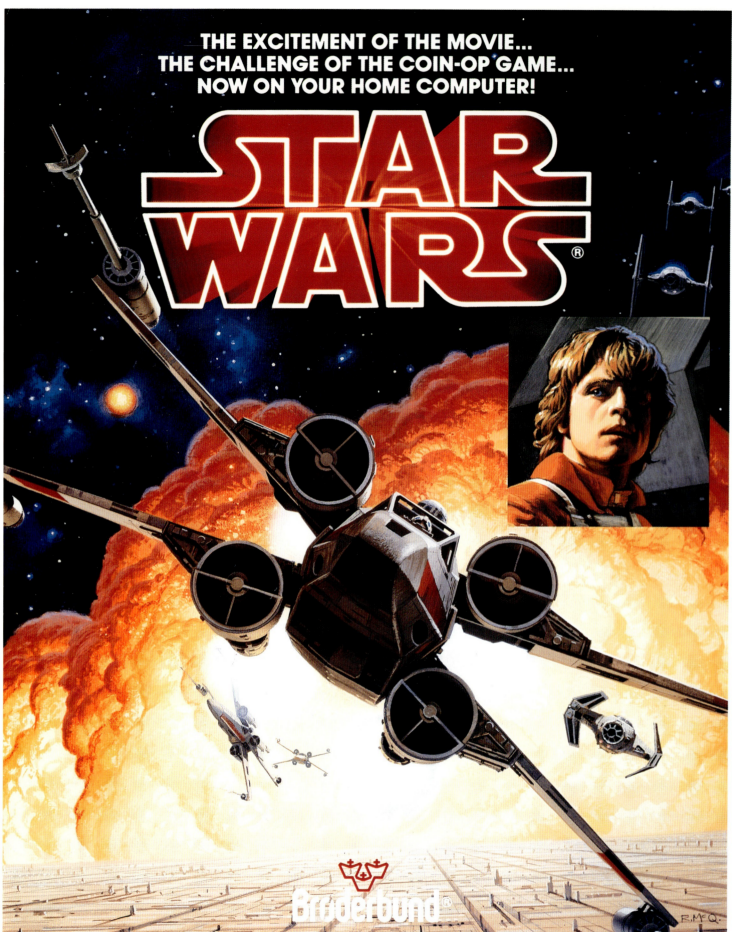

BRODERBUND *STAR WARS* VIDEO GAME United States / 1987 / 22 × 28
Star Wars concept artist Ralph McQuarrie created this dramatic artwork for Broderbund's 1987 *Star Wars* video game cartridge; the design was also used on the promotional poster. According to McQuarrie, the key art of the X-wing battle unfortunately was stolen shortly after completion.

THE EMPIRE STRIKES BACK TENTH ANNIVERSARY: LUKE MYLAR
United States / 1990 / 27 × 41
While this isn't the rarest of the anniversary Mylar posters produced by Kilian Enterprises, the stylized "Luke on Tauntaun" graphic denoting *Empire*'s tenth anniversary has made this poster among the most sought after. Designed by Dayna Stedry.

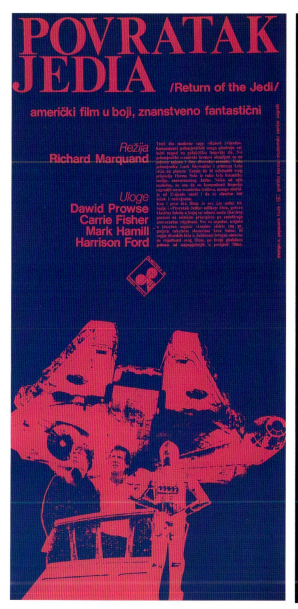
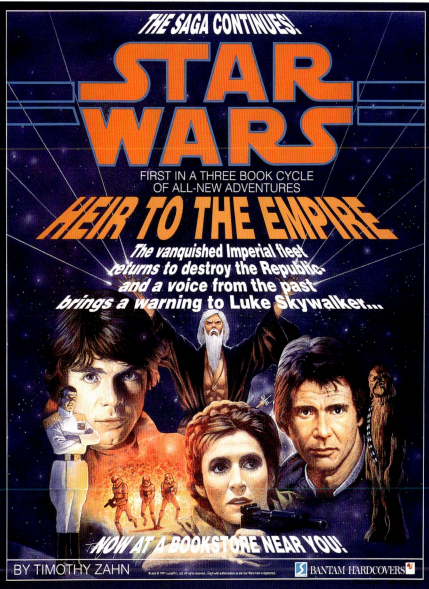

above left

ZAGREB FILM FESTIVAL Croatia / 1991 / 13 × 27

This hot pink and purple poster for *Jedi* was used to promote a showing of the movie in Zagreb for an annual festival known as Filmoteka 16. It's even odder with the *Millennium Falcon* flying upside down and only a rear view of C-3PO. And it gives top billing to David Prowse, the man in the Vader suit, even though the actor personally had less screen time in *Jedi* than in either of the first two movies.

above right

HEIR TO THE EMPIRE United States / 1991 / 17 × 22

Timothy Zahn restarted the *Star Wars* engine in 1991 with his *Heir to the Empire* novel published by Bantam Books. *Star Wars* stalwart Tom Jung appropriately provided the cover art and posters. The hardcover novel zoomed to top place in the *New York Times* bestseller list.

opposite

THE EMPIRE STRIKES BACK TENTH ANNIVERSARY: NOBLE

United States / 1990 / 27 × 41

Although not used for the original release of *The Empire Strikes Back* in 1980, Lawrence Noble's concept artwork grabs the viewer. The image was used on a small promotional poster by the artist and achieved fame ten years later as an anniversary poster.

the Indiana Jones properties were the most well known in Japan, they were displayed prominently on the posters. There were even a couple produced with George Lucas' visage, one of which was made available to fan club members in the United States. For American fans, where little was happening on the *Star Wars* front in 1992, the show's Japanese exclusivity was disappointing news.

Books and video games filled the void for most fans during the years between the films, with the United States and Japan producing most of the posters to advertise them. These were the first *Star Wars* posters to use computer-generated imagery. Since the level of graphic sophistication was a strong selling point for *Star Wars* games, it was natural for the posters to display the graphics prominently. Traditional artwork still had a place, however. Ralph McQuarrie painted a striking poster for Broderbund's *Star Wars* video game from 1987, and Greg Winters painted a visceral cockpit perspective for 1993's *Rebel Assault*.

Computer graphics found an unexpected place on 1993's *George Lucas Exhibition* poster, which was hosted by Japan's Sezon Museum of Art. The image displayed *Star Wars* hardware with wire-frame graphics, suggesting the progressive nature of the exhibit. The 1994 *Art of Star Wars* show in San Francisco used traditional photography for its large bus stop posters. A few years later, the Smithsonian Institution would step up to host a full-fledged *Star Wars: Magic of Myth* exhibit, which produced separate posters of Yoda, Vader, and C-3PO. The

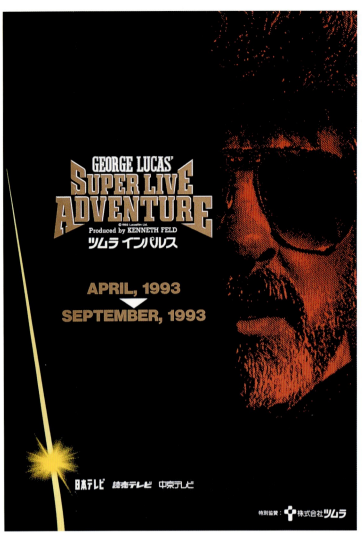

above left

GEORGE LUCAS SUPER LIVE ADVENTURE: PORTRAIT Japan / 1992 / 29 × 40
George Lucas himself was the focus of this limited poster—only twenty-eight were said to have been made—for Japan's George Lucas Super Live Adventure arena show.

above right

GEORGE LUCAS SUPER LIVE ADVENTURE: HIRO Japan / 1992 / 20 × 29
This busy montage by Hiro for the George Lucas Super Live Adventure has *Star Wars* as the predominant theme. But it also had to squeeze in Indiana Jones and characters from *Tucker* and *American Graffiti*.

golden droid's image ended up being used for several venue posters throughout the show's multi-year tour across the United States, with its final destination Sydney, Australia.

In addition to video games and museum shows, the films themselves were released several times on video throughout the late 1980s and 1990s to keep the *Star Wars* flame alive. By the late 1980s, the films could be purchased as a trilogy set, and early posters featured mixed montages of the original release posters. For the 1995 release, however, an expansive domestic and international campaign was designed for the original trilogy's final appearance in unaltered form.

While the U.S. campaign opted to go with photo art for the cassette sleeves and posters, the international marketing was done with original artwork designed or executed by artists with strong ties to the classic trilogy. Posters used in England, Germany, Australia, and other countries featured artwork designed and conceived by Drew Struzan, although scheduling conflicts required the finished artwork to be handled by a different artist, Greg Roman.

In Germany and a few other countries, John Alvin designed an elegant lightsaber threesome to reference each film in the trilogy. Originally conceived as art covers for slipcased editions of the trilogy, the graphics translated well to posters. For the final release of the original trilogy, Alvin also created the artwork covers for the standard cassettes. "That was the last piece of art done to represent the original saga because the next art was for the Special Edition," Alvin points out. "'The Original One Last Time' was true for the artwork itself."

The arrival of the *Star Wars* Special Editions in 1997 ended a hiatus that had been at least partly

"YOURS TRULY," YODA

United States / 1992 / 19.5 × 22

Famed fantasy illustrator Michael Whelan produced this image of Yoda for the cover of a diary, *My Jedi Journal*, in 1983. It later was released as a limited edition lithograph. The artist fondly refers to the painting as "Yours Truly."

left, top
SEZON MUSEUM OF ART: GEORGE LUCAS
Japan / 1993 / 14 × 20
For an exhibit of concept art, costumes, matte paintings, and props, Japan's Sezon Museum of Art came up with two main posters. This one uses silhouettes of the letters of George Lucas' name to show scenes from the original trilogy.

left, bottom
SEZON MUSEUM OF ART: LIGHTSABER
Japan / 1993 / 29 × 40
A computer-generated lightsaber blade slices diagonally through this 1993 George Lucas Exhibit poster from the Sezon Museum of Art in Japan. It also uses wireframe models of R2-D2, a TIE fighter, and an X-wing fighter.

opposite
THE ART OF *STAR WARS* AT YERBA BUENA GARDENS
United States / 1994 / 14 × 24
The Art of *Star Wars* at Yerba Buena Gardens in San Francisco was the first large-scale exhibit of *Star Wars* props and costumes to be staged in the United States. A few years later, the Smithsonian Institution took another large show on the road with the Magic of Myth tour.

filled by original fiction, games, and multiple video releases. Additionally, the updated trilogy edition would introduce the first universal image campaign ever staged for a *Star Wars* release. The "Ingot" poster was originally conceived as the sole image to launch the global campaign. But because George Lucas decided that he'd also like an artwork poster in the traditional sense, Drew Struzan was called in.

Struzan remembers being inspired at the prospect of a trilogy release. "I said, 'When in history has there ever been an opportunity to do three paintings for a series of films? Why not do a triptych, you know, where we have a poster for each of the three movies, but they all relate to each other? When you put them side by side, they'll make one big painting.'"

Intrigued, Lucasfilm bought the concept. Struzan set to work designing the triptych, establishing a color scheme for each. "I just had feelings about the color of each film," explains Struzan. "You know, the first one was in the desert a lot, . . . and *Empire*, because of Vader and a lot of space stuff, was blue. What was different about *Return of the Jedi* was the forest, so I made it green."

Finally, Struzan worked out the composition. "By that time we knew Vader was kind of the cornerstone of the story, so I put him in the center. I have him dominate everything, with the good guys

on both sides." The three Struzan posters and/or the Ingot poster were the only images used worldwide. For a "quiet" decade-plus, there still had been plenty of posters and a decent helping of Star Wars.

ART OF *STAR WARS*: MCQUARRIE PAINTING
United States / 1994 / 26 × 60
Ralph McQuarrie's matte painting of the Death Star shaft where Darth Vader throws the Emperor lends graphic interest to this artful banner used to promote the 1994 Art of *Star Wars* show in San Francisco. The lettering at the bottom is deliberately cut off.

REBEL ASSAULT II United States / 1995 / 27 × 36
LucasArts' Rebel Assault II video game was given the cinematic treatment in this theatrical style promotional poster.

opposite
RETURN OF THE JEDI 10TH ANNIVERSARY United States / 1994 / 27 × 41
For *Return of the Jedi*'s tenth anniversary, Kazu Sano's unused concept art for the 1985 theatrical rerelease poster was blown up to one-sheet size. Sano had designed the composition loosely around the letter "S," with the logo to be placed on the center explosion.

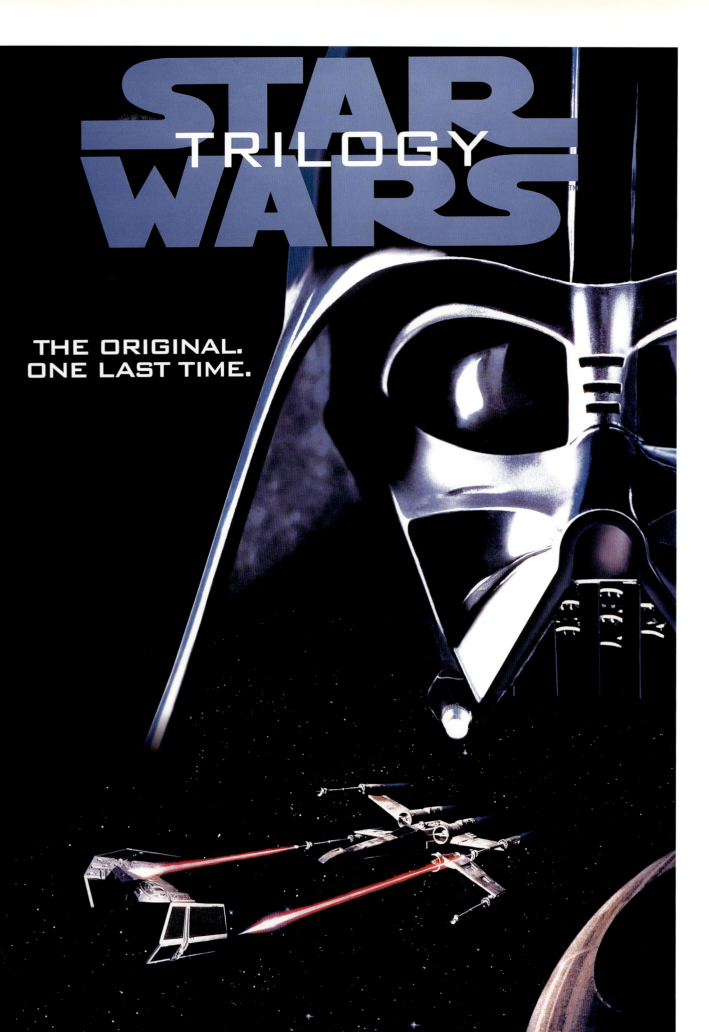

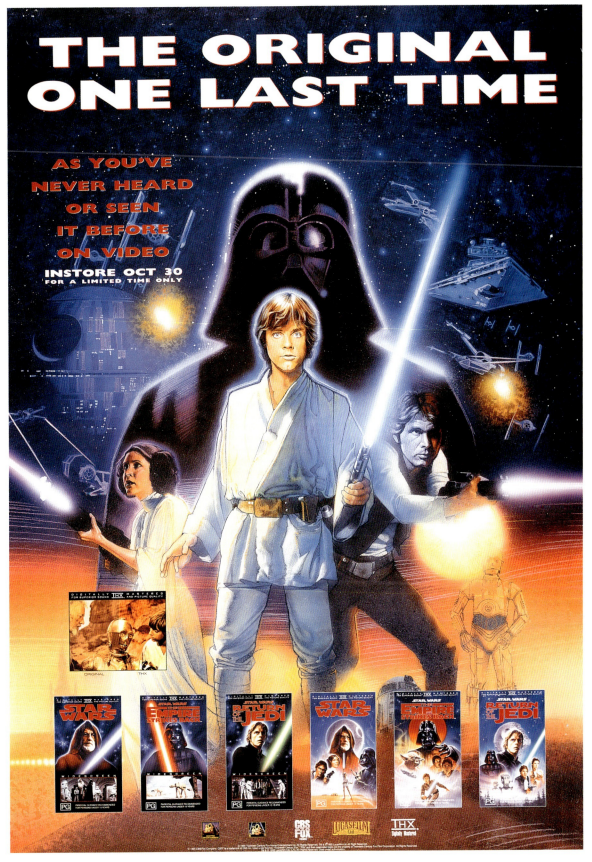

FOX HOME VIDEO INTERNATIONAL Australia / 1995 / 28 × 39
For the international video poster campaign, Drew Struzan conceived and designed an original artwork that was then painted by Greg Roman.

opposite

FOX HOME VIDEO: "ONE LAST TIME" United States / 1995 / 36 × 48
Darth Vader's iconic mask and helmet were used as the primary compositional element in this poster to promote the U.S. release of "The Original Trilogy One Last Time" on video. After this release came the Special Editions.

190

top
FOX HOME VIDEO GERMANY: BANNER Germany / 1995 / 15 × 54
left
FOX HOME VIDEO GERMANY: *STAR WARS* Germany / 1995 / 15 × 54
center
FOX HOME VIDEO GERMANY: *THE EMPIRE STRIKES BACK* Germany / 1995 / 15 × 54
right
FOX HOME VIDEO GERMANY: *RETURN OF THE JEDI* Germany / 1995 / 15 × 54
For this video poster ensemble from Germany, John Alvin created three distinct lightsaber images to suggest each film from the original trilogy. Looking closely at the hands holding the lightsabers, it is possible to identify their owners as Obi-Wan Kenobi, Darth Vader, and Luke Skywalker.

***THE EMPIRE STRIKES BACK* FIFTEENTH ANNIVERSARY** United States / 1995 / 27 × 41
The visage of the galaxy's most notorious bounty hunter, Boba Fett, graced the fifteenth anniversary Mylar poster for *The Empire Strikes Back* from Kilian Enterprises.

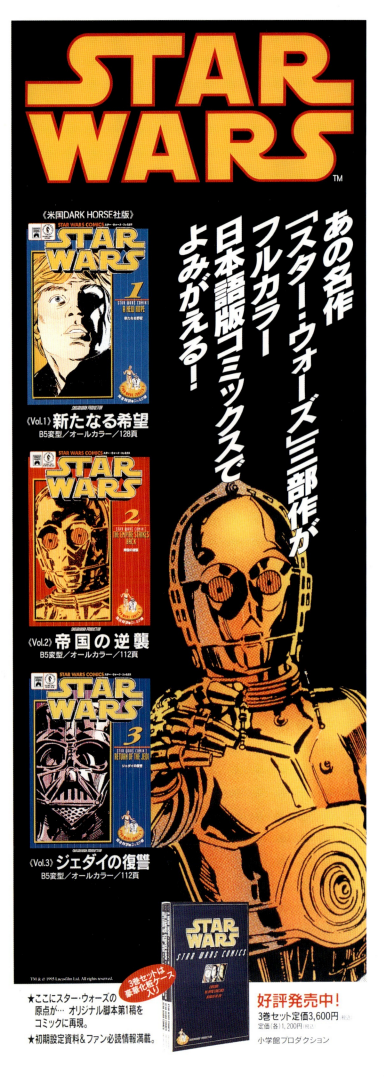

DARK HORSE COMICS JAPAN
Japan / 1995 / 8 × 23
The original Marvel comics for the classic trilogy were reprinted as graphic novels in Japanese.

READ THIS OR I SHOOT!
United Kingdom / 1995 / 14 × 21
Princess Leia plans on taking no prisoners in her crusade to eradicate illiteracy. Well, she'd really just like you to buy a book in this cheeky British in-store poster.

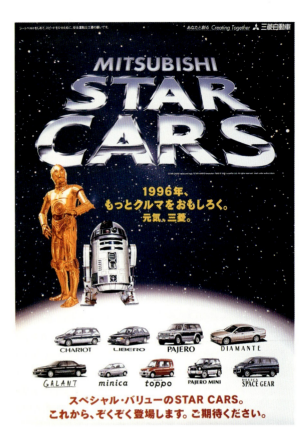

left
MITSUBISHI STAR CARS: DROIDS
Japan / 1996 / 29 × 40
Mitsubishi Motors did a months-long Star Cars promotion using C-3PO and R2-D2.

below
MITSUBISHI STAR CARS: CHERRY BLOSSOMS
Japan / 1996 / 29 × 40
R2-D2 seems quite at home amid the cherry blossoms in this campaign for Mitsubishi cars. Meanwhile C-3PO takes time to ponder the car of his choice.

opposite
"ALL I NEED TO KNOW...."
United States / 1996 / 24 × 36
This poster, cobbled together by author Steve Sansweet, offered all the credentials necessary to become a member of the *Star Wars* generation. The majority of the art is from Tom Jung's *Return of the Jedi* 1985 rerelease theatrical one-sheet. It was printed by Portal Publications.

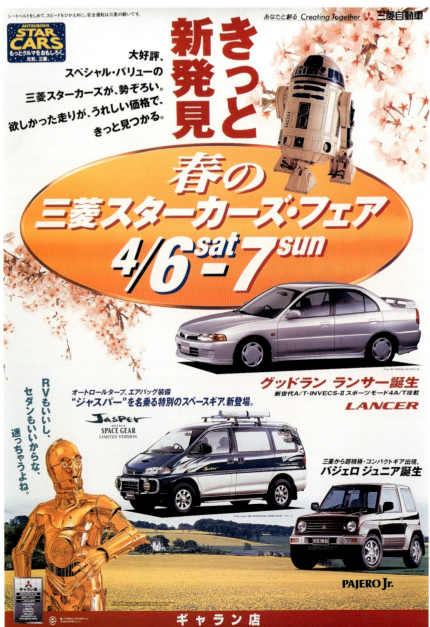

OHRAI: VEHICLES Germany / 1996 / 22 × 40
This sprawling 1978 work by Japan's Noriyoshi Ohrai, reprinted by ZigZag in 1996, includes the *Tantive IV Blockade Runner* as it appeared before designers rotated the cockpit cone sideways.

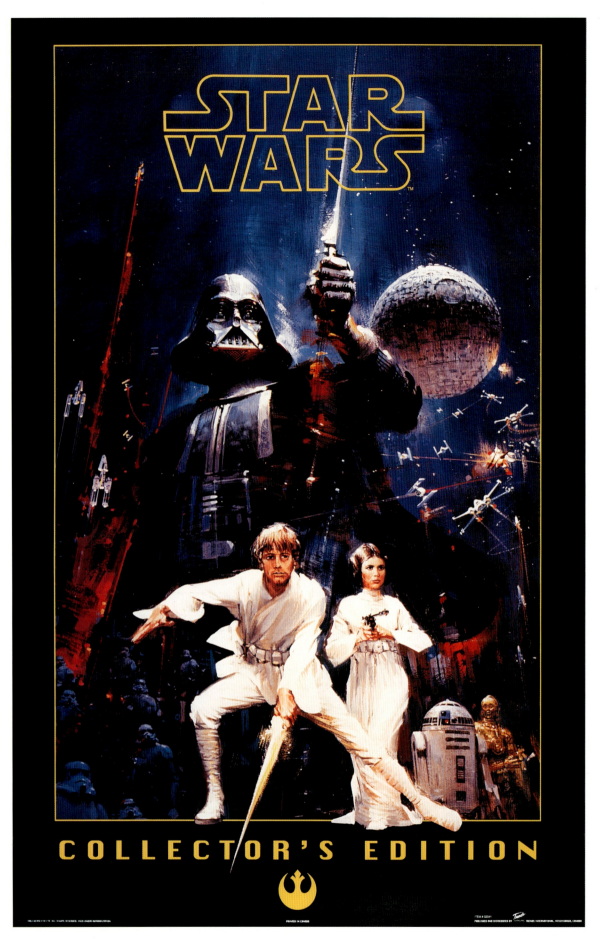

BERKEY NOVELIZATION COVER ART Canada / 1996 / 22 × 35
John Berkey's classic cover art for the *Star Wars* novelization wasn't formally showcased on a poster until Trends International printed it exclusively. Note that in this version, Luke Skywalker is left-handed.

opposite
***STAR WARS* TRILOGY SPECIAL EDITION: INGOT** United States / 1997 / 27 × 40
Before Drew Struzan created the three artwork posters for the Special Edition trilogy, the so-called Ingot poster was to be the sole poster image released worldwide.

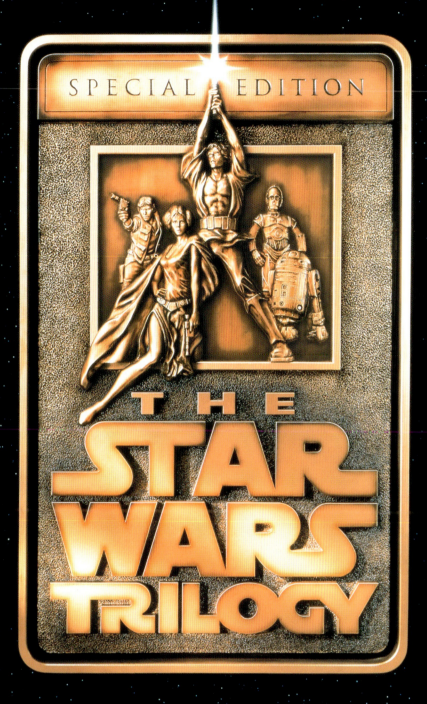

previous spread, left
***STAR WARS* SPECIAL EDITION: STYLE "B"**
United States / 1997 / 27 × 40
Though some fans may recognize Leia's portrait as derived from *The Empire Strikes Back,* all can agree that Struzan's composition for the *Star Wars* Special Edition poster is striking.

previous spread, right
***THE EMPIRE STRIKES BACK* SPECIAL EDITION: STYLE "C"**
United States / 1997 / 27 × 40
Because of Vader's prominent role in *The Empire Strikes Back,* Drew Struzan made him a central figure on the Special Edition poster. When placed in the triptych, Vader becomes the center of the overall composition as well.

opposite
***RETURN OF THE JEDI* SPECIAL EDITION: MARCH 7TH**
United States / 1997 / 27 × 40
Before *Return of the Jedi* Special Edition was released on March 14, 1997, most of the posters in print carried the originally slated release date of March 7. The film was pushed back a week because of the overwhelming success of the first two films in the trilogy. There is both a poster and a paste-on snipe with the March 14 date.

above
***STAR WARS* TRILOGY SPECIAL EDITION: TRIPTYCH**
United States / 1997 / 16 × 26
The only U.S. poster to feature all three Special Edition artworks in a single tapestry, this was distributed to lucky fans at select theaters.

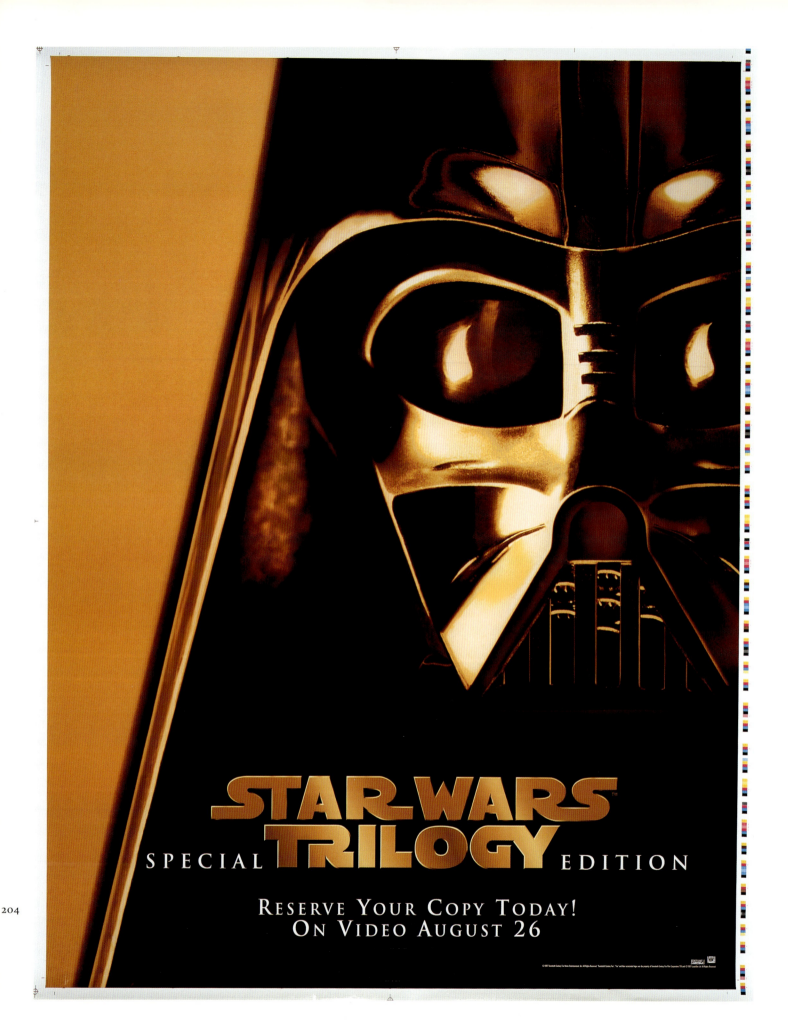

FOX HOME VIDEO: *STAR WARS TRILOGY SPECIAL EDITION*
United States / 1997 / 40 × 51.5
Darth Vader's helmet was photographed in a blaze of glory for this stunning poster for the Special Edition trilogy on video. This version is an untrimmed printer's proof.

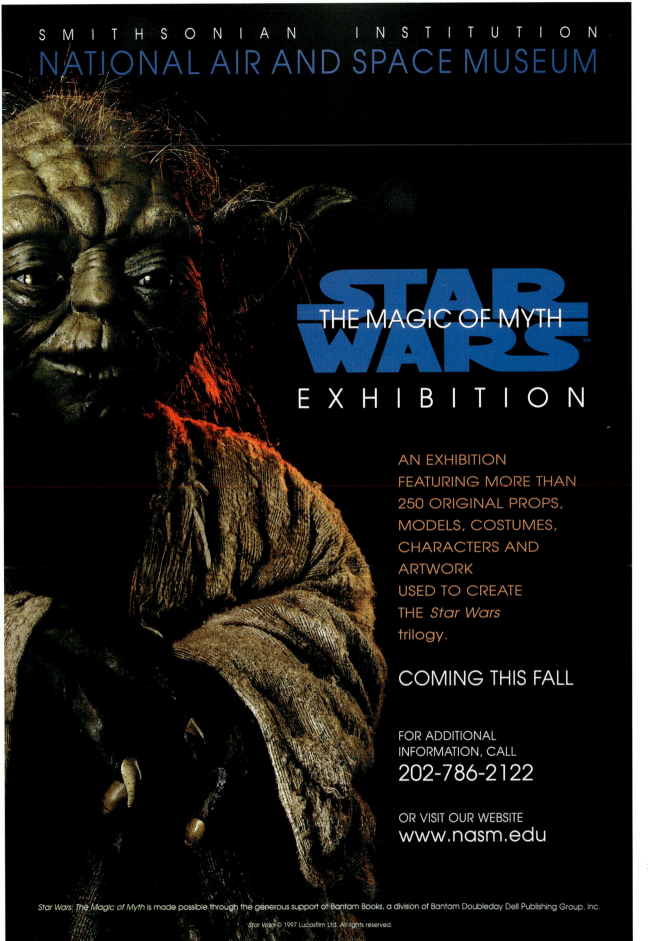

***STAR WARS:* THE MAGIC OF MYTH: YODA**
United States / 1997 / 36 × 53
Fewer than ten of the large Yoda Advance posters for the Smithsonian Institution's *Star Wars: The Magic of Myth* exhibit were said to have been printed.

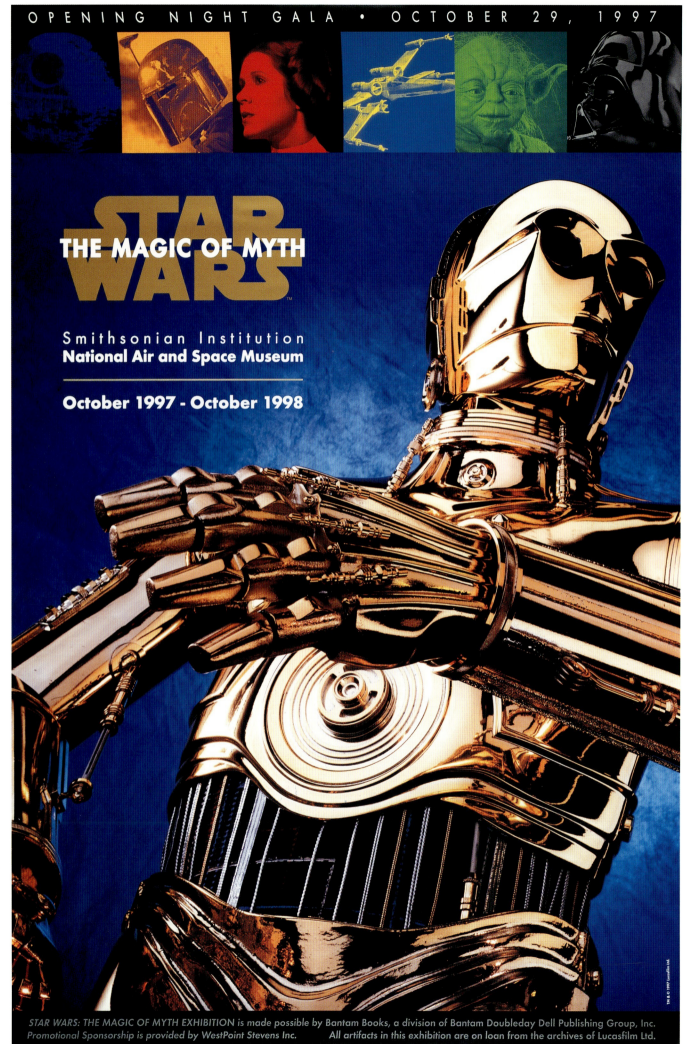

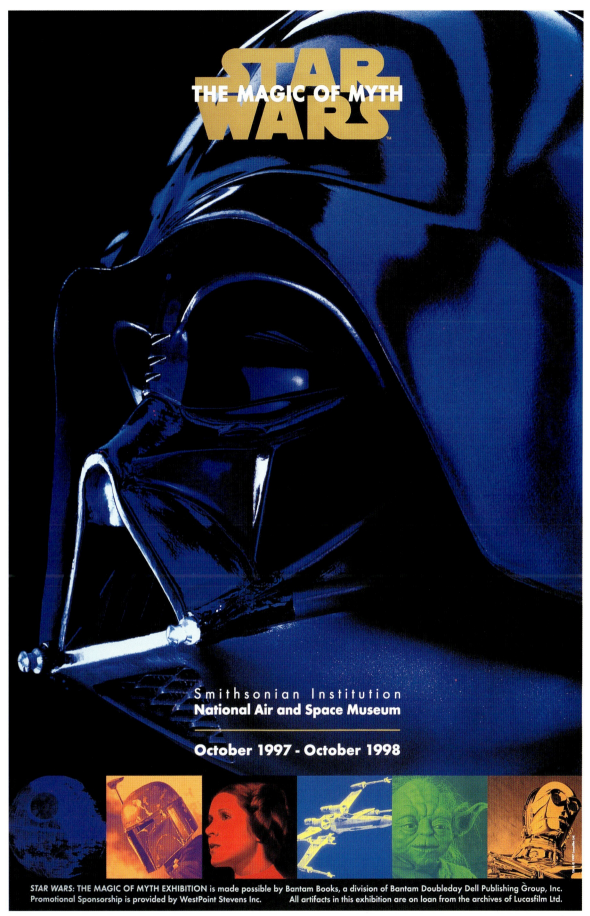

***STAR WARS:* THE MAGIC OF MYTH: DARTH VADER** United States / 1997 / 23 × 35
The Darth Vader poster for *Star Wars:* The Magic of Myth was sold only at the Washington D.C. venue of the national tour organized by the Smithsonian Institution. Design by Troy Alders.

opposite
***STAR WARS:* THE MAGIC OF MYTH "GALA PREMIERE"** United States / 1997 / 23 × 35
A rare Gala Premiere version of the *Star Wars:* The Magic of Myth C-3PO poster was given to invited guests on the opening night of the Smithsonian exhibit. Design by Troy Alders.

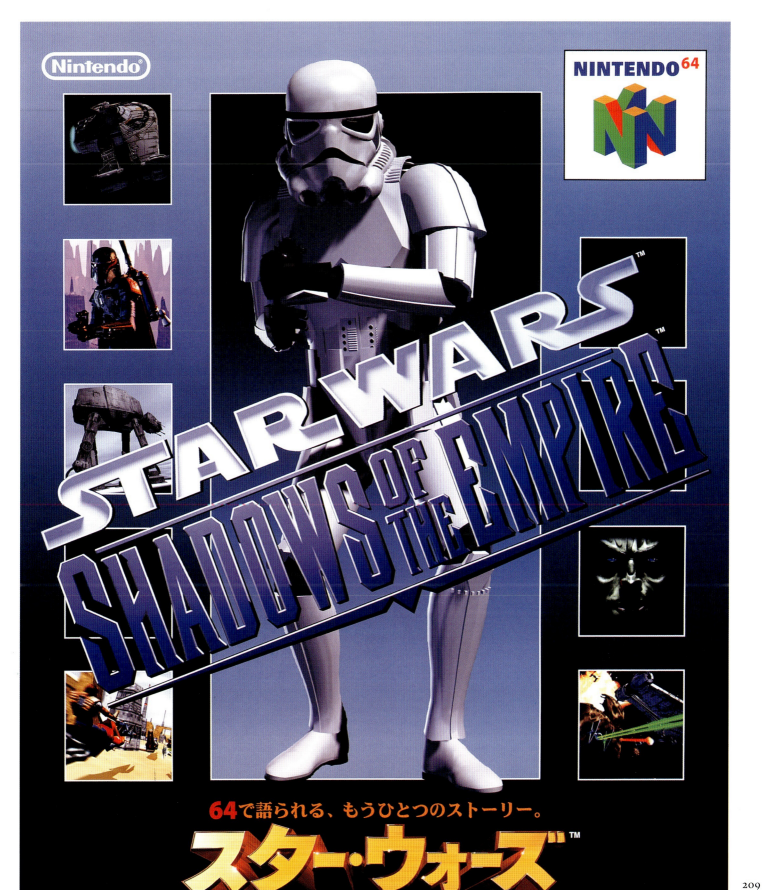

previous spread, left

SPACE WORLD *STAR WARS* EXHIBIT: C-3PO

Japan / 1997 / 29 × 40

C-3PO was the symbol of a *Star Wars* exhibition at the Space World theme park in Fukuoka Prefecture on Kyushu, the southernmost island of Japan.

previous spread, right

NINTENDO: *SHADOWS OF THE EMPIRE*

Japan / 1997 / 20 × 29

Nintendo used images from its game to promote its part in the worldwide multimedia event that was *Star Wars: Shadows of the Empire*. *Shadows* consisted of a novel, comics, toys, even a "soundtrack" CD—in short, everything except a movie. It was set in the time period between *The Empire Strikes Back* and *Return of the Jedi*.

BANTAM BOOKS C-3PO United States / 1997 / 26 × 66
Bantam Books, which published *Star Wars* novels, showed C-3PO in all his glory for this unusual life-size poster.

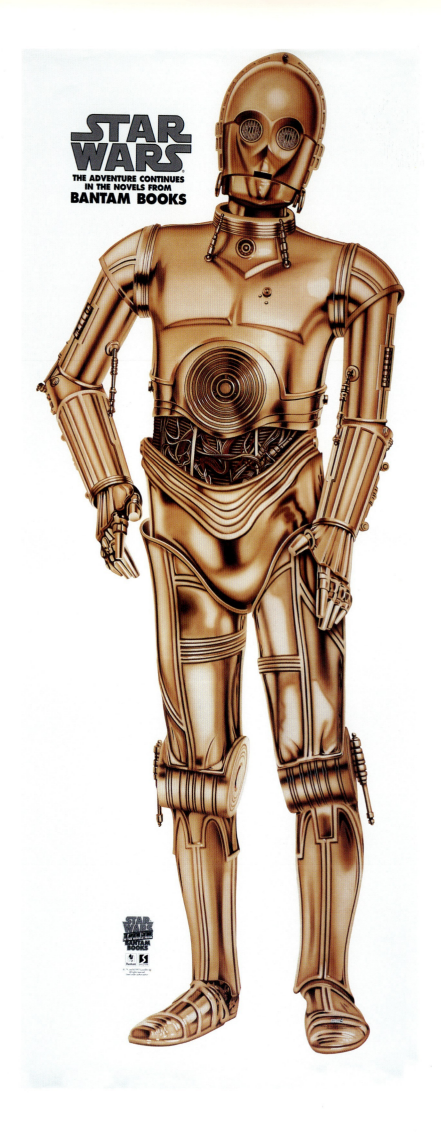

TRANSPLANTATION Canada / 1997 / 18 × 23
The droids C-3PO and R2-D2 help out in a public service campaign for the Canadian Association of Transplantation and the Kidney Foundation, playing off of a line of Threepio's dialog near the end of *Star Wars*.

above
DECIPHER: BOBA FETT United States / 1997 / 25 × 33
The danger and romance of Cloud City are successfully captured in this Decipher Inc. customizable card game poster depicting Boba Fett.

opposite
FRITO LAY: YODA United States / 1997 / 24 × 36
Yoda was the clear choice from the start to promote the Pepsi/Frito Lay *Star Wars* tie-in.

OFFICIAL *STAR WARS* FAN CLUB: 20TH ANNIVERSARY

United States / 1997 / 24 × 36

Tsuneo Sanda created this special anniversary montage to celebrate the first film's first twenty years.

opposite

OFFICIAL *STAR WARS* FAN CLUB: BOBA FETT

United States / 1997 / 24 × 36

Boba Fett shamelessly holds the smoking gun in this *Star Wars* Fan Club exclusive by Tsuneo Sanda.

OFFICIAL *STAR WARS* FAN CLUB: YODA United States / 1997 / 24 × 36
Before we see Yoda deflect Count Dooku's force lightning in *Attack of the Clones*, artist Tsuneo Sanda gave the Jedi Master something to practice with in this *Star Wars* Fan Club exclusive.

opposite

MAX REBO AND THE BAND United States / 1997 / 23 × 35
The Max Rebo Band finally got a concert poster fourteen years after it arrived on the scene in Jabba's Palace for *Return of the Jedi*. Artist William Brent imbued the poster with a retro look, like a poster from a Bill Graham concert at the Fillmore Auditorium. Published by Western Graphics.

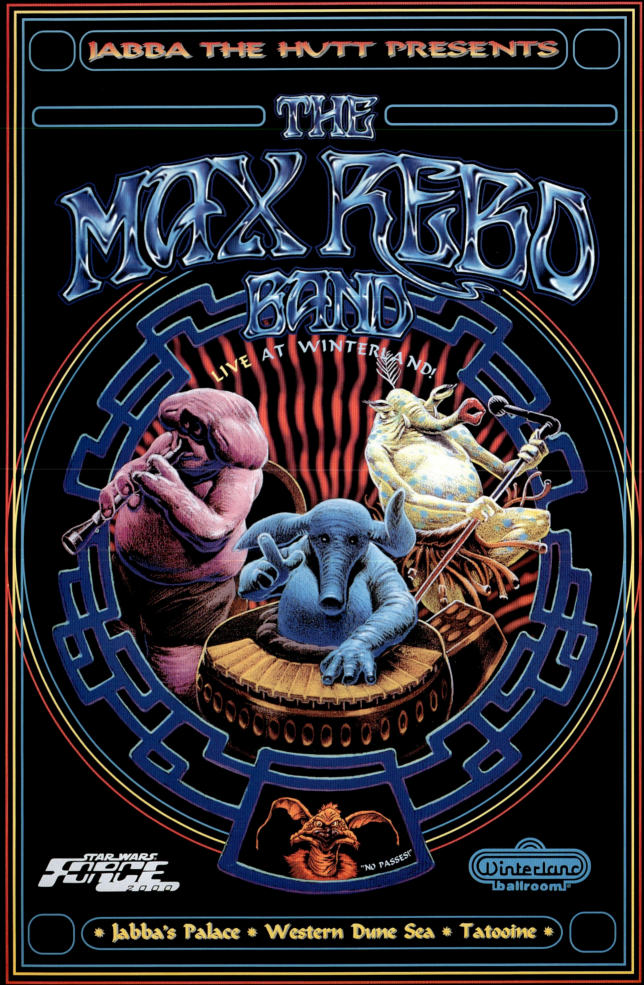

THE PREQUELS

**THE PHANTOM MENACE
THEATRICAL ADVANCE BANNER**

United States / 1998 / 48 × 96

The Episode I teaser poster had to draw people back into the storyline with a singular image, which it achieved beyond a shadow of a doubt. The theatrical banner was horizontal and large enough to play out Vader's shadow in the sand. The concept was developed at Lucasfilm by Ellen Lee of the Episode I Art Department, who worked with Jim Ward, vice president of marketing.

EPISODE I

In the movie business, five years can be a lifetime.

Sixteen years is an entire generation. And that was the challenge facing Lucasfilm and its newly invigorated marketing division. The division had faded away in the years after *Return of the Jedi,* and the company spent nearly a year searching for the right candidate to start it up again.

Eschewing marketers from Hollywood, Lucasfilm found the right man in Jim Ward, who had spent fifteen years in the advertising business, where he was involved with some of the most significant consumer-product launches in recent history. As senior vice president and general manager of BBDO/Los Angeles, Ward led the global launch of Apple's PowerBook. At Wieden + Kennedy, as global account director, he spearheaded the worldwide introduction of Microsoft Windows '95 and oversaw Nike's participation in the 1996 Olympics. And he was passionate about movies.

So it fell to Ward, vice president of marketing and distribution, to get the public reacquainted

THE PHANTOM MENACE THEATRICAL ADVANCE ONE-SHEET
United States / 1998 / 27 × 40
The Episode I teaser poster had to be reformatted for this regular-size theater poster. A Tatooine hut had to be added to cast Vader's shadow.

opposite and following spread
THE PHANTOM MENACE THEATRICAL ONE-SHEET
United States / 1999 / 27 × 40
Thailand / 1999 / 24 × 35
Hong Kong / 1999 / 21 × 30
Japan / 1999 / 29 × 40
Korea / 1999 / 27 × 39
Finland / 1999 / 16 × 24
France / 1999 / 27 × 39
Denmark / 1999 / 16 × 24
Germany / 1999 / 23 × 33
Greece / 1999 / 27 × 38
Norway / 1999 / 24.5 × 33
Spain / 1999 / 27 × 39
Sweden / 1999 / 27 × 39
Israel / 1999 / 27 × 39
Italy / 1999 / 39 × 55
Brazil/Portugal / 1999 / 25 × 36
Artist Drew Struzan was called in to do the worldwide theatrical release poster in the same manner as the art that he did for the Special Edition trilogy. Only the sizes and language changed in each of thirty-two countries where the poster was customized.

with the *Star Wars* universe. "One of the things that was a big key for Episode I was to communicate that this little boy, Anakin Skywalker, was ultimately going to become Darth Vader," says Ward. "We experienced a very long time between the films and needed to remind people that yes, this was the storyline, and we needed to do it in a very quick and succinct way."

Approaching the same art department that had spent three years developing the look for Episode I, Ward enlisted the help of Ellen Lee. With a year and a half to go before the film's release, Ward asked Lee to start exploring possible concepts for a teaser poster. "I said, 'Ellen, go explore transitions, you know, go explore communicating that this little boy somehow becomes Darth Vader,'"

Thailand

Hong Kong

Japan

Korea

Finland

France

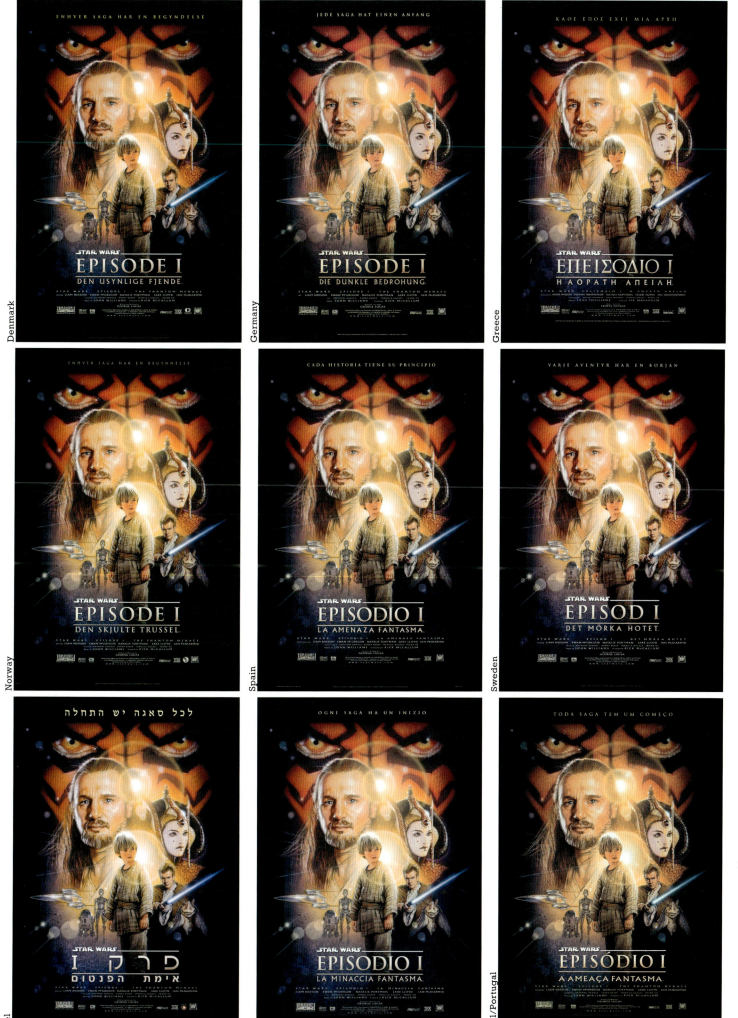

explains Ward. Lee came up with about a hundred different concepts and variations. "Over the course of about a month and a half she got to a point where there were a number of great ideas on the table, and one of them was [the final teaser]. I think once we saw it and everybody saw it, we knew, boy, that's the one."

The image of a young Anakin Skywalker casting the shadow of the iconic Darth Vader, whom he would become, was instantly readable by even the casual fan. While the teaser sought to reintroduce the public to the saga, it also introduced something new to *Star Wars* posters in general—photo art. "That's some new ground," says Ward, who credits the idea to Lucas' openness. "George gave us that latitude."

The teaser was released to theaters and fans on November 10, 1998, in the form of a one-sheet and a banner. The design of each was modified to accommodate their respective formats. The vertical one-sheet showed Anakin's shadow upon a wall, while the banner took advantage of its broad canvas to cast his shadow lengthways across the sand. Both were made available to *Star Wars* Fan Club members.

For the release poster, the campaign stuck to tradition. Not only would the theatrical one-sheet be illustrated, but Lucasfilm turned to an artist

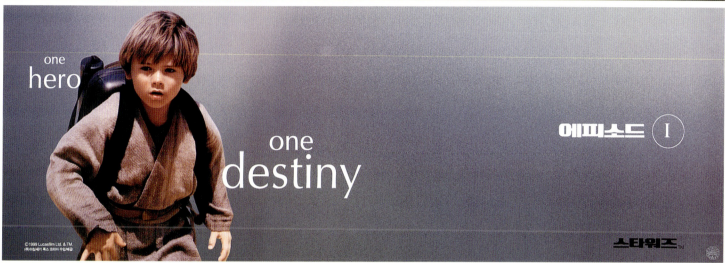

opposite

***THE PHANTOM MENACE* INTERNATIONAL CAMPAIGN: BATTLEDROID** Korea / 1999 / 10 × 30
***THE PHANTOM MENACE* INTERNATIONAL CAMPAIGN: QUI-GON** Korea / 1999 / 10 × 30
***THE PHANTOM MENACE* INTERNATIONAL CAMPAIGN: OBI-WAN** Korea / 1999 / 10 × 30

above

***THE PHANTOM MENACE* INTERNATIONAL CAMPAIGN: AMIDALA** Korea / 1999 / 10 × 30
***THE PHANTOM MENACE* INTERNATIONAL CAMPAIGN: ANAKIN** Korea / 1999 / 10 × 30
***THE PHANTOM MENACE* INTERNATIONAL CAMPAIGN: MACE** Korea / 1999 / 10 × 30

overleaf

***THE PHANTOM MENACE* INTERNATIONAL CAMPAIGN: JAR JAR** Korea / 1999 / 10 × 30
***THE PHANTOM MENACE* INTERNATIONAL CAMPAIGN: WATTO** Korea / 1999 / 10 × 30
***THE PHANTOM MENACE* INTERNATIONAL CAMPAIGN: DARTH MAUL** Korea / 1999 / 10 × 30

Korea released a series of small horizontal transit posters featuring nine of the characters from Episode I as part of the international "One" campaign: One Love, One Hate, etc. Other countries had the same, or a more limited, campaign, but the posters varied in size from country to country.

who was already considered a *Star Wars* standard. Drew Struzan was charged with the coveted task of rendering the poster that would launch the prequel trilogy, and he was asked to do so in what many consider the quintessential *Star Wars* style.

The design started in-house at Lucasfilm, where Ellen Lee and Design Director Doug Chiang blocked out a composition to roughly establish the placement of characters and other elements in the poster. Struzan instantly recognized a trend. "It developed based on the Special Edition posters," he says. "Everything's in that black frame sort of breaking out. It looks like it's bigger than reality, like you can't hold it in." As the black space allowed the Special Edition triptych posters to seamlessly combine, so it appeared Lucas had similar plans for the prequel posters.

Because Lucasfilm intended to launch the campaign worldwide with this single image, many refinements were requested of the artist. Obi-Wan's pose needed adjusting to suggest more action; Jar Jar's expression was changed twice—first from playful to surprised, and then to amiable; the droids were added in place of a droid control ship;

THE PHANTOM MENACE TRANSIT AD: OBI-WAN Japan / 1999 / 14 × 20
This uncommon image of Obi-Wan peering past the viewer saw more limited use abroad than the standard full-figure depiction of Obi-Wan as a Jedi Knight.

and Darth Maul's initial purple skin cast was repainted to red. The painting, from first pencil sketch to final modification, was completed in a week.

The Phantom Menace had a traditional launch, opening in the United States on May 19, 1999, with subsequent openings all over the world until the final November 5 opening in China. The Struzan artwork was used worldwide, but the expanded international campaign included a variety of special posters that used a number of the prequel's characters. This was another first for a *Star Wars* campaign.

"Internationally, *Star Wars* is at varying degrees of maturity," explains Ward. "Particularly in non-English speaking countries, we have to work a little harder in terms of communicating what the films are about. Therefore, from a media mix standpoint, outdoor and posters become a very important way for us to quickly communicate a message." U.S. fans have wondered why they don't get to see the often striking character posters that appear on international billboards and at transit stations. "In the U.S.," Ward says, "we get so saturated with everything *Star Wars* . . . that we don't really need to go out and make the expenditure in doing outdoor and similar things."

Episode II presented Ward and the marketing team with a totally different marketing challenge, one somewhat reminiscent of the start of *The Empire Strikes Back* campaign. "We wanted very much to communicate that there was this relationship, in fact a love story, pure and simple," says Ward. "But there are many different ways to do that. We explored traditional romance kinds of poses and postures. We explored a lot of different ideas that created some sense of angst that would exist as a result of that relationship. It seemed that what consumers really responded to was the tension that would exist in that kind of relationship."

With about fifty pieces of teaser poster concept art in hand (Ward had hired Venables, Bell & Partners for the job), focus groups helped narrow the choices for the right romantic angle to use. "That was some new territory for us in the *Star Wars* world," Ward says. "We needed to go out and

top left
POWER OF MYTH EUROPEAN TOUR
United Kingdom / 1999 / 25 × 35
The *Star Wars* characters share space with some of myth and legend's best-known figures in this poster for the proposed European Power of Myth tour, which was canceled. However, posters already had been printed for as many as five European venues, with each country highlighting a legendary character from its own past.

top right
FRENCH LOTTO: AMIDALA
France / 1999 / 22 × 59
The French national lottery licensed *The Phantom Menace* for a successful scratch-off game. Street kiosks were covered with posters, banners, and other point-of-purchase material.

opposite
STAR WARS CELEBRATION I
United States / 1999 / 24 × 36
John Alvin created a menacing Darth Maul looking over young Anakin Skywalker in this poster created for the first *Star Wars* Celebration fan event in Denver, Colorado.

see how people were going to respond, and pretty much hands down everyone kept coming back to the poster that we ended up with."

Lucasfilm ultimately chose the image of Anakin and Padmé facing away from each other, suggesting the friction that emerged from their forbidden relationship. And for the first time since the first *Star Wars* teaser, a telling line of copy was added to a *Star Wars* theatrical poster: "A Jedi Shall Not Know Anger. Nor Hatred. Nor Love." Again, the teaser was released as both a one-sheet and banner, as well as in a myriad of international languages. The large horizontal banner works best because it allows even more space between Anakin Skywalker and Padmé Amidala.

For the release poster, Struzan was again called upon to provide the artwork, this time designed in a more collaborative fashion. Lucasfilm and the artist traded ideas back and forth until the final

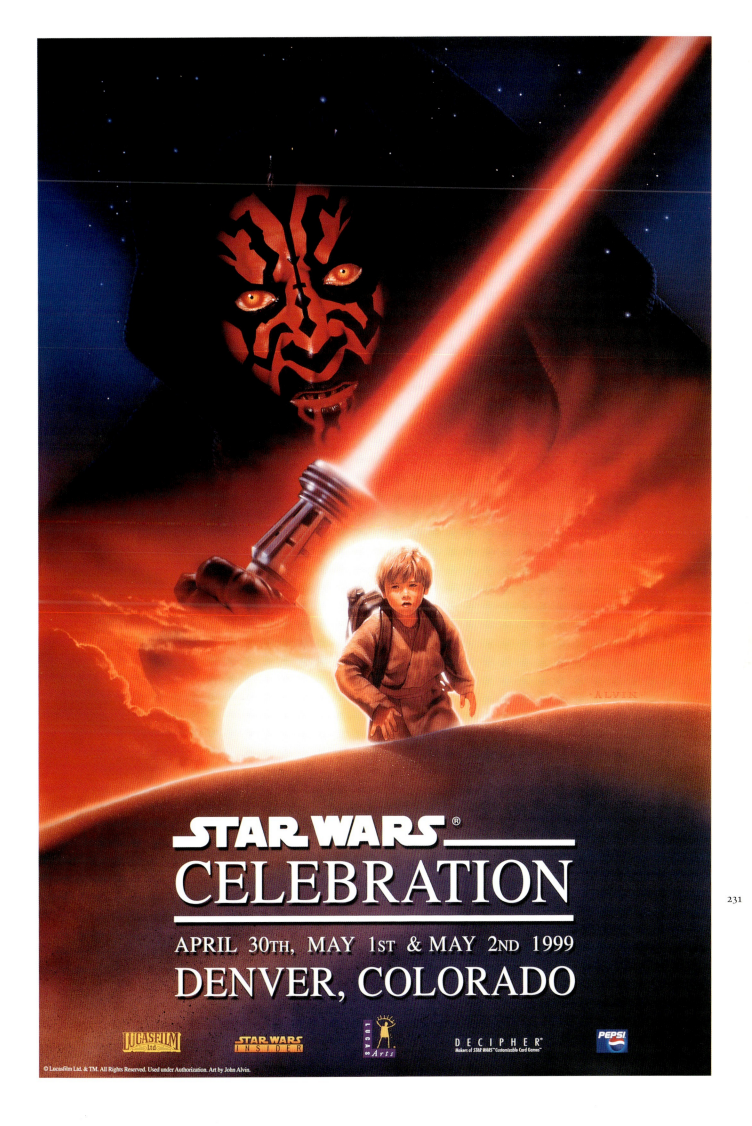

THE ART OF *STAR WARS*: DARTH MAUL
United Kingdom / 2000 / 20 × 30

opposite

THE ART OF *STAR WARS*: C-3PO United Kingdom / 2000 / 20 × 30
C-3PO has been framed in this clever image used for the Art of *Star Wars* exhibit, which started at the Barbican Centre in London. In the companion poster, Darth Maul looks like he's ready to fight an early concept sketch of himself by artist Iain McCaig.

opposite

JEDI-CON: SANDA ART Germany / 2001 / 23 × 33
Tsuneo Sanda produced an original artwork for Germany's Jedi-Con 2001, an event produced by the official fan club there.

below left

THE ART OF *STAR WARS*: DARTH MAUL FACE Finland / 2002 / 27 × 39
The devil is in the details of this Iain McCaig concept portrait of Darth Maul, which served as a poster for the Finnish Art of *Star Wars* exhibit.

below right

THE ART OF *STAR WARS*: C-3PO HEAD Finland / 2002 / 27 × 39
Rather than use the posters that had been developed for the European Art of *Star Wars* tour, the Taidemuseo Tennispalatsi, or Tennis Palace Art Museum, in Helsinki, used a blow-up of C-3PO's head at an angle to imply movement.

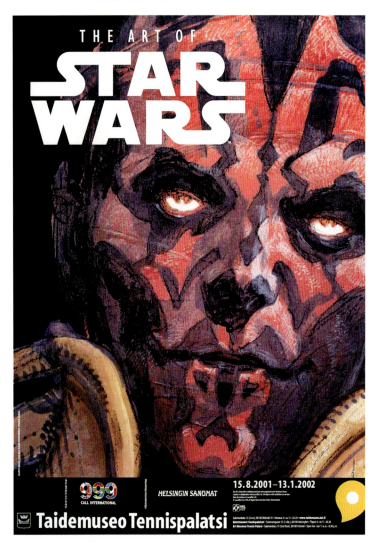
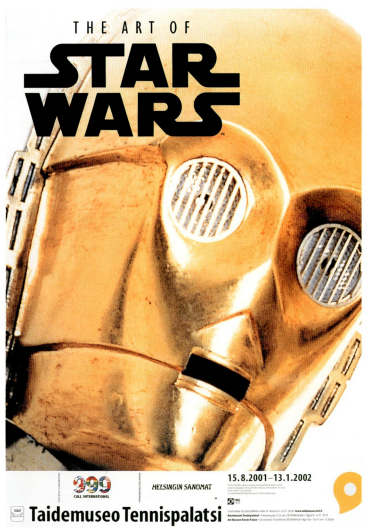

design was settled upon, one that easily evokes the romantic tone the campaign was after. The design was built around the paired image of Anakin and Padmé, which had been photographed specifically for the poster at one of the late pick-up filming sessions, since none of the photos already in hand were quite right to use as a model.

The international campaign again used an extensive array of imagery, all carrying the common motif of Jedi Knights or clone troopers lined up on the horizon with a major character or characters front and center. The images proved very popular worldwide. *Attack of the Clones* was released simultaneously worldwide on May 16 and 17, 2002—with a few exceptions. The release coincided with the quadrennial Soccer World Cup being played in Korea and Japan, so in those countries along with soccer-mad Latin America, the release was delayed until after the Cup finals. Taking advantage of Cup fever, some of the international campaigns were tweaked with soccer-appropriate taglines.

There also was a special photomontage poster for outdoor use in Italy, a country that has always been a hard sell for *Star Wars* movies. This over-

left
THE PHANTOM MENACE ON TV: AMIDALA
Germany / 2000 / 47 × 69
For Germany's debut of *The Phantom Menace* on television, three large transit station posters were designed, including this uncommon portrait of Queen Amidala in black. There was also a large lenticular poster on which Yoda fades into Darth Maul.

opposite
SHOWTIME "MAN IN BLACK"
United States / 1998 / 27 × 39.5
This poster for Showtime's 1998 debut of the *Star Wars* Special Edition makes an unusual request of its viewers.

sized sheet had a gauzy, romantic feel to it and featured a lovey-dovey Anakin and Padmé.

Episode II marked another first. Lucasfilm released a version of the film to IMAX large-screen theaters in North America starting November 1. Because at the time those theaters were capable of showing only two hours of film, some twenty minutes had to be cut from *Clones*. Another poster was called for, and this time the creative direction came from the Lucasfilm Marketing team. The poster shows a huge Yoda brandishing a lightsaber astride North America, with various landmarks at his feet. It was created by artist David McMacken, a Connecticut illustrator who specializes in posters that have the feel of the 1930s and 1940s.

For the final film of the saga, there was no question that Struzan would complete his own sextuple play by painting the main release poster. That left the teaser image, which was developed by New Wave Entertainment, one of Hollywood's leading

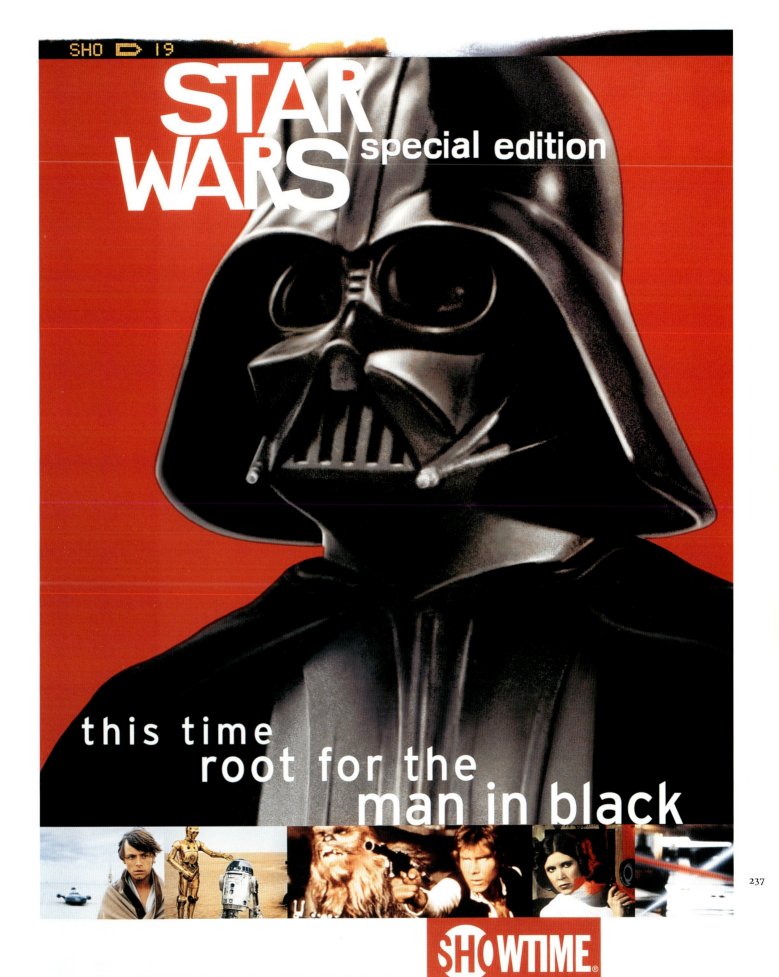

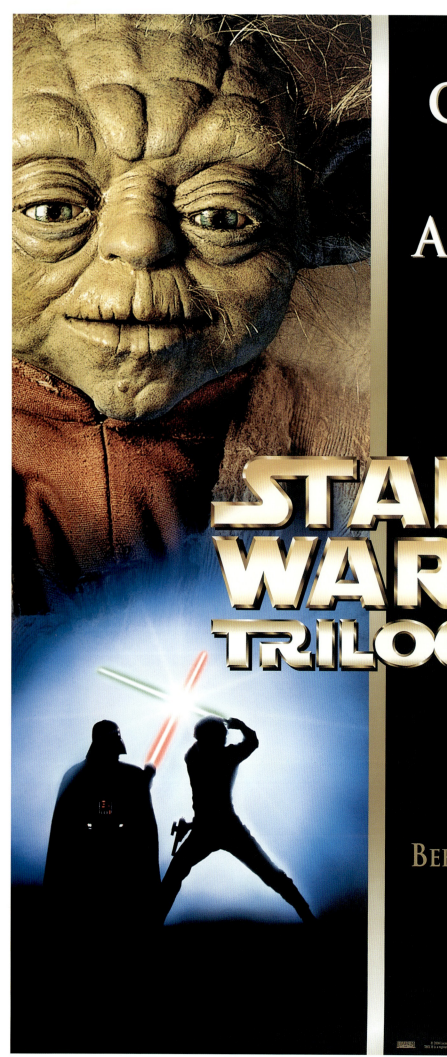

opposite

FOX HOME VIDEO SAGA RELEASE
United States / 2000 / 27 × 40
This rather formal poster for the 2000 *Star Wars* Trilogy video release focuses on the Jedi Knights of the story.

right

FOX HOME VIDEO JAPAN: DROIDS
Japan / 2000 / 13 × 28
This unique Japanese poster for the saga video release in 2000 elegantly juxtaposes technology with nature.

left
FOX HOME VIDEO GERMANY: DROIDS
Germany / 1997 / 23 × 33
Enhanced photos of C-3PO and R2-D2 practically jump off the front of this luminous German video store poster.

opposite
SEGA: *STAR WARS* TRILOGY ARCADE
Japan / 1998 / 29 × 40
This clever Sega poster quickly imparts the information that its *Star Wars* Trilogy arcade game is fast and furious.

motion picture and television marketing companies. The company came up with nearly two hundred different concepts, some just slight variations, but many starkly different. Some had taglines. Others featured Anakin Skywalker and his new Master, Emperor Palpatine. But the one that focus groups—representing broader audiences than just core fans—consistently picked harks back to the Episode I teaser. It shows a partially seen Anakin Skywalker gazing straight at the viewer, with his cape flying. The folds of the cape, which occupies most of the poster, form an image of the mask and helmet that Anakin is destined to wear by the end of *Revenge of the Sith*: that of Darth Vader. George Lucas, given a choice among a number of finalists, picked the same poster.

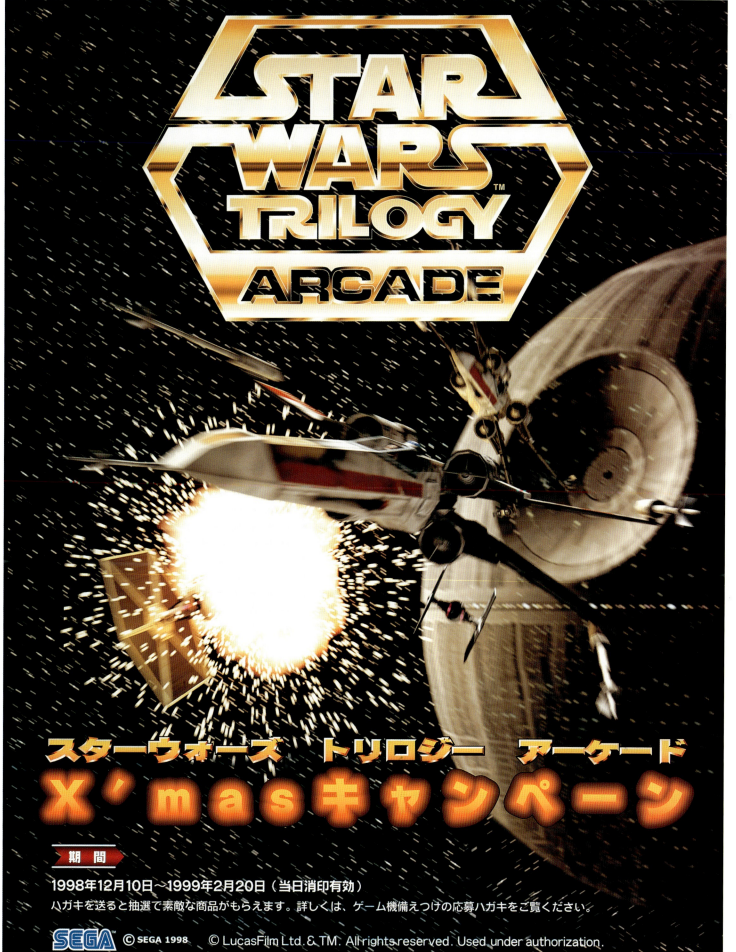

TERÄS KÄSI 1: ARDEN LYN Japan / 1998 / 12 × 33
TERÄS KÄSI 2: LUKE SKYWALKER Japan / 1998 / 12 × 33
TERÄS KÄSI 3: BOBA FETT Japan / 1998 / 12 × 33

The state of the art of video-game computer graphics was advanced enough that large blow-ups of three of the fighters in this PlayStation game were used by Sony. They are Arden Lyn, a master of an ancient martial art known as Teräs Käsi, Luke Skywalker, and Boba Fett.

opposite

JAPANESE MANGA Japan / 1999 / 14 × 20

Famous Japanese Manga artist Kia Asamiya of Studio Tron illustrated the Manga version of *The Phantom Menace* for Tentomushi Comics. This is a reproduction of the cover art with added characters and vehicles.

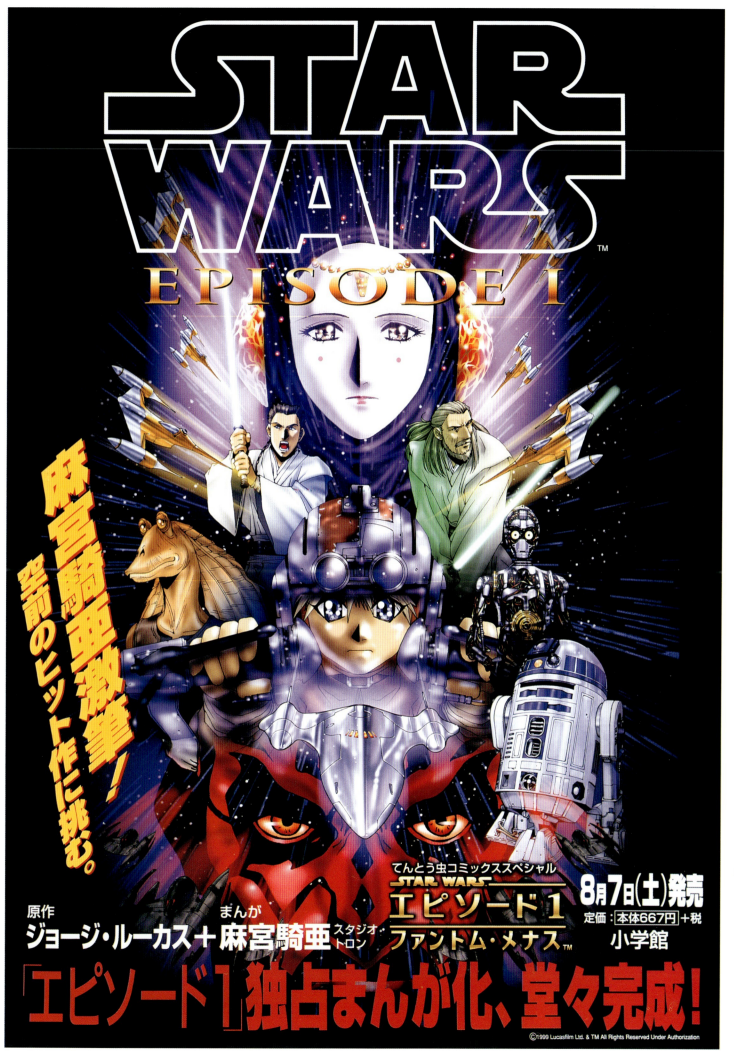

OFFICIAL *STAR WARS* FAN CLUB: "*STAR WARS* ROCKS"

United States / 1999 / 24 × 36

For this 1999 *Star Wars* Fan Club exclusive poster by Australian artist Hugh Fleming, the bearded artist featured himself as one of the *Star Wars* groupies in the audience. The piece originally was commissioned to accompany a story in *Star Wars Insider,* the official fan club magazine in the United States, about rock bands and music influenced by the original trilogy.

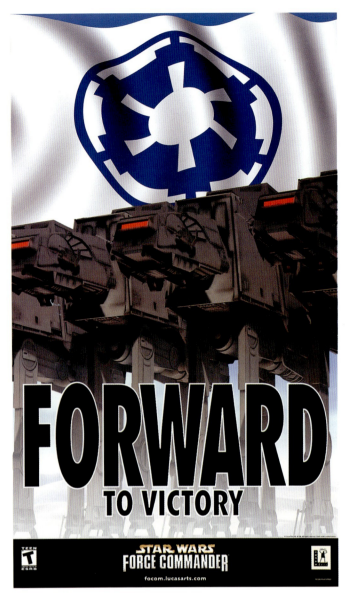
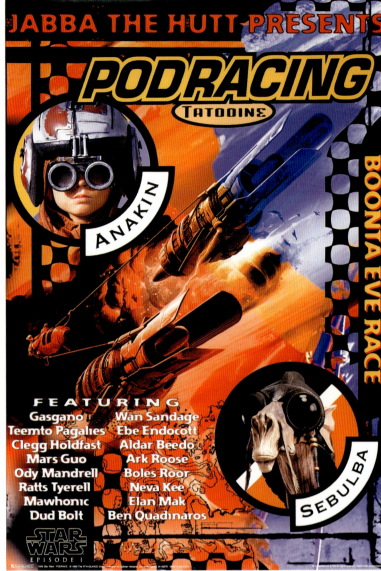

above left
FORCE COMMANDER VIDEO GAME: AT-ATS United States / 2000 / 13 × 22
This wonderful computer-generated imagery of a line of AT-ATs harks back to the Axis propaganda posters of the 1940s.

above right
BOONTA EVE PODRACE United States / 1999 / 24 × 36
The excitement of the Boonta Eve Race is successfully captured in this period-style illustration by artist Ken Phipps for At-a-Glance.

opposite, top left
LEGO: NABOO STARFIGHTER United States / 1999 / 24 × 36
LEGO *Star Wars* vehicles have taken flight on many of the advertising posters for the licensee.

opposite, bottom left
EPISODE I PLAYSTATION GAME Japan / 1999 / 20 × 28
This attractive photomontage was used by Sony for its Episode I PlayStation game.

opposite, right
FOX HOME VIDEO JAPAN: PODRACERS Japan / 2000 / 13 × 41
The vertical format of this Japanese poster for the release of Episode I on video gives this oft-used image a fresh look.

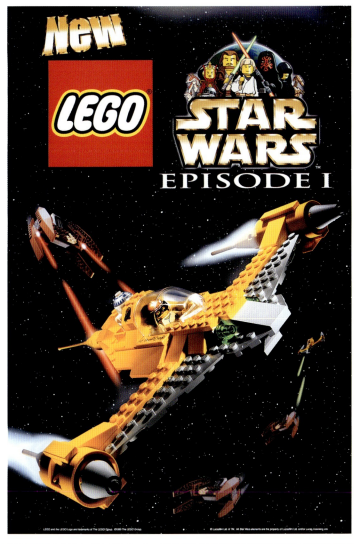

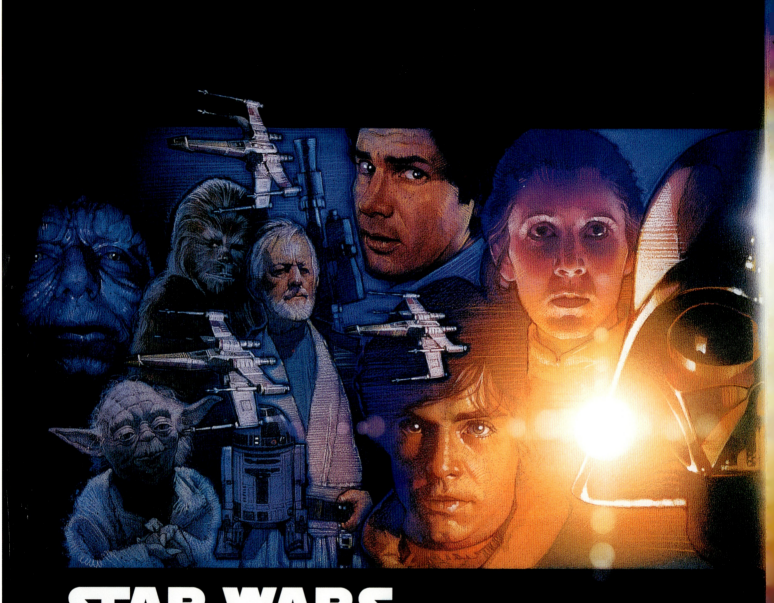

WIZARDS OF THE COAST: *STAR WARS* ROLEPLAYING GAME
United States / 2000 / 16 × 28
Darth Vader becomes the fulcrum between the two *Star Wars* trilogies in this poetic image created by Drew Struzan for Wizards of the Coast.

EPISODE I

DON'T PANIC
YOU'VE GOT FLIPPERS

WILLIAMS EPISODE I PINBALL United States / 1999 / 22 × 34
A simple but effective poster promotes Williams' Episode I pinball arcade game. It's likely to become a game-room fixture in years to come.

opposite, top left

DARTH MAUL PHOTO-MOSAIC

United Kingdom / 1999 / 25 × 36
This Darth Maul photomosaic was printed as a premium for the British edition of the *Star Wars* Fact Files in 1999. The technique uses hundreds or thousands of tiny photos to make up the shape and coloring of objects or people when viewed from a bit of a distance.

opposite, top right

UNISOURCE PAPERS: DARTH MAUL

Canada / 1999 / 21 × 33
Darth Maul's stare stole many glances in this unusual 1999 poster to promote Unisource Papers.

opposite, bottom left

DARTH MAUL BLACK LIGHT

United States / 1999 / 22 × 33
Darth Maul's tattooed face becomes an artful mosaic in this somewhat anachronistic 1999 black light poster. And it's flocked, too! Art by Johnny Kwan for At-a-Glance.

opposite, bottom right

THE PHANTOM MENACE ON TV: DARTH MAUL

Australia / 2001 / 30 × 40
Hide the kids! This photographic portrait of Darth Maul is enough to scare the folks Down Under into watching the first television broadcast of *The Phantom Menace*.

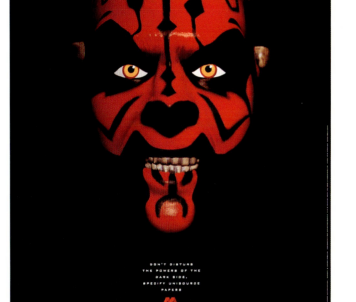
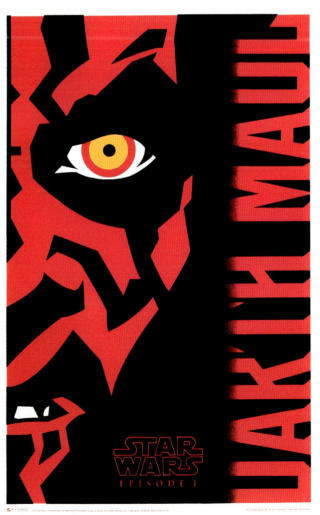

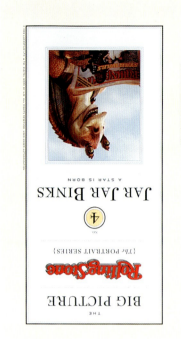
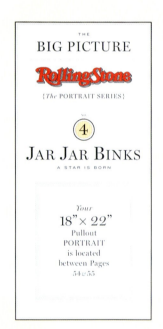

JAR JAR IN *ROLLING STONE* United States / 1999 / 22 × 24
Jar Jar Binks discovers his heritage in this pull-out poster from a 1999 issue of *Rolling Stone* magazine. The Jar Jar image was specially composed by Industrial Light + Magic. Poster © 1999 by RollingStone LLC.

opposite

FOX HOME VIDEO MEXICO: BART WARS Mexico / 1999 / 24 × 36
A collection of *Simpsons* episodes that featured one show heavy with *Star Wars* references was released in Mexico and other countries, using a clever spin on the epic duel between father and son for its advertising. The art originally had been developed for a 1998 cover story in *Star Wars Insider*. The Simpsons™ & © Twentieth Century Fox Film Corp. All Rights Reserved.

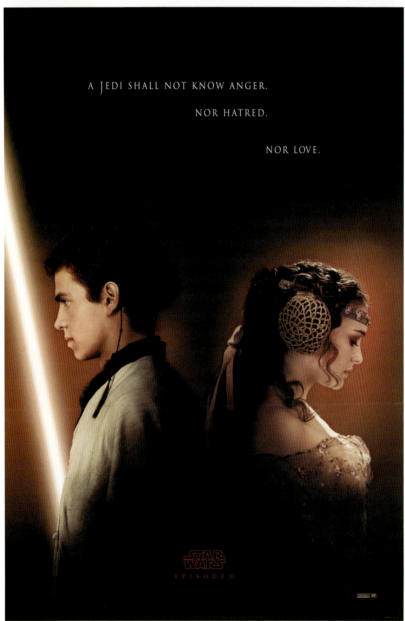

above
ATTACK OF THE CLONES ADVANCE THEATRICAL BANNER
United States / 2001 / 60 × 108
For Episode II, copy was again used on a *Star Wars* teaser, as this banner shows. The banner is even more effective than the standard one-sheet in showing tension—and distance—between the two lovers.

left
ATTACK OF THE CLONES THEATRICAL ADVANCE
United States / 2001 / 27 × 40
Anakin and Padmé's bristling relationship is clearly defined in this effective teaser produced for Episode II by Venables, Bell & Partners, a San Francisco agency.

opposite
ATTACK OF THE CLONES THEATRICAL ONE-SHEET
United States / 2002 / 27 × 40
Hayden Christensen and Natalie Portman were photographed in a pose exclusively as a reference for this Episode II poster. That and other images formed the basis of Drew Struzan's art.

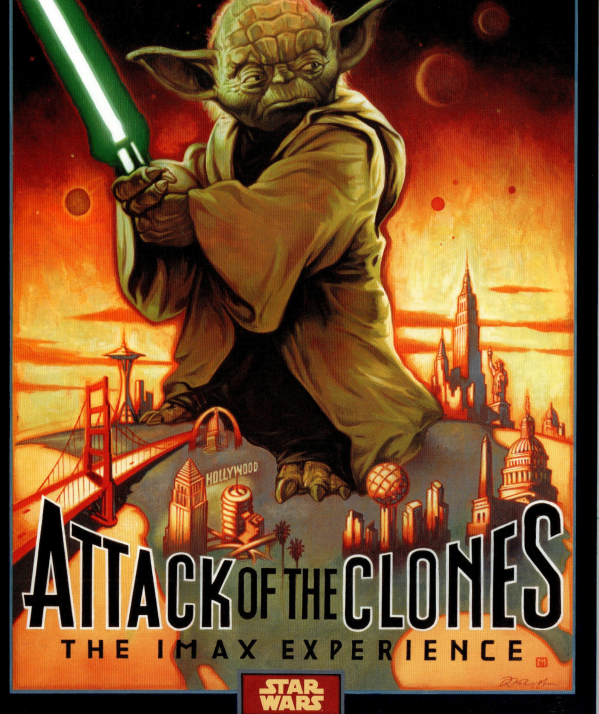

***ATTACK OF THE CLONES*: ROMANCE OUTDOOR** Italy / 2002 / 39 × 55
The romantic pose seen on the Italian *Attack of the Clones* poster was shot specifically for this piece of outdoor advertising and used nowhere else in the world. It was, however, the basis for the Struzan painted poster. Design by Scott Erwert.

opposite

YODA IMAX CAMPAIGN THEATRICAL ONE-SHEET AND BANNER United States / 2002 / 27 × 40, 48 × 60 Banner
The IMAX poster for *Attack of the Clones* is a wonderful diversion from a traditional modern movie campaign with this period-style rendering by artist David McMacken. The image was also used on a large vinyl banner for theaters. A few even-larger banners were made for the most important venues.

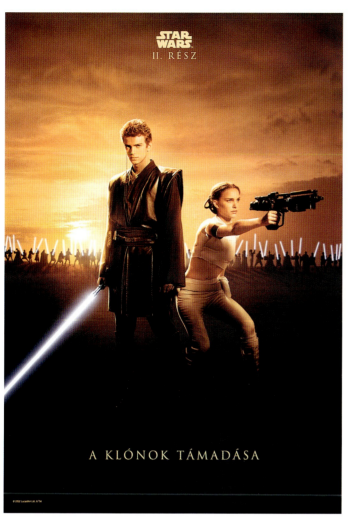

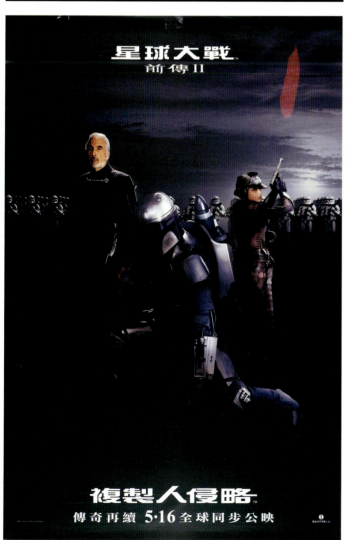

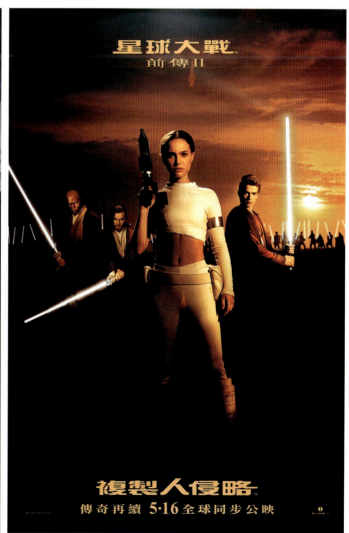

opposite
ATTACK OF THE CLONES: JANGO FETT ONE-SHEET
Hungary / 2002 / 27 × 39
The cool and elegant nature of the photograph belies the true grit of the bounty hunter Jango Fett in this one-sheet poster.

left
ATTACK OF THE CLONES: ANAKIN AND PADMÉ ONE-SHEET
Hungary / 2002 / 27 × 39
Anakin and Padmé are on the defensive in this posed battlefield image from a Hungarian one-sheet.

below left
ATTACK OF THE CLONES: VILLAINS OUTDOOR
Hong Kong / 2002 / 40 × 60

below right
ATTACK OF THE CLONES: HEROES OUTDOOR
Hong Kong / 2002 / 40 × 60
The heroes and villains of Episode II are given some exotic flare on these posters from Hong Kong used for outdoor advertising. Though not featured in this version, some of the large international posters using the image of Padmé hoisting her blaster clearly show the engraved prop serial number on the base of the grip. [See inset detail from German version.]

みんなで守ろう、みんなの地球。

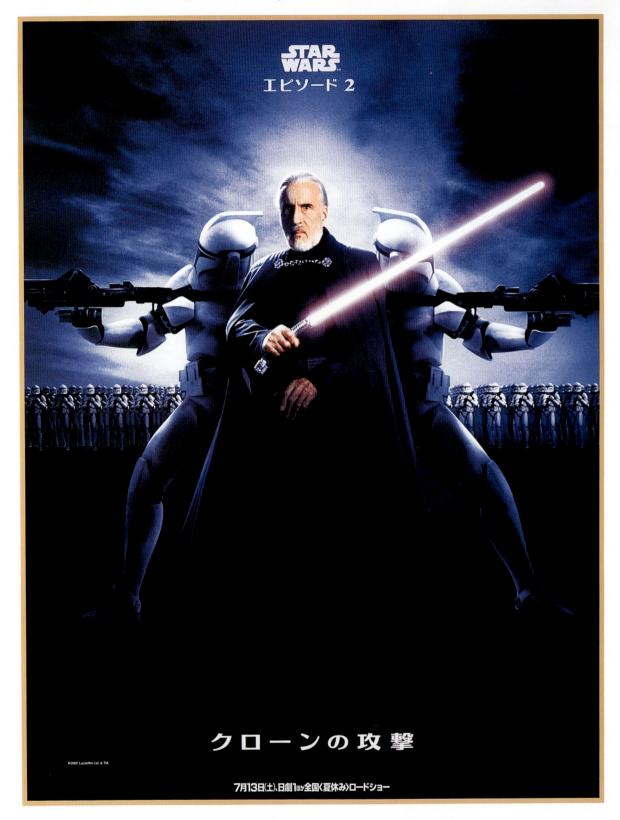

6月は環境月間です。
ルーカスフィルムと20世紀フォックス映画は地球温暖化と闘います。

環境月間は環境省が主唱しています。

opposite
***ATTACK OF THE CLONES*: DOOKU AND CLONES TRANSIT**
Japan / 2002 / 20 × 29
The perfectly matched clone troopers behind Count Dooku in this Japanese transit poster lend an uncommon symmetry to a *Star Wars* poster.

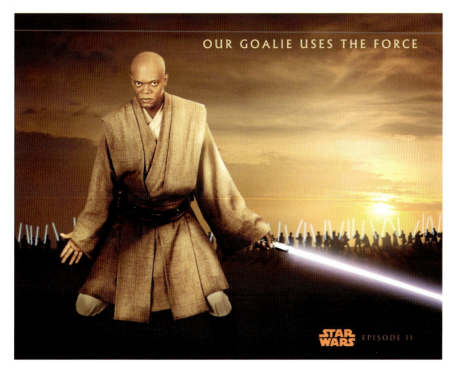

***ATTACK OF THE CLONES* WORLD CUP: OUR GOALIE USES THE FORCE OUTDOOR** United Kingdom / 2002 / 48 × 60
***ATTACK OF THE CLONES* WORLD CUP: THE OTHER "GROUP OF DEATH" OUTDOOR** United Kingdom / 2002 / 48 × 60
***ATTACK OF THE CLONES* WORLD CUP: FORCE-FORCE-TWO OUTDOOR** United Kingdom / 2002 / 48 × 60
***ATTACK OF THE CLONES* WORLD CUP: GIRLS PLAY ON OUR TEAM OUTDOOR** United Kingdom / 2002 / 48 × 60
Because the release of *Attack of the Clones* coincided with the quadrennial World Cup soccer tournament, a special program of cross-advertising was devised to showcase the *Star Wars* characters with terms familiar to soccer fans. The campaign was used for outdoor advertising in varied sizes in the UK, Brazil, and a number of other countries.

left

FOX HOME VIDEO ***ATTACK OF THE CLONES*: YODA**

United States / 2002 / 18 × 59

For the DVD and tape release of Episode II, Yoda's famous battle-ready pose was used to great effect in the campaign.

opposite

***CREA* MAGAZINE COVER POSTER**

Japan / 2002 / 29 × 40

The ill-fated lovers embrace for a cover of *Crea* magazine, which also served as an enlarged advertisement for the issue.

CREA

「恋する映画」スペシャル！

6月号発売中！

http://www.CYBERCREA.com

CINEMA_SECRET LOVE!

スターサイングッズ特別プレゼント！
ジョシュ・ハートネット
永瀬正敏／妻夫木聡
宮沢りえ／井川遥

- 金城武「映画の夢」語ります！
- 窪塚洋介の「ピンポン」直筆原稿
- 私のジョシュ独り占め体験！
- 「STAR WARS」噂のヘイデン直撃
- パリ発「アメリ」の舞台に潜入
- 「ブラピが告白」14年前の失恋秘話
- ジュリアのギャラが安い理由
- 激撮！ニコラス・ケイジの禿頭
- 「千と千尋」宮崎駿監督の意外な趣味
- ラッセル・クロウのオスカー自慢
- 韓国の新星ウォンビンの大好物
- マドンナの"ゾンビ写真"を入手!?
- レスリー・チャンのこだわり風水
- 「ディカプ最新作」公開延期の真相
- ウィノナ「万引きの瞬間」……他全100本!!

夏のおすすめ映画 30本完全ガイド

試写会&劇場ご招待
読者1000名様に！

Skincare_Project X
25歳からの美肌大作戦！
スキンケア「プロジェクトX」

㊙スクープ全100本一挙公開!!
映画の秘密！

***STAR WARS* CELEBRATION II: ANAKIN/VADER** United States / 2002 / 22 × 28
Star Wars Celebration II, an official gathering that attracted twenty-six thousand fans just weeks before the release of Episode II, used the images of Anakin Skywalker and Darth Vader to celebrate "25 Years of the Force." Design by Troy Alders.

opposite
***ATTACK OF THE CLONES*: "POD" PREMIUM** Singapore / 2002 / 30 × 43
Photocollage was the method of choice for many Episode II promotional and premium posters, including this one for SingTel Mobile from Singapore. The "pod" in the poster refers to SingTel's business segment that caters to the "young and trendy."

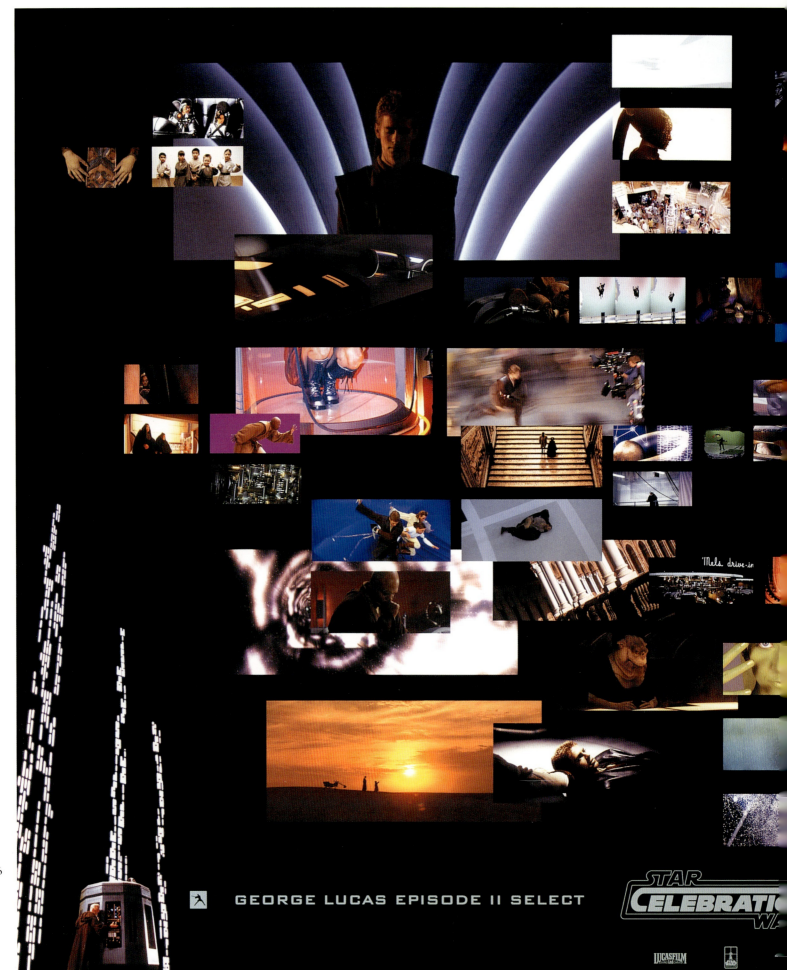

STAR WARS CELEBRATION II: GEORGE LUCAS SELECTS

United States / 2002 / 22 × 28

This Celebration II souvenir poster is a collage of unusual images from *Attack of the Clones* that George Lucas personally selected to run once a week on the official Web site, www.starwars.com.

JEDI STARFIGHTER VIDEO GAME United Kingdom / 2002 / 16.5 × 23
The Jedi starfighter gets bathed in the limelight for this video game poster from England.

opposite

STAR WARS CELEBRATION II: RUSS WALKS MONTAGE United States / 2002 / 22 × 34
A *Star Wars* Celebration II fan event exclusive poster by Russell Walks lends a symmetrical perspective to the two trilogies.
It was printed by Trends International.

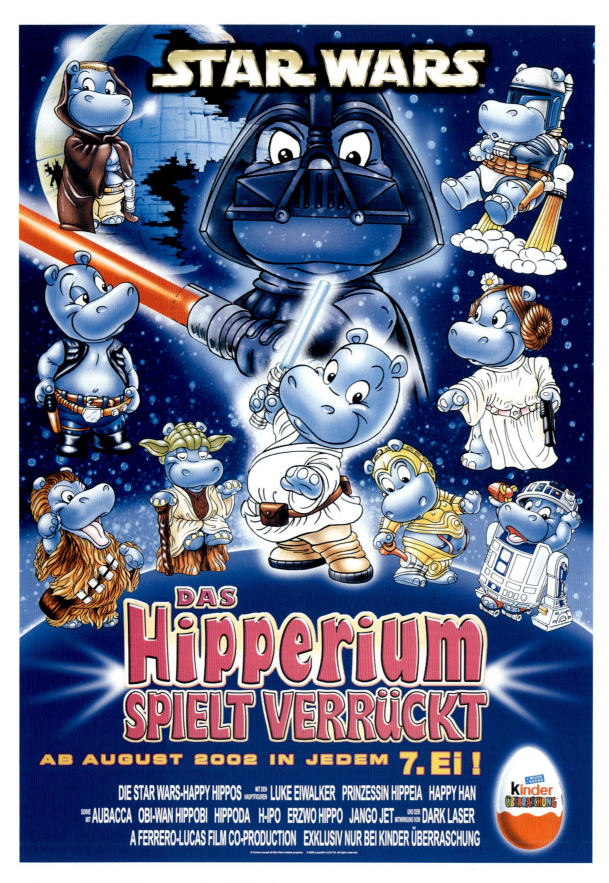

270 **STAR WARS HAPPY HIPPOS** Germany / 2002 / 23 × 33
Ferrero of Germany, part of a worldwide candy company, came up with a promotion using their trademarked Happy Hippos and the *Star Wars* characters. It was anyone's guess which character was in which chocolate-enrobed Kinder Egg.

opposite
JANGO FETT PIN-UP United States / 2002 / 22 × 34
Just as Boba Fett achieved pin-up status in 1980, so does father Jango in this retail poster from Trends International.

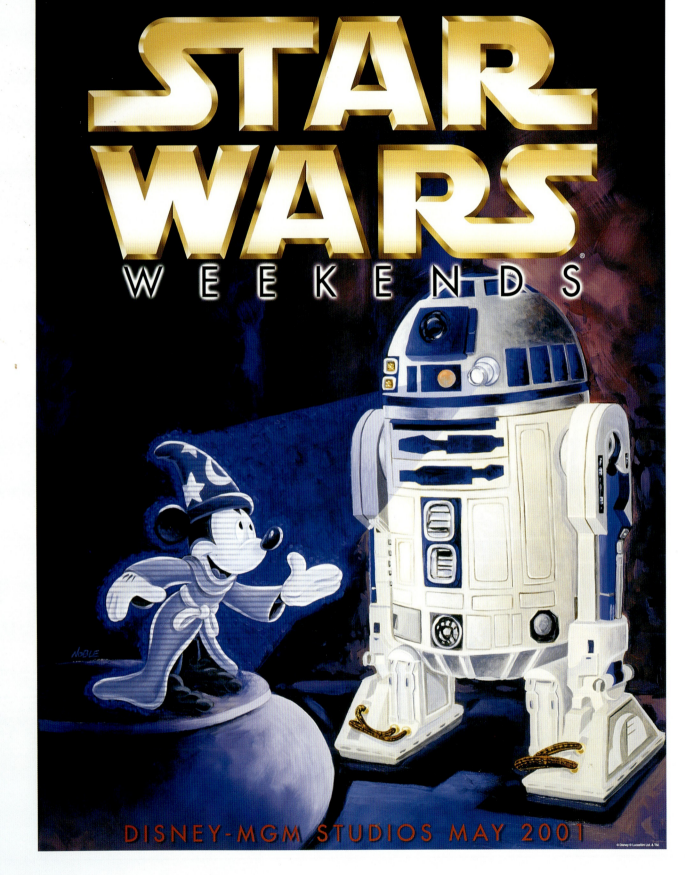

DISNEY *STAR WARS* WEEKENDS United States / 2001 / 18 × 24
Disney Design Group artist Randy Noble cleverly combined two icons of entertainment in this limited edition print produced for Disney's *Star Wars* Weekends event.

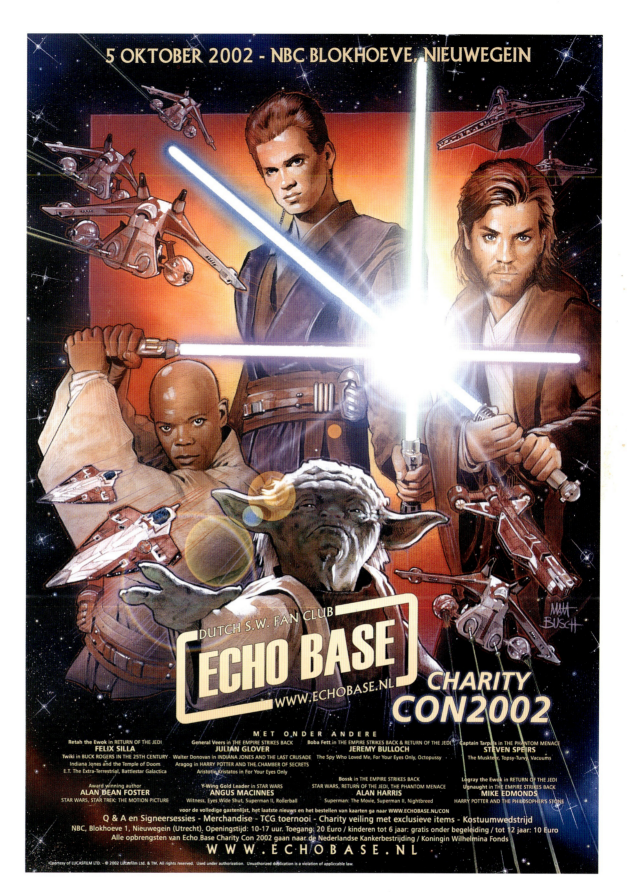

ECHO BASE CHARITY CON The Netherlands / 2002 / 19 × 28
Artist Matt Busch created this poster for the annual Echo Base Charity Con. Echo Base is an unofficial *Star Wars* fan club in The Netherlands.

STAR WARS: SCIENCE AND ART PART 2 Japan / 2004 / 20 × 29
Queen Amidala's Asian-influenced regalia was the perfect image to advertise the second part of Japan's *Star Wars*: Science and Art exhibit, which covered the first two prequels.

opposite

STAR WARS: SCIENCE AND ART PART 1 Japan / 2003 / 20 × 29
Japan's *Star Wars:* Science and Art exhibit was divided into two sections. The first, titled "The Art of *Star Wars*," is advertised in this poster of C-3PO and R2-D2 standing in the middle of a sea of props from the original trilogy. Scores of photos were taken after this impressive display was set up years ago, including a famous one of George Lucas himself in the spot occupied here by the droids.

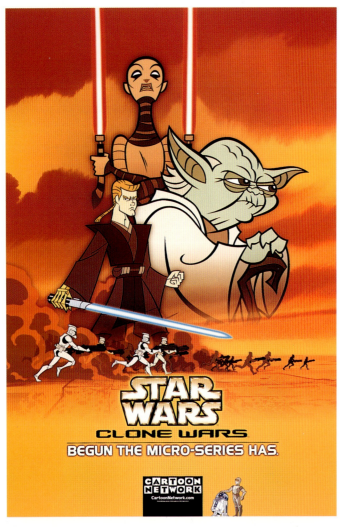
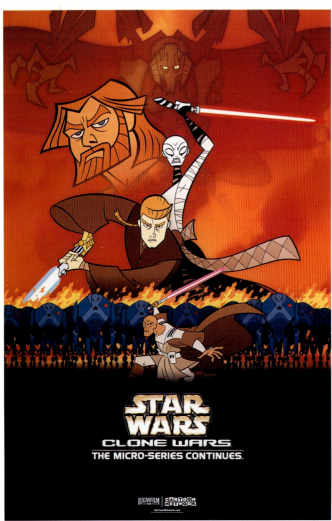

opposite, top left
CLONE WARS PART ONE
United States / 2003 / 24 × 36
Cartoon Network's *Clone Wars* micro-series debuted in 2003, helping to bridge the gap between the saga's second and third cinematic chapters.

opposite, bottom left
CLONE WARS PART TWO
United States / 2004 / 24 × 36
General Grievous, an Episode III villain, made his first appearance in this poster for the next ten episodes of the *Clone Wars* animated series.

opposite, right
CLONE WARS HYPERSPACE EXCLUSIVE
United States / 2003 / 18 × 24
Hyperspace, the premium Web site of the Official *Star Wars* Fan Club, offered this exclusive *Clone Wars* poster to members and new enrollees at San Diego's 2003 Comic-Con International.

above
HUNGRY JACKS PREMIUM OFFER
Australia / 2002 / 25 × 27.5
They look cool whatever they are. Hungry Jacks tells customers how to get these Episode II premiums, but not exactly what they are. Hint: Does the phrase "3D character frames" help?

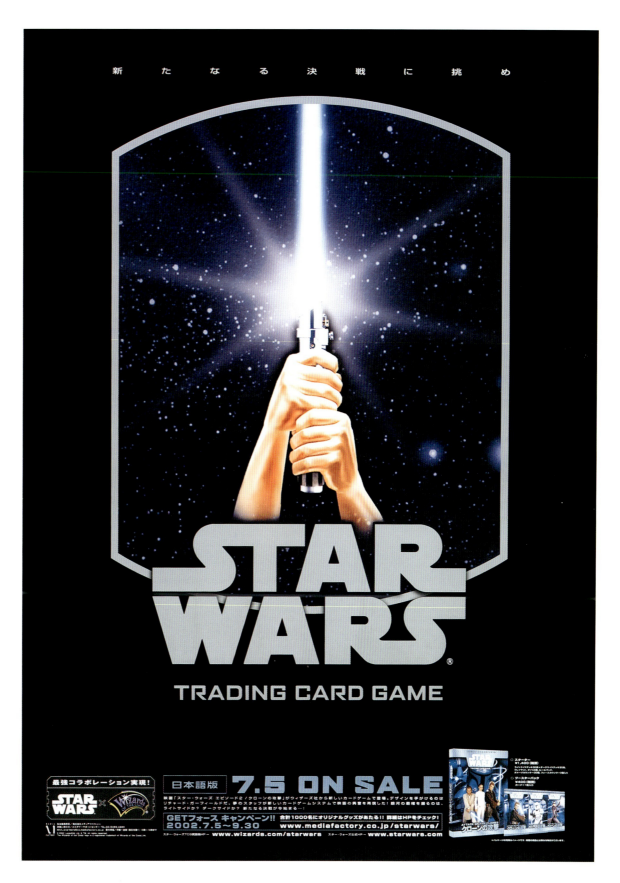

***STAR WARS* TRADING CARD GAME: LIGHTSABER** Japan / 2002 / 20 × 29
The hands with lightsaber image was used yet again for much of the merchandising of Episode II, including this poster for Wizards of the Coast's *Star Wars* Trading Card Game.

opposite

BOUNTY HUNTER VIDEO GAME France / 2002 / 17 × 23
This image of Jango Fett's T-shaped visor is used to menacing effect in this promotional poster for the Bounty Hunter video game.

OFFICIAL *STAR WARS* FAN CLUB: VANDER STELT PRINT

United States / 2003 / 24 × 30

Star Wars Fan Club members were the only ones who could purchase one of the five hundred prints of this remarkable *Attack of the Clones* lithograph by Jerry Vander Stelt.

ILM: YODA AND THE HULK United States / 2003 / 18 × 23
It's not easy being green. Pairing the ILM version of the Hulk from the Universal Pictures movie with the diminutive Jedi Master may not have made them two peas in a pod, but the fit seemed a natural for this 2003 poster by Ellen Pasternack and Jamy Wheless for the Siggraph convention. The Hulk and Related Comic Book Characters™ & © Marvel Characters, Inc. © 2003 Universal Studios.

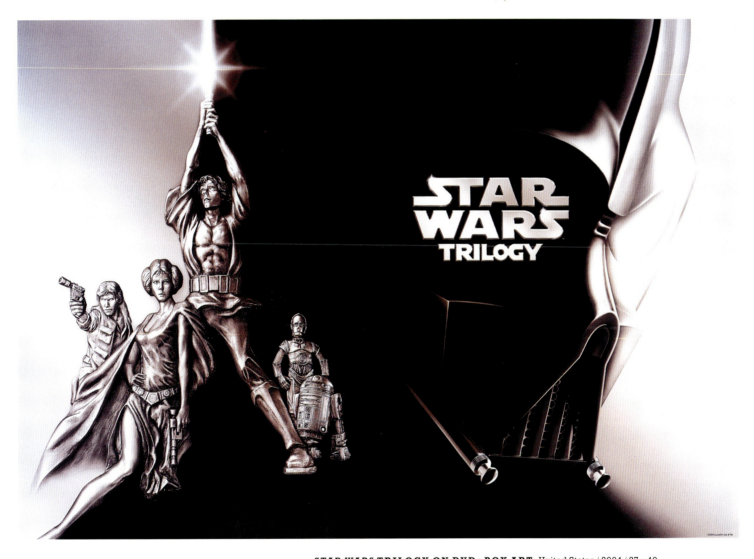

STAR WARS TRILOGY ON DVD: BOX ART United States / 2004 / 27 × 40
This embossed poster produced exclusively for the official StarWarsShop.com uses both sides of the DVD packaging art skillfully blended into one piece.

opposite

STAR WARS EN CONCIERTO Mexico / 2004 / 25.5 × 36
Erich Kunzel, who directed the 1982 Cincinnati *Star Wars* concert, returned for this Mexican encore in 2004, sponsored by the Official Mexican Fan Club.

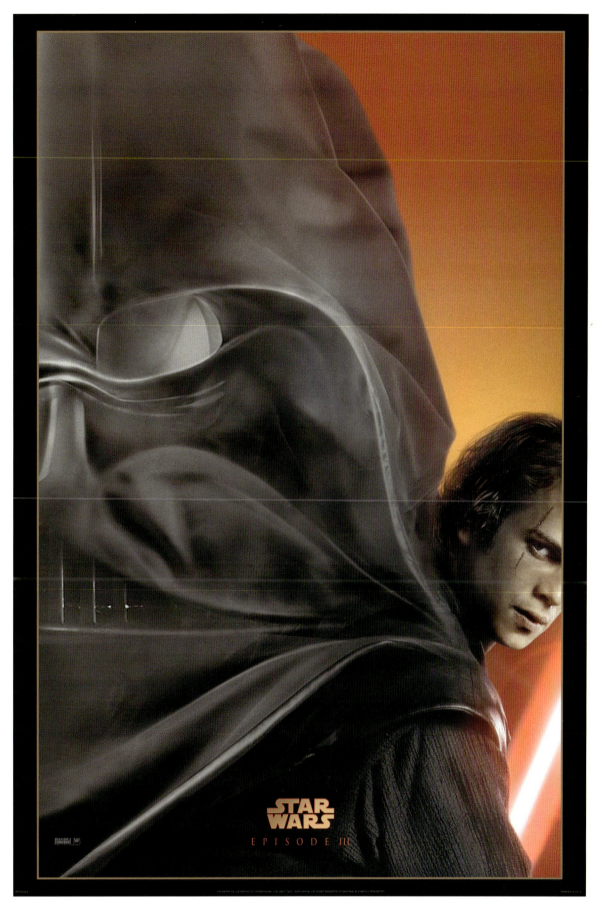

***REVENGE OF THE SITH* THEATRICAL ADVANCE AND BANNER**
United States / 2004 / 27 × 40, 60 × 96
One of nearly two hundred concepts developed by New Wave Entertainment, this Episode III Advance poster brings to mind the shadow of Darth Vader cast by the nine-year-old Anakin Skywalker on the Episode I Advance. This time, the combination of photo and art let us know that Anakin's transformation would be complete. The large vinyl banner was meant for display for up to five months until the final key art was released.

opposite
LUCASFILM MAGAZINE: OBI-WAN France / 2003 / 16 × 23
Obi-Wan's Episode III appearance was first glimpsed in this French Fan Club members' poster.

REVENGE OF THE SITH ADVANCE LARGE THEATRICAL BANNER
United States / 2004 / 120 × 180
This large vinyl banner, printed in very limited numbers, let Anakin's cape make an even bigger impact because of its horizontal format.

REVENGE OF THE SITH THEATRICAL ONE-SHEET United States / 2005 / 27 × 40
Artist Drew Struzan completes the circle with this stirring art for the final *Star Wars* movie.

APPENDIX

Bootlegs and Reprints

As with *Star Wars* itself, there is a dark side to the poster-collecting hobby. Sellers will knowingly or unknowingly pass off a poster as an original when it is a reprint or, worse, a bootleg.

First, to clarify, a reprint is a legitimate copy of a poster published by a sanctioned Lucasfilm Ltd. licensee. Reprints may resemble the originals in appearance and size but almost always will have the publisher's information accompanied by the printing date near the Lucasfilm copyright line.

Bootlegs, on the other hand, are deliberately designed to mislead. Because *Star Wars* bootlegs have been in heavy circulation since the early 1990s, serious collectors know what to look for. The following telltale characteristics can give away a bootleg poster:

Star Wars Style "A" one-sheet: A "hair" (a thin scratch-like line on the printed poster) exists on Luke's belt. Because the artwork on the bootleg poster is slightly smaller than on the original, the line "©1977 Twentieth Century Fox" at the bottom left side is flush with the left border; on the original, the copyright line is indented about one-eighth inch from the left border.

Star Wars Teaser "B" one-sheet: The GAU logo, or union "bug," is missing from the lower border near the National Screen Service (NSS) disclaimer.

Star Wars Style "C" one-sheet: A "hair" exists on the white gown on Leia's back.

Revenge of the Jedi with May 25 release date: There are at least two different bootlegs. On one, fold lines are apparent in the print, even though the poster may be rolled. Some sellers will actually fold over these lines to obscure them. On the other, a "cloud" exists in the black area near the Twentieth Century Fox logo. It is well disguised to the casual viewer because it appears appropriate to the style of the illustration. The area around the Fox logo, however, should be totally black.

Revenge of the Jedi with no date: Measurements are closer to 27 × 40 inches than the correct 27 × 41. Also, the Twentieth Century Fox logo in the lower right corner is a deeper shade of blue than that found on the original.

Star Wars Trilogy triple bill: The real poster is a photographic blowup with three lines of copy at the top. The bootleg is printed (and can smear) and has only two lines of copy on top.

Star Wars Style "D" one-sheet: Kilian Enterprises legitimately reprinted a 1992 commemorative poster, but the 1992 copyright information wasn't included. Most were printed with a serial number directly over the "Style D" in the lower right-hand corner, but some escaped without one. To ensure that this reprint would not be confused with an original, quotation marks were omitted around the letter D. But to confuse the matter further, National Screen Service printed a legitimate version of this poster *without* the quotation marks. To determine if a Style "D" is an original, it must possess either of the two following sets of conditions: It lacks a NSS disclaimer and has quotation marks around the letter D; it has the NSS disclaimer with no quotation marks around the letter D. Several images of bootleg posters can be viewed at www.movieposterauthentication.com.

Star Wars Poster List

The following list comprises a large majority of known posters printed for the *Star Wars* saga from 1976 through the launch of Episode III. It includes relatively few non-authorized posters. For ease of use, we've separated the list into four broad categories: Theatrical, Event, Advertising, and Commercial.

Posters can fluctuate widely in price, so rather than try to assign a value to each, the authors have attempted to rate each poster based on a combination of scarcity and value. To use an example, an Episode I video poster from Hungary, although rare, is not highly sought after, so it receives a rating of three stars on a scale of one to ten. Additionally, posters with equal ratings in different categories may not command the same market value. For example, although both the 1978 *Star Wars* Concert poster and the Chaykin "Poster 1" are rare and highly prized, the concert poster sells for more than twice the price of the Chaykin. Each, however, is considered a "10" in their respective categories of Events and Advertising. There is a fair amount of subjectivity that goes into the ratings, but the authors hope that this guide will help give a general sense of the desirability of a specific poster. There are several good *Star Wars* posters fan Web sites, chief among them www.starwarsmovieposter.com. But for more general information on poster collecting, we recommend www.learnaboutmovieposters.com.

THEATRICAL POSTERS

	Film	Year	Size	Rating	Description
ARGENTINA					
	SW	1978	27.5 × 41.5	•••••••	Like US Style "C," printed like a stone litho
	ESB	1980	58 × 42	••••••	Style "B" art in horizontal format; large white border
	ESB	1980	29 × 43	•••••••	Japanese Ohrai art
	ROTJ	1983	29 × 43	•••••	Like US Style "B," blurred, non-gloss
	EWOK1	1984	29 × 43	•••••	Style "B" Drew Struzan art; *Caravana Del Valor*
	AOTC	2001	27 × 39	••••	Advance teaser
	AOTC	2002	27 × 39	••••	Drew Struzan artwork
AUSTRALIA					
	SW	1978	27 × 40	••••••••	Like US Style "A"; small logo, blue NRC rating
	SW	1978	27 × 40	••••••••	Like US Style "A"; large logo, pink NRC rating
	SW	1978	13 × 27	•••••	Daybill of Style "A" artwork; small logo, blue NRC rating
	SW	1978	13 × 27	••••••	Daybill of Style "A" artwork; large logo, pink NRC rating
	SW	1978	27 × 40	••••••	Like US Style "C" sheet with superscript: "A long time ago in a galaxy far, far away . . ."
	SW	1978	13 × 27	••••••	Daybill of Style "C" artwork
	ESB	1980	13 × 27	•••••	Advance daybill of Vader head with Yoda/Luke below
	ESB	1980	27 × 40	••••••••	Japanese Ohrai art
	ESB	1980	13 × 27	••••••	Daybill of Japanese Ohrai art
	ESB	1980	13 × 27	•••••••	Daybill of Japanese Ohrai art; blue cast to silver logo
	SW	1981	27 × 40	••••••	Like US 1981 rerelease, but yellow banner says, "The Force will be with you"
	SW	1981	13 × 27	•••••	Daybill of 1981 rerelease
	ROTJ	1983	27 × 40	••••••	Like US Style "A" art
	ROTJ	1983	13 × 27	•••••	Daybill of US Style "A" art
	ROTJ	1983	27 × 40	••••••	Like US Style "B" art
	ROTJ	1983	13 × 27	•••••	Daybill of US Style "B" art
	TRIL	1985	27 × 40	••••••••	Black, white, silver and red with all three logos and art from *Star Wars* and *Empire* posters
	TRIL	1985	13 × 27	•••••	Daybill of triple-bill
	TRILSE	1997	27 × 40	•••	Ingot art
	SWSE	1997	27 × 40	•••	Drew Struzan art
	ESBSE	1997	27 × 40	•••	Drew Struzan art
	ROTJSE	1997	27 × 40	•••	Drew Struzan art
	TPM	1998	27 × 40	•••	Two-sided Advance
	TPM	1999	27 × 40	••••	Drew Struzan art; two-sided
	AOTC	2001	27 × 39	••••	Advance teaser
	AOTC	2002	46 × 70	••••••	One-sided Anakin and Padmé
	AOTC	2002	27 × 39	•••	Drew Struzan art
BELGIUM					
	SW	1978	14 × 21	•••••••	Miniature of US "A" sheet in French
	SW	1978	14 × 21	•••••••	Miniature of US "A" sheet in Flemish
	ESB	1980	14 × 21	•••••	Miniature of US "B" sheet in French
	ESB	1980	14 × 21	•••••	Miniature of US "B" sheet in Flemish
	ROTJ	1983	14 × 21	•••••	Jouin art, Flemish title, all else in English
	ROTJ	1983	14 × 21	•••••••	Jouin art, French title, with "Clipper" toys superscript in Flemish
	EWOK1	1985	14 × 21	•••••	*Caravan of Courage*; Struzan art in Flemish and French
	SWSE	1997	13 × 20	•••	Drew Struzan art
	ESBSE	1997	13 × 20	•••	Drew Struzan art
	ROTJSE	1997	13 × 20	•••	Drew Struzan art
BRAZIL					
	SW	1978	25 × 36	•••••••	Like US "C" sheet
	ESB	1980	25 × 36	•••••••	Like Japanese Ohrai art
	ROTJ	1983	25 × 36	••••••	Like US "A" sheet
	ROTJ	1983	25 × 36	••••••	Like US "B" sheet
	TPM	1998	25 × 36	•••	Advance, one-sided; "Episodio I"
	AOTC	2002	48 × 60	••••••••	"Yodinho!" Yoda against Jedi horizon
	AOTC	2002	48 × 96	••••••••	"Yodinho!" Yoda against Jedi horizon; horizontal
	AOTC	2002	25 × 37	•••	Drew Struzan art
BULGARIA					
	TPM	1999	27 × 38	•••	Drew Struzan art; "Hebuauma. . . ."
	AOTC	2002	27 × 38	•••	Drew Struzan art
CANADA					
	SW	1977	27 × 41	•••••••	Teaser "B" white on blue; Canadian seal over PG rating box
	SW	1977	23.5 × 31.5	•••••••	French Style "A" poster with Quebec sticker
	SW	1979	27 × 41	•••••••••	US "It's Back!" silver and blue with red band; Canadian seal next to credits
	ESB	1980	15 × 21	•••••••	Like French "A" version with Quebec sticker
	SW	1981	22 × 28	•••••••	US rerelease with yellow stripe; white label over PG rating box
	TRIL	1985	27 × 41	•••••••••+	Triple-bill one-sheet; Uptown Theater, Toronto; printed on photographic paper
	AOTC	2001	27 × 40	••••	Two-sided Advance; in French
CROATIA					
	TPM	1999	18 × 26	•••	Drew Struzan art; "Epizoda I: Fantomska Prijetnja"
CZECHOSLOVAKIA					
	SW	1990	23 × 33	•••••••	Tom Jung "A" sheet art with logo in Czech and English with "Lucernafilm Beta"
	SW	1990	12 × 16.5	••••••	Tom Jung "A" sheet art with logo in Czech and English with "Lucernafilm Beta"
	TPM	1999	23 × 33	•••	Drew Struzan art: "Epizoda I: Skryta Hrozba"
DENMARK					
	SW	1978	24 × 33	••••••	Like US "A" sheet
	ESB	1980	24 × 33	••••••	Like US "B" sheet
	ESB	1980	12 × 18	•••••••	Horizontal with US "B" art at left and title at right; premieres August 15, 1980
	ROTJ	1983	24 × 33	••••••	Like US "B" sheet
	TPM	1998	24 × 33	•••	Advance, one-sided
	TPM	1999	24 × 33	•••	Drew Struzan art; "Den Usynlige Fjende"
	AOTC	2001	24 × 33	•••	Advance teaser
	AOTC	2002	24 × 33	•••	Drew Struzan art
ESTONIA					
	TPM	1999	19 × 28	••••	Drew Struzan art; "Osa I: Mahtamatu Oht"
FINLAND					
	SW	1978	16 × 24	••••••	Like US "C" sheet; both Finnish and Swedish languages
	ESB	1980	16 × 24	••••••	Like US "B" sheet
	ROTJ	1983	16 × 24	••••••	Like US "B" sheet
	TPM	1999	16 × 24	•••	Drew Struzan art
	AOTC	2002	16 × 24	•••	Drew Struzan art
FRANCE					
	SW	1978	120 × 144	••••••••	Eight sheet; artwork inside French title against white
	SW	1978	63 × 94	••••••••	Two sheet; artwork inside French title against white

THEATRICAL POSTERS

Film	Year	Size	Rating	Description
FRANCE, CONT.				
SW	1978	59 × 78	•••••••	Two sheet & artwork inside French title against white
SW	1978	47 × 62	•••••	Like US "A" sheet in French
SW	1978	23.5 × 31.5	•••••	Like US "A" sheet in French; white border, blue title
ESB	1980	27 × 108	••••••••	Advance "Le 20 Aout" in two sheets, Vader on left, droids on right
ESB	1980	47 × 62	••••••••	Like US "A" sheet but in French and with Lando and Boba Fett at right
ESB	1980	15 × 21	••••••	Like US "A" sheet but in French and with Lando and Boba Fett at right
ESB	1980	120 × 160	•••••••••	Like US "B" sheet; horizontal eight sheet, English title
ESB	1980	47 × 62	•••••••	Like US "B" sheet but in French
ESB	1980	23 × 31.5	•••••••	Black, white, purple Advance with copies of media reviews
ROTJ	1983	23 × 63	•••••	Door poster like US "A" sheet with superscript "Le 19 Octobre"
ROTJ	1983	144 × 240	••••••••	Jouin montage art billboard in eight sections
ROTJ	1983	59 × 78	•••••••	Jouin montage art in two sheets
ROTJ	1983	47 × 63	••••••	Jouin montage art
ROTJ	1983	15 × 21	•••••	Jouin montage art
EWOK1	1984	47 × 63	•••••	Like US "B" sheet
EWOK1	1984	23 × 30.5	•••••	Like US "B" sheet
TRIL	1985	23 × 62	•••••••	Triple bill with three small poster artworks on tall vertical format
TRIL	1985	23 × 62	•••••••	Triple bill with three small poster artworks on tall vertical format, white time blocks
TRILSE	1997	47 × 63	••••	Ingot art sealed on stiff card
TRILSE	1997	47 × 63	•••	Ingot art not sealed on card
SWSE	1997	47 × 63	•••••	Drew Struzan art sealed on stiff card
SWSE	1997	47 × 63	••••	Drew Struzan art not sealed on card
ESBSE	1997	47 × 63	•••••	Drew Struzan art sealed on stiff card
ESBSE	1997	47 × 63	••••	Drew Struzan art not sealed on card
ROTJSE	1997	47 × 63	•••••	Drew Struzan art sealed on stiff card
ROTJSE	1997	47 × 63	••••	Drew Struzan art not sealed on card
TRILSE	1997	16 × 21	••	Ingot art
SWSE	1997	16 × 21	•••	Drew Struzan art
ESBSE	1997	16 × 21	•••	Drew Struzan art
ROTJSE	1997	16 × 21	•••	Drew Struzan art
TPM	1998	47 × 63	••••	Advance; sealed folded on stiff card "Affiche Originale"
TPM	1998	47 × 63	•••	Advance; "UFD" in corner
TPM	1999	47 × 63	•••••	Drew Struzan art; sealed folded on stiff card "Affiche Originale"
TPM	1999	47 × 63	••••	Drew Struzan art
TPM	1999	27 × 39	••••	Drew Struzan art, two-sided
TPM	1999	93 × 136	•••••••	Maul; vertical, two sheets; "NRJ" in corner
TPM	1999	46 × 67	•••••••	Maul; two-sided; "NRJ" in corner
TPM	1999	15 × 21	••••••	Maul ("NRJ" below, October 13 start)
TPM	1999	93 × 136	•••••••	Qui-Gon; vertical, two sheets; "NRJ" in corner
TPM	1999	46 × 67	•••••••	Qui-Gon; two-sided; "NRJ" in corner
TPM	1999	93 × 136	•••••••	Amidala; vertical, two sheets; "NRJ" in corner
TPM	1999	46 × 67	•••••••	Amidala; two-sided; "NRJ" in corner
TPM	1999	15 × 21	••••••	Amidala ("NRJ" below, October 13 start)
TPM	1999	46 × 67	•••••••	Watto; two-sided; "NRJ" in corner
TPM	1999	15 × 21	••••••	Watto ("NRJ" below, October 13 start)
TPM	1999	46 × 67	•••••••	Obi-Wan; two-sided; "NRJ" in corner
TPM	1999	15 × 21	••••••	Obi-Wan ("NRJ" below, October 13 start)
TPM	1999	46 × 67	•••••••	Battle droid; two-sided; "NRJ" in corner
TPM	1999	15 × 21	••••••	Battle droid; ("NRJ" below, October 13 start)
TPM	1999	46 × 67	•••••	Jar Jar; two-sided; "NRJ" in corner
TPM	1999	15 × 21	••••	Jar Jar ("NRJ" below, October 13 start)
TPM	1999	46 × 67	•••••	Anakin; two-sided; "NRJ" in corner
TPM	1999	46 × 67	•••••••	Mace; two-sided; "NRJ" in corner
AOTC	2001	46 × 62	••••	Anakin and Padmé Advance like US
AOTC	2002	46.5 × 72	•••••••	Drew Struzan art on banner with rods, string hanger; two-sided
AOTC	2002	46 × 62	••••••	Drew Struzan art
AOTC	2002	15 × 21	••••	Drew Struzan art
AOTC	2002	90 × 124	•••••••	Anakin and Padmé on landscape; four sheets, "NRJ" in corner
AOTC	2002	47 × 69	•••••••	Anakin and Padmé on landscape; NRJ in corner, "Hit Music Only"; halftone reverse
AOTC	2002	90 × 124	•••••••	Dooku and troopers; four sheets, "NRJ" in corner
AOTC	2002	47 × 69	•••••••	Dooku and troopers, "NRJ" in corner, halftone reverse
AOTC	2002	90 × 124	•••••••	Jango; four sheets, "NRJ" in corner
AOTC	2002	47 × 69	•••••••	Jango, "NRJ" in corner, halftone reverse
AOTC	2002	47 × 69	•••••••	Mace and Obi-Wan, "NRJ" in corner, halftone reverse
AOTC	2002	47 × 136	•••••••	Anakin, vertical two sheets; "NRJ" in corner, halftone reverse
AOTC	2002	47 × 136	•••••••	Padmé, vertical two sheets; "NRJ" in corner, halftone reverse
AOTC	2002	47 × 136	•••••••	Jango, vertical two sheets; "NRJ" in corner, halftone reverse
AOTC	2002	47 × 136	•••••••	Yoda, vertical two sheets; "NRJ" in corner with critic comments, halftone reverse
GERMANY				
SW	1977	25 × 35	•••••••••	Instruction sheet for 10-sheet Deko display: "Das Display-Material fur Ihre Theaterdekoration"
SW	1977	23 × 33	••••••••••	A. TIE fighter
SW	1977	23 × 33	••••••••••	B. C-3PO and R2-D2
SW	1977	23 × 33	••••••••••	C. Two X-wing fighters
SW	1977	23 × 33	••••••••••	D. Jawa and "Tusken-Bandit"
SW	1977	23 × 33	••••••••••	E. Large blue planet
SW	1977	23 × 33	••••••••••	F. Luke and Leia
SW	1977	23 × 33	••••••••••	G. Star Destroyer
SW	1977	23 × 33	••••••••••	H. Obi-Wan and Darth Vader
SW	1977	23 × 33	••••••••••	I. X-wing and "broken" red planet
SW	1977	23 × 33	••••••••••	J. Chewbacca and Han Solo
SW	1977	19.5 × 46.5	••••••••••	Krieg der Sterne logo in blue star-field letters on silver with *Star Wars* under, part of Deko display
SW	1977	13 × 23	•••••••	Krieg der Sterne logo in blue star-field letters on silver with *Star Wars* under, part of Deko display
SW	1977	19.5 × 23	••••••••••	Silver paper insert for Deko display: "Es War Einmal . . ."
SW	1977	16 × 27.5	•••••••••	Illustration of battle scene, miniature of Deko display
SW	1978	46 × 67	••••••••	Like US "A" sheet with silver background; two sheets
SW	1978	33 × 46	•••••••	Like US "A" sheet with silver background
SW	1978	23 × 33	••••••	Like US "A" sheet with silver background
SW	1978	33 × 46	•••••••	Like US "C" sheet with silver background
SW	1978	23 × 33	••••••	Like US "C" sheet with silver background
SW	1978	11.5 × 16.5	••••••	Like US "C" sheet with silver background
SW	1978	23.5 × 33	•••••	Uncut sheet of six paper lobby cards with blue borders and perforations (Set A)
SW	1978	23.5 × 33	•••••	Uncut sheet of six paper lobby cards with blue borders and perforations (Set B)

THEATRICAL POSTERS

Film	Year	Size	Rating	Description
GERMANY, CONT.				
ESB	1980	7 × 94	●●●●●●	Banner: "The *Star Wars* Continues" (white on blue)
ESB	1980	3 × 38	●●●●	Banner: "The *Star Wars* Continues" (white on blue) with adhesive backing
ESB	1980	33 × 46	●●●●●●	Luke in flight outfit with Yoda on shoulder
ESB	1980	23 × 33	●●●●●●	Luke in flight outfit with Yoda on shoulder; black logo
ESB	1980	11.5 × 16	●●●●●	Luke in flight outfit with Yoda on shoulder
ESB	1980	23 × 33	●●●●●●	Like US "B" sheet
ESB	1980	47 × 67	●●●●●●●●●	Luke on Tauntaun; centerpiece to Deko display in two sheets
ESB	1980	18 × 33	●●●●●●●●●	A. Han Solo: Character photo Deko display with large blue caption bands
ESB	1980	18 × 33	●●●●●●●●●	B. Darth Vader
ESB	1980	18 × 33	●●●●●●●●●	C. Yoda
ESB	1980	18 × 33	●●●●●●●●●	D. AT-AT
ESB	1980	18 × 33	●●●●●●●●●	E. Chewbacca
ESB	1980	18 × 33	●●●●●●●●●	F. Luke
ESB	1980	18 × 33	●●●●●●●●●	G. Leia
ESB	1980	18 × 33	●●●●●●●●●	H. C-3PO and R2-D2
ESB	1980	23.5 × 33	●●●●●	Uncut sheet of six paper lobby cards (Set A)
ESB	1980	23.5 × 33	●●●●●	Uncut sheet of six paper lobby cards (Set B)
ROTJ	1983	33 × 46	●●●●●●	Like US "A" sheet art: Opening Dec. 9
ROTJ	1983	23 × 33	●●●●●	Like US "A" sheet art: Opening Dec. 9
ROTJ	1983	11.5 × 19	●●●●●	Like US "A" sheet art: Opening Dec. 9
ROTJ	1983	23 × 33	●●●●●●	*Jedi* Advance with all three logos and art from US "A" sheet
ROTJ	1983	12 × 16.5	●●●●●	*Jedi* Advance with all three logos and art from US "A" sheet
ROTJ	1983	33 × 46	●●●●●●	Like US "B" sheet art
ROTJ	1983	23 × 33	●●●●●	Like US "B" sheet art
ROTJ	1983	12 × 16.5	●●●●	Like US "B" sheet art
ROTJ	1983	16 × 34	●●●●●●●●●	A. All three logos: Deko display of continuous posters tied by lightsabers
ROTJ	1983	16 × 34	●●●●●●●●●	B. Darth Vader
ROTJ	1983	16 × 34	●●●●●●●●●	C. Luke and Leia
ROTJ	1983	16 × 34	●●●●●●●●●	D. Gamorrean Guard
ROTJ	1983	16 × 34	●●●●●●●●●	E. Yoda and heroes
ROTJ	1983	16 × 47	●●●●●●●●●	F. Horizontal ROTJ logo banner
ROTJ	1983	23.5 × 33	●●●●●	Uncut sheet of six paper lobby cards (Set A)
ROTJ	1983	23.5 × 33	●●●●●	Uncut sheet of six paper lobby cards (Set B)
TRIL	1985	23 × 33	●●●●●●●●●	A. *Star Wars*—Torn out news headlines on the "Star Wars" defense plan: *Star Wars* Belongs Only in the Movies
TRIL	1985	23 × 33	●●●●●●●●●	B. *The Empire Strikes Back* logo, otherwise the same as above
TRIL	1985	23 × 33	●●●●●●●●●	C. *Return of the Jedi* logo, otherwise the same as above
EWOK1	1985	47 × 66	●●●●●●●	Two sheets with unique art by Rob
EWOK1	1985	16.5 × 23.5	●●●●●●	Horizontal art by Rob
EWOK1	1985	33 × 46	●●●●●●	*Caravan of Courage:* Struzan art
EWOK1	1985	23 × 33	●●●●●	*Caravan of Courage:* Struzan art
EWOK1	1985	11.5 × 16.5	●●●●	*Caravan of Courage:* Struzan art
EWOK1	1985	16.5 × 23.5	●●●●●●●	A. Painting of Ewok with *Caravan* logo on bright yellow background
EWOK1	1985	16.5 × 23.5	●●●●●●●	B. Painting of different Ewok with *Caravan* logo on bright yellow background
EWOK2	1986	33 × 47	●●●●●●	Battle for Endor (R. Casaro art)
EWOK2	1986	23 × 33	●●●●●	Battle for Endor (R. Casaro art)
TRILSE	1997	47 × 66	●●●	Ingot art in two sheets
TRILSE	1997	33 × 47	●●●	One-sided Ingot art
TRILSE	1997	23 × 33	●●●	One-sided Ingot art
SWSE	1997	33 × 47	●●●●	One-sided Drew Struzan art
SWSE	1997	23 × 33	●●●	One-sided Drew Struzan art
ESBSE	1997	47 × 66	●●●●	Drew Struzan art in two sheets
ESBSE	1997	33 × 47	●●●●	One-sided Drew Struzan art
ESBSE	1997	23 × 33	●●●	One-sided Drew Struzan art
ROTJSE	1997	47 × 66	●●●●	Two sheets; Drew Struzan art
ROTJSE	1997	33 × 47	●●●●	One-sided Drew Struzan art
ROTJSE	1997	23 × 33	●●●	One-sided Drew Struzan art
TPM	1998	33 × 46	●●●●	Advance with Anakin and shadow; all English
TPM	1998	23 × 33	●●●	Advance with Anakin and shadow; all English
TPM	1999	33 × 46	●●●●	Drew Struzan art
TPM	1999	23 × 33	●●●	Drew Struzan art
TPM	1999	46 × 99	●●●●●●	Three sheets; Anakin "One" campaign
TPM	1999	47 × 66	●●●●●●	Two sheets; Watto "One" campaign
AOTC	2001	33 × 47	●●●●	Advance like US
AOTC	2001	23 × 33	●●●	Advance like US
AOTC	2002	47 × 68	●●●●●●	Jango; "Vanaf 17 Mei in de Bioscoop"; two-sided
AOTC	2002	33 × 47	●●●●●●	Jango "Vanaf 17 Mei in de Bioscoop"
AOTC	2002	47 × 68	●●●●●●	Anakin and Padmé "Vanaf 17 Mei in de Bioscoop," two-sided
AOTC	2002	33 × 47	●●●●●●	Anakin and Padmé "Vanaf 17 Mei in de Bioscoop"
AOTC	2002	47 × 68	●●●●●●	Mace and Obi-Wan; "Vanaf 17 Mei in de Bioscoop," two-sided
AOTC	2002	47 × 68	●●●●●●	Dooku and troopers; "Vanaf 17 Mei in de Bioscoop," two-sided
AOTC	2002	47 × 100	●●●●●●	Jango photo in three sheets (vertical)
AOTC	2002	47 × 100	●●●●●●●	Anakin in three sheets (vertical)
AOTC	2002	47 × 100	●●●●●●●	Padmé in three sheets (vertical)
AOTC	2002	47 × 100	●●●●●●●	Mace and Obi-Wan in three sheets (vertical)
AOTC	2002	33 × 47	●●●●	Drew Struzan art
AOTC	2002	23 × 33	●●●	Drew Struzan art
GREECE				
SWSE	1997	12 × 16	●●●●●	Drew Struzan art
ESBSE	1997	12 × 16	●●●●●	Drew Struzan art
TPM	1999	27 × 38	●●●●	Drew Struzan art; "Haopath Aneiah"
AOTC	2002	27 × 38	●●●●	Drew Struzan art
HONG KONG				
SW	1978	21.5 × 31	●●●●●●●●●	Like US "C" sheet; coated stock
ESB	1980	21.5 × 31	●●●●●●●●●	Like US "A" sheet with AT-ATs
ESB	1980	21.5 × 31	●●●●●●●●●	Elements of US "B" sheet, but mostly Chinese characters
ROTJ	1983	21.5 × 31	●●●●●●●●●	Like US "B" sheet with writing around borders and "rainbow" logo
ROTJ	1983	21.5 × 31	●●●●●●●●●	Like US "B" sheet with soft drink contest below; transit
TPM	1998	21 × 30	●●●	Advance, one-sided; printed in US
TPM	1999	21 × 30	●●●●	Drew Struzan art
TPM	1999	40 × 60	●●●●●●●	Transit "One" campaign: Darth Maul
TPM	1999	40 × 60	●●●●●●	Transit "One" campaign: Obi-Wan
TPM	1999	40 × 60	●●●●●●	Transit "One" campaign: Qui-Gon

THEATRICAL POSTERS

Film	Year	Size	Rating	Description
HONG KONG, CONT.				
TPM	1999	40 × 60	••••••	Transit "One" campaign: Anakin
AOTC	2002	27 × 38	••••	Drew Struzan art
AOTC	2002	40 × 60	••••••	Transit: Villains
AOTC	2002	40 × 60	••••••	Transit: Heroes
HUNGARY				
SW	1977	16 × 22	•••••••••	Monotone image of Vader-like character, R2-D2, X-wing, etc.
ESB	1980	16 × 22	•••••••••	Monotone image of Vader-like character, AT-AT, Star Destroyer, etc.
ROTJ	1984	16 × 22	•••••••••	Vader-like head with Death Star in eye, Star Destroyer, speeder bike, shuttle, etc.
TPM	1999	27 × 39	•••	Drew Struzan art; "I. Resz: Baljos Arnyak"
AOTC	2002	23 × 33	•••	Drew Struzan art; "Epizoda II: Klony Utoci"
AOTC	2002	27 × 39	••••••	Jango; "II Resz: A Klonok Tamadasa"
AOTC	2002	27 × 39	••••••	Anakin and Padmé; "II Resz: A Klonok Tamadasa"
AOTC	2002	27 × 39	••••••	Obi-Wan and Mace; "II Resz: A Klonok Tamadasa"
INDIA				
SW	1977	30 × 40	•••••••	Like US Style "C," printed on thin paper by Tamiland Printers in Madras
ESB	1980	27 × 40	••••••	Ohrai art with cast photos along top; on newsprint
TRILSE	1997	27 × 40	•••••	Ingot art with Hindi language logo
ROTJSE	1997	27 × 40	••••	Drew Struzan art with Hindi language logo
INDONESIA				
TPM	1998	27 × 40	•••	Advance
ISRAEL				
SW	1977	25 × 37.5	•••••••••	Like US "A" sheet
ROTJ	1983	25 × 37.5	••••••••	Like US "B" sheet, matte
TPM	1999	27 × 39	••••	Drew Struzan art; coated stock
ITALY				
SW	1978	53 × 78	•••••	Two-sheet like US "A" sheet
SW	1978	13 × 27.5	•••••	Vertical like US "A" sheet
SW	1978	13 × 27.5	•••••	Vertical like US "A" sheet; wider bottom border with venue information
SW	1978	39 × 55	•••••••	Cartoon art by Papuzza
SW	1978	26.5 × 37.5	•••••••	Stormtrooper on bantha surrounded by white, artwork, and credits
SW	1978	26.5 × 37.5	•••••••	Leia comforting Luke surrounded by white, artwork, and credits
SW	1978	18.5 × 26.5	•••••••	Photobusta set A; logo lower left, two images: Stormtrooper firing, Luke on Tatooine
SW	1978	18.5 × 26.5	•••••••	Photobusta set A; logo lower left, two images: Leia and R2-D2, Obi-Wan on Death Star
SW	1978	18.5 × 26.5	•••••••	Photobusta set A; logo lower left, two images: Escape pod, Jawa
SW	1978	18.5 × 26.5	•••••••	Photobusta set A; logo lower left, two images: Rebel hangar, Tusken Raider
SW	1978	18.5 × 26.5	•••••••	Photobusta set A; logo lower left, two images: sandcrawler, droids and landspeeder
SW	1978	18.5 × 26.5	•••••••	Photobusta set B; logo upper right, single large image: Troopers stop speeder
SW	1978	18.5 × 26.5	•••••••	Photobusta set B; logo upper right, single large image: Vader entering Blockade Runner
SW	1978	18.5 × 26.5	•••••••	Photobusta set B; logo upper right, single large image: Luke in garage
SW	1978	18.5 × 26.5	•••••••	Photobusta set B; logo upper right, single large image: Luke and Leia on Death Star bridge
SW	1978	18.5 × 26.5	•••••••	Photobusta set B; logo upper right, single large image: Crew in *Falcon* cockpit
SW	1978	18.5 × 26.5	•••••••	Photobusta set B; logo upper right, single large image: Vader threatens Leia
SW	1978	18.5 × 26.5	•••••••	Photobusta set B; logo upper right, single large image: Han in Death Star corridor
SW	1978	18.5 × 26.5	•••••••	Photobusta set B; logo upper right, single large image: Luke in garage with inset of Luke as trooper
SW	1978	18.5 × 26.5	•••••••	Photobusta set B; logo upper right, single large image: Luke and Leia on Death Star bridge with inset of Luke
ESB	1980	27.5 × 39	•••••••••	Like US Advance, Italian title; starts in September
ESB	1980	53 × 78	•••••••	Like US "B" sheet in two pieces
ESB	1980	39 × 55	•••••••	Like US "B" sheet
ESB	1980	13 × 27	•••••	Like US "B" sheet
ESB	1980	18.5 × 26.5	••••••	Photobusta A: C-3PO, Luke, Leia, *Falcon* and Hoth (silver backgrounds with large photos)
ESB	1980	18.5 × 26.5	••••••	Photobusta B: Luke emerges from Dagobah swamp
ESB	1980	18.5 × 26.5	••••••	Photobusta C: C-3PO and R2-D2 in ice cave
ESB	1980	18.5 × 26.5	••••••	Photobusta D: Luke on Tauntaun
ESB	1980	18.5 × 26.5	••••••	Photobusta E: Luke vs. Vader
ESB	1980	18.5 × 26.5	••••••	Photobusta F: Darth, Lando, Fett
ESB	1980	18.5 × 26.5	••••••	Photobusta G: Chewie, C-3PO, Leia, Han on *Falcon*
ESB	1980	18.5 × 26.5	••••••	Photobusta H: Lando, Leia, Han, Chewie
ESB	1980	18.5 × 26.5	••••••	Photobusta I: Luke and R2 on Dagobah
ESB	1980	18.5 × 26.5	••••••	Photobusta J: C-3PO looks through clear plotting chart
ESB	1980	18.5 × 26.5	••••••	Photobusta K: Stormtroopers and Lobot
ESB	1980	18.5 × 26.5	••••••	Photobusta L: Darth Vader with hand outstretched
ROTJ	1983	53 × 78	•••••••••	Red ROTJ title in Italian against dark blue
ROTJ	1983	53 × 78	••••••	Like US "B" sheet
ROTJ	1983	39 × 55	••••••	Like US "B" sheet
ROTJ	1983	13 × 27	•••••	Like US "B" sheet
ROTJ	1983	18 × 26	••••••	Photobusta A: Skiff; *Millennium Falcon* (blue star field backgrounds with two photos)
ROTJ	1983	18 × 26	••••••	Photobusta B: Jabba; Lando fighting
ROTJ	1983	18 × 26	••••••	Photobusta C: Surrounded by Ewoks; Yoda
ROTJ	1983	18 × 26	••••••	Photobusta D: Star Destroyer; heroes in forest
ROTJ	1983	18 × 26	••••••	Photobusta E: Droids and Ewok; Luke, Leia on skiff
ROTJ	1983	18 × 26	••••••	Photobusta F: Inside Death Star; Darth Vader
ROTJ	1983	18 × 26	••••••	Photobusta G: Rebels' council; Gamorrean Guard
ROTJ	1983	18 × 26	••••••	Photobusta H: Heroes captured; Han defrosting
ROTJ	1983	18 × 26	••••••	Photobusta I: Heroes in *Falcon*; speeder bike rider
ROTJ	1983	18 × 26	••••••	Photobusta J: Forest battle; Han
EWOK1	1985	53 × 78	•••••	*Caravan of Courage* like US "B" sheet
EWOK1	1985	39 × 55	•••••	*Caravan of Courage* like US "B" sheet
EWOK1	1985	13 × 27	•••••	*Caravan of Courage* like US "B" sheet
EWOK2	1987	53 × 78	••••••	*Battle for Endor;* art by Berrett
EWOK2	1987	39 × 55	••••••	*Battle for Endor;* art by Berrett
EWOK2	1987	13 × 27	•••••	*Battle for Endor;* art by Berrett
SWSE	1997	39 × 55	••••	Drew Struzan art (smooth paper)
SWSE	1997	39 × 55	••••	Drew Struzan art (coarse paper)
SWSE	1997	13 × 28	•••	Drew Struzan art; white space above
ESBSE	1997	54 × 78	••••	Two sheets; Drew Struzan art
ESBSE	1997	39 × 55	••••	Drew Struzan art (coarse paper)
ESBSE	1997	39 × 55	••••	Drew Struzan art (smooth paper)
ESBSE	1997	13 × 28	•••	Drew Struzan art; blue outline box above
ROTJSE	1997	39 × 55	••••	Drew Struzan art (coarse paper)
ROTJSE	1997	39 × 55	••••	Drew Struzan art (smooth paper)
ROTJSE	1997	13 × 28	•••	Drew Struzan art; blue outline box above
TPM	1998	39 × 55	••••	Like US Advance

THEATRICAL POSTERS

	Film	Year	Size	Rating	Description
ITALY, CONT.					
	TPM	1999	39 × 55	●●●●	Drew Struzan art
	TPM	1999	13 × 28	●●●	Drew Struzan art
	AOTC	2002	39 × 55	●●●●	Photo montage with Anakin and Padmé in center
	AOTC	2002	39 × 55	●●●●	Drew Struzan art
	AOTC	2002	13 × 28	●●●	Drew Struzan art
JAPAN					
	SW	1977	29 × 41	●●●●●●●●	Advance; mostly Japanese; "SW" in silver on blue/star background
	SW	1977	20 × 29	●●●●●●●	Advance; mostly Japanese; "SW" in silver on blue/star background
	SW	1978	39 × 62	●●●●●●●●	"May the Force...." but mostly Japanese. Good guy photos in front of illustrated Vader. Academy Awards
	SW	1978	29 × 41	●●●●●●●●	"May the Force...." but mostly Japanese. Good guy photos in front of illustrated Vader. Academy Awards
	SW	1978	20 × 29	●●●●●	"May the Force...." but mostly Japanese. Good guy photos in front of illustrated Vader. Academy Awards (yellow); flat stock
	SW	1978	20 × 29	●●●●●	"May the Force...." but mostly Japanese. Good guy photos in front of illustrated Vader. Academy Awards (black); coated stock
	SW	1978	14 × 20	●●●●●	"May the Force...." but mostly Japanese. Good guy photos in front of illustrated Vader. Academy Awards (transit)
	SW	1978	39 × 62	●●●●●●●●	Seito version of US "A" sheet with illustration of seven Academy Awards
	SW	1978	29 × 41	●●●●●●●●	Seito version of US "A" sheet
	SW	1978	20 × 29	●●●●●	Seito version of US "A" sheet
	SW	1978	20 × 29	●●●●●	Like US "A" sheet, but mostly Japanese with Oscar in lower left corner
	SW	1978	20 × 29	●●●●●	Like US "A" sheet, all English
	SW	1978	14 × 20	●●●●●●	Two posters 14 × 20 each with theater listings including *Star Wars*
	SW	1979	20 × 29	●●●●●●●	"It's Back!" blue and red rerelease like US version
	ESB	1979	29 × 41	●●●●●●●	Advance Darth head photo; no text at top, red title text below
	ESB	1979	29 × 41	●●●●●●●	Advance Darth head photo; text at top and "2" added to red title text below
	ESB	1980	29 × 41	●●●●●●●●	"SW 2" but mostly Japanese; Ohrai art
	ESB	1980	20 × 29	●●●●●●●	"SW 2" but mostly Japanese; Ohrai art; coated stock
	ESB	1980	20 × 29	●●●●●●●	"SW 2" but mostly Japanese; Ohrai art; flat stock
	ESB	1980	20 × 29	●●●●●●●	Ohrai art; all Japanese, not same as coated and flat versions above
	ESB	1980	29 × 41	●●●●●●●	"SW 2" but mostly Japanese; Photo of cast in front of Bespin City and Darth head
	ESB	1980	20 × 29	●●●●●●	"SW 2" but mostly Japanese; photo of cast in front of Bespin City and Darth head; coated stock
	ESB	1980	20 × 29	●●●●●●	"SW 2" but mostly Japanese; photo of cast in front of Bespin City and Darth head; flat stock
	ESB	1980	14 × 20	●●●●●●	Photo montage art, horizontal
	SW	1982	20 × 29	●●●●●●●	Ohrai art of *Falcon:* "In Commemoration of Japanese-dubbed Version"
	SW	1982	14 × 20	●●●●●●	Horizontal transit with Jung art, "It's Back." For Japanese dubbed version
	ROTJ	1982	29 × 41	●●●●●●●●●●	Revenge logo Advance (on star field)
	ROTJ	1983	29 × 41	●●●●●●	US "A" sheet with Japanese in top and bottom borders
	ROTJ	1983	22 × 33	●●●●●	US "A" sheet with Japanese in lower and right borders; reverse is black-and-white forest cast photo
	ROTJ	1983	21 × 34	●●●●●	US "A" sheet with Japanese in top and bottom borders; backed by Kung Fu poster
	ROTJ	1983	20 × 29	●●●●●	US "A" sheet; mostly in Japanese
	ROTJ	1983	14.5 × 20	●●●●●	Horizontal US "A" sheet illustration on left and three photos on top; blank white space beneath for theater name
	ROTJ	1983	14.5 × 20	●●●●●	Horizontal US "A" sheet illustration and printing in lower margin
	ROTJ	1983	39 × 62	●●●●●●●	Like US "B" sheet, but smaller Lando than US version
	ROTJ	1983	21 × 34	●●●●	Like US "B" sheet backed by photo of Japanese teenager
	ROTJ	1983	20 × 29	●●●●●	Like US "B" sheet, but smaller Lando than US version (coated stock)
	ROTJ	1983	20 × 29	●●●●●	Like US "B" sheet, but smaller Lando than US version (flat stock)
	ROTJ	1983	21 × 34	●●●●●	Like US "B" sheet; all English except Japanese in top and bottom white borders
	ROTJ	1983	20 × 29	●●●●●	Like US "B" sheet; all English except Japanese in top and bottom white borders
	ROTJ	1983	29 × 41	●●●●●●	Vertical photo-collage with large Star Destroyer and Death Star
	ROTJ	1983	20 × 29	●●●●●	Vertical photo-collage with large Star Destroyer and Death Star
	ROTJ	1983	29 × 41	●●●●●●●	Horizontal photo-collage with large Star Destroyer and Death Star (different configuration than vertical version)
	ROTJ	1983	29 × 41	●●●●●●●	Photos of heroes set against Death Star, Vader, etc.
	ROTJ	1983	20 × 29	●●●●●●	Photos of heroes set against Death Star, Vader, etc.
	EWOK1	1984	20 × 29	●●●●	Like US "A" sheet with small photo inset; coated stock
	EWOK1	1984	20 × 29	●●●●	Like US "A" sheet with small photo inset; flat stock
	EWOK1	1984	20 × 29	●●●●	Like US "B" sheet
	EWOK1	1984	20 × 29	●●●●	Photo illustration with Gorax in background
	ESB/ROTJ	1986	20 × 28	●●●●●	For double bill, Morikouji-Million Theatre in Osaka; Jedi photo-collage with Japanese text
	EWOK2	1987	20 × 29	●●●●	Photo of girl at center with ENDOR in cutout photo-filled letters at top (coated stock)
	EWOK2	1987	20 × 29	●●●●	Photo of girl at center with ENDOR in cutout photo-filled letters at top (flat stock)
	EWOK2	1987	20 × 29	●●●●	Different photo of girl, more abstract sky in background, no Endor (flat stock)
	TRILSE	1997	29 × 40	●●●●	Ingot art
	TRILSE	1997	20 × 29	●●●	Ingot art
	SWSE	1997	29 × 40	●●●●	Drew Struzan art
	SWSE	1997	20 × 29	●●●	Drew Struzan art
	SWSE	1997	29 × 40	●●●●	"Children's Day Special Cinema Preview" poster; Drew Struzan artwork framed in white with text
	SWSE	1997	14 × 20	●●●●	Horizontal Drew Struzan art framed in white; "Children's Day Special Cinema Preview" on left
	SWSE	1997	29 × 40	●●●●	Drew Struzan artwork with Japanese writing all over
	SWSE	1997	20 × 29	●●●●	Drew Struzan artwork with Japanese writing all over
	ESBSE	1997	29 × 40	●●●●	Drew Struzan art
	ESBSE	1997	20 × 29	●●●	Drew Struzan art
	ROTJSE	1997	29 × 40	●●●●	Drew Struzan art (copper ink for credits)
	ROTJSE	1997	20 × 29	●●●	Drew Struzan art (copper ink for credits)
	TPM	1998	29 × 40	●●●	Two-sided Advance
	TPM	1998	20 × 29	●●●	Advance
	TPM	1999	29 × 40	●●●●	Two-sided Drew Struzan art
	TPM	1999	20 × 29	●●●	Drew Struzan art
	TPM	1999	29 × 40	●●●●●●	Transit; Anakin against blue, white border with Japanese writing
	TPM	1999	29 × 40	●●●●●●	Transit; Qui-Gon against black, white border with Japanese writing
	TPM	1999	29 × 40	●●●●●●	Transit; Amidala against white, white border with Japanese writing
	TPM	1999	29 × 40	●●●●●●	Transit; Anakin against blue above, several pictures of city locations below
	TPM	1999	29 × 40	●●●●●●	Transit; Amidala against white above, several pictures of city locations below
	TPM	1999	29 × 40	●●●●●●	Transit; Qui-Gon against black above, several pictures of city locations below
	TPM	1999	29 × 40	●●●●●●●	Transit; Obi-Wan (looking left) against blue above, several pictures of city locations below
	TPM	1999	29 × 40	●●●●●●	Transit; Anakin against blue above, several pictures of city locations below; green border
	TPM	1999	29 × 40	●●●●●●	Transit; Amidala against white above, several pictures of city locations below; green border
	TPM	1999	29 × 40	●●●●●●	Transit; Qui-Gon against black above, several pictures of city locations below; green border
	TPM	1999	29 × 40	●●●●●●	Transit; Obi-Wan (standing) against black above, several pictures of city locations below; green border
	TPM	1999	29 × 40	●●●●●●	Transit; Anakin/shadow image above; transit information below
	TPM	1999	14 × 20	●●●●●	Transit; Anakin against blue; "Crime Prevention" in upper left corner
	TPM	1999	14 × 20	●●●●●	Transit; Obi-Wan; "Crime Prevention" in upper left corner
	TPM	1999	14 × 20	●●●●●	Transit; Amidala; "Crime Prevention" in upper left corner
	TPM	1999	14 × 20	●●●●●	Transit; Amidala photo, writing at right (horizontal)
	TPM	1999	14 × 20	●●●●●	Transit; Darth Maul image with white bar at bottom (horizontal)
	TPM	1999	14 × 20	●●●●●	Transit; Anakin photo, writing at right (horizontal)
	TPM	1999	14 × 20	●●●●●	Transit; Qui-Gon photo, writing at right (horizontal)

THEATRICAL POSTERS

	Film	Year	Size	Rating	Description
JAPAN, CONT.					
	TPM	1999	14 × 20	•••••	Transit; Obi-Wan photo, writing at right (horizontal)
	TPM	1999	14 × 20	•••••	Transit; Amidala image with white bar at bottom (horizontal)
	TPM	1999	14 × 20	••••••	Transit; Anakin image with white bar at bottom (horizontal)
	TPM	1999	14 × 20	•••••	Transit; Obi-Wan image with white bar at bottom (horizontal)
	TPM	1999	14 × 20	•••••	Transit; Qui-Gon image with white bar at bottom (horizontal)
	TPM	1999	14 × 20	•••••	Transit; Anakin/shadow image at left, writing at right
	AOTC	2001	29 × 40	••••	One-sided Advance like US poster
	AOTC	2001	29 × 40	••••	Two-sided Advance like US poster
	AOTC	2001	20 × 29	•••	Advance like US poster
	AOTC	2002	29 × 40	••••	One-sided Drew Struzan art
	AOTC	2002	29 × 40	••••	Two-sided Drew Struzan art
	AOTC	2002	20 × 29	•••	Drew Struzan art
	AOTC	2002	20 × 29	••••••	Transit; Anakin and Padmé photo, white border with red text above, green text below
	AOTC	2002	20 × 29	••••••	Transit; Dooku and Clones photo, white border with red text above, green text below
	AOTC	2002	20 × 29	••••••	Transit; Obi-Wan and Mace photo, white border with red text above, green text below
	AOTC	2002	20 × 29	••••••	Transit; Jango photo, white border with red text above, green text below
	AOTC	2002	14 × 20	•••••	Transit; horizontal, Obi-Wan and Mace on left, text on right
	AOTC	2002	14 × 20	•••••	Transit; horizontal, Jango on left, text on right
	AOTC	2002	14 × 20	•••••	Transit; horizontal, Anakin and Padmé on left, text on right
	AOTC	2002	14 × 20	•••••	Transit; horizontal, Dooku and Clones on left, text on right
	AOTC	2002	14 × 20	•••••	Transit; horizontal, top/bottom borders white, photo of Anakin and Padmé in middle
	AOTC	2002	14 × 20	•••••	Transit; horizontal, top/bottom borders white, photo of Jango in middle
	AOTC	2002	14 × 20	•••••	Transit; horizontal, top/bottom borders white, photo of Dooku and Clones in middle
	AOTC	2002	14 × 20	•••••	Transit; horizontal, top/bottom borders white, photo of Obi-Wan and Mace in middle
KOREA					
	TPM	1998	27 × 39	•••	Advance, one-sided; all English, with "KF" at bottom
	TPM	1999	27 × 39	•••	Drew Struzan art
	TPM	1999	10 × 30	•••••	Horizontal "One" campaign: Battle droid
	TPM	1999	10 × 30	•••••	Horizontal "One" campaign: Qui-Gon
	TPM	1999	10 × 30	•••••	Horizontal "One" campaign: Obi-Wan
	TPM	1999	10 × 30	•••••	Horizontal "One" campaign: Amidala
	TPM	1999	10 × 30	•••••	Horizontal "One" campaign: Anakin
	TPM	1999	10 × 30	•••••	Horizontal "One" campaign: Mace
	TPM	1999	10 × 30	•••••	Horizontal "One" campaign: Jar-Jar
	TPM	1999	10 × 30	•••••	Horizontal "One" campaign: Watto
	TPM	1999	10 × 30	•••••	Horizontal "One" campaign: Darth Maul
	AOTC	2002	13 × 21	•••	Drew Struzan art
	AOTC	2002	27 × 39	••••	Drew Struzan art
LITHUANIA					
	TPM	1999	27 × 39	••••	Drew Struzan art; "I DALA: Launu Vestosa Iluzija"
MEXICO					
	TRILSE	1996	27 × 37	••••	Passport for trilogy with triptych art; one-sided
NETHERLANDS					
	SWSE	1997	13 × 19.5	•••	Drew Struzan art with "Het Laatste Niews"
	ESBSE	1997	13 × 19.5	•••	Drew Struzan art with "Het Laatste Niews"
	ROTJSE	1997	13 × 19.5	•••	Drew Struzan art with "Het Laatste Niews"
NEW ZEALAND					
	ESB	1980	27 × 41	••••••	US style "B" one sheet with "GY" sticker applied
	EWOK1	1985	27 × 41	•••••	Like US "B" sheet
	EWOK1	1985	13 × 27	••••	Like US "B" sheet
	EWOK2	1986	27 × 40	••••••	Ewoks and the Marauders of Endor; Berrett art
	EWOK2	1986	13 × 26	•••••	Ewoks and the Marauders of Endor daybill; Berrett art
NORWAY					
	TPM	1999	24.5 × 33	•••	Drew Struzan art; "Den Skjulte Trussel"
	AOTC	2002	24.5 × 33	•••	Drew Struzan art
PAKISTAN					
	SW	1977	29 × 40	•••••••	Copy of US "C" sheet on thin paper stock; Mughal Process
	ESB	1980	29 × 40	••••••	Copy of US "B" sheet on thin paper stock; Mughal Process
	ROTJ	1983	29 × 40	••••••	Uses US "B" artwork with Luke/Leia added at top; Mughal Process
POLAND					
	SW	1979	26 × 38	ereeeeee	Yellow C-3PO on black background
	ESB	1982	26 × 38	••••••••	Yellow, black, and red on blue background with indistinguishable head
	ROTJ	1984	26.5 × 38	•••••••••	Exploding head Vader
	ROTJ	1984	26.5 × 38	••••••••	Luke, Leia, Han, and C-3PO
	TRILSE	1997	27 × 38	•••	One-sided Ingot art "Gwiezdne Wojny"
	SWSE	1997	27 × 38	••••	One-sided Drew Struzan art
	ESBSE	1997	27 × 38	••••	One-sided Drew Struzan art
	ROTJSE	1997	27 × 38	••••	One-sided Drew Struzan art
	TPM	1998	27 × 38	••••••	Advance; photos of Amidala, Qui-Gon, Maul
	TPM	1998	27 × 38	•••	Advance like US, one-sided
	TPM	1999	27 × 38	•••	Drew Struzan art
	AOTC	2001	27 × 38	••••	Like US Advance
	AOTC	2002	27 × 38	••••	Anakin and Padmé "Atak Klonow"
	AOTC	2002	27 × 38	••••	Drew Struzan art "Atak Klonow"
PORTUGAL					
	TPM	1999	27 × 38	•••	Drew Struzan art; "Episodio I: A Ameaca Fantasma"
ROMANIA					
	SW	1977	19 × 26	••••••	Style "C" artwork in black-and-white; orange circle with credits
	SW	1978	13 × 19	••••••	Style "C" art in black-and-white with title and credits in red circle
	ESB	1980	18 × 26	••••••	US "B" art in black-and-white with red box for logo
	SWSE	1997	18 × 26	•••	Drew Struzan art; "Razbouil Stelelor"; Guild Film
	ESBSE	1997	18 × 26	•••	Drew Struzan art; "Razbouil Stelelor"; Guild Film
	ROTJSE	1997	18 × 26	•••	Drew Struzan art; "Razbouil Stelelor"; Guild Film
	TPM	1999	27 × 39	•••	Drew Struzan art; "Episodul I: Amenintarea Fantomei"
	TPM	1999	27 × 39	••••••	Photo art of Darth Maul, Amidala, and Qui-Gon
RUSSIA					
	SW	1990	21.5 × 33.5	•••••••••	Strange puma-like Vader head with small glyphs surrounding the head
	SW	1990	25 × 41	•••••••••	Face made of stone flying through space
	SW	1991	33 × 62	••••••••••	Three sheets; cowboy figure shooting pistol in form of circuit-board montage
	SW	1991	17 × 25	••••••••	Three abstract alien-type creatures against a space backdrop; flat paper stock, one line of copyright text
	SW	1991	17 × 25	••••••••	Three abstract alien-type creatures against a space backdrop; coated paper stock, two lines of copyright text
	AOTC	2002	n/a	•••••	Drew Struzan art "Ataka Krohob"

THEATRICAL POSTERS

	Film	Year	Size	Rating	Description
S. AFRICA					
	SW	1978	28 × 40	●●●●●●	Black-and-white with yellow overlay; US "A" sheet art
	ROTJ	1983	33 × 46	●●●●●●	US Style "B" artwork with "May the Force Be With You" at top; two sheets
	TPM	1998	27 × 39	●●●	Advance, two-sided; "Ster-Kinekor Pictures" at bottom
	TPM	1999	27 × 39	●●●●	Drew Struzan art; two-sided, like US but "Ster-Kinekor Pictures"
SINGAPORE					
	AOTC	2002	27 × 40	●●●●	Padmé and heroes; in English
	AOTC	2002	27 × 40	●●●●	Jango and villains; in English
SLOVAKIA					
	TPM	1999	26 × 38	●●●	Drew Struzan art; "Epizoda I: Grozeca Prikazen"
SPAIN					
	SW	1978	27.5 × 39	●●●●●●●	US "C" sheet art, no border; marked Grobes S.A.-Paris & Barcelona DLB
	SW	1978	27.5 × 39	●●●●●●●	Mostly white with logo "cut out" from "A" sheet with *Time* magazine quote at top
	SW	1979	27.5 × 39	●●●●●●●●	Like US "D" sheet with Spanish title
	ESB	1980	27.5 × 39	●●●●●●●	Ohrai art, bleed border
	ESB	1980	27.5 × 39	●●●●●●●	Like US "A" sheet with Lando and Boba Fett
	ESB	1980	27.5 × 39	●●●●●●	Like US "B" sheet
	ROTJ	1983	27.5 × 39	●●●●●●	Jouin art with "Retorno"
	ROTJ	1983	27.5 × 39	●●●●●●●	Jouin art with "Retorn" and slightly different credits, printed in the Catalan language; used in select regions of Spain
	EWOK1	1985	27.5 × 39	●●●●●	Like US "B" sheet
	SW	1986	27.5 × 39	●●●●●	Rerelease; Like US "C" sheet art version, but with white border and "boxed" Fox logo; marked Grobes S.A.-Paris & Barcelona DLB
	ESB	1987	27.5 × 39	●●●●●	For rerelease; Like Ohrai art version, but with white border
	TRILSE	1997	27 × 39	●●●	Ingot art with Spanish title
	SWSE	1997	47 × 69	●●●●	Drew Struzan art; "Estreno 21 de Marzo"; halftone reverse
	SWSE	1997	27 × 39	●●●●	Drew Struzan art
	ESBSE	1997	27 × 39	●●●●	Drew Struzan art
	ROTJSE	1997	27 × 39	●●●●	Drew Struzan art
	TPM	1998	27 × 39	●●●	Advance like US; two-sided
	TPM	1999	27 × 39	●●●●	Drew Struzan art; two-sided; "La Amenaza Fantasma"
	TPM	1999	47 × 68.5	●●●●●●●	Qui-Gon, plastic transit sheet; "Un Maestro, Un Rebelde"
	TPM	1999	47 × 68.5	●●●●●●●	Obi-Wan, plastic transit sheet; "Una Fuerza, Una Opción"
	TPM	1999	47 × 68.5	●●●●●●●	Jar Jar, plastic transit sheet; "Un Amigo, Un Payaso"
	TPM	1999	47 × 68.5	●●●●●●●	Anakin, plastic transit sheet; "Un Héroe, Un Destino"
	TPM	1999	47 × 68.5	●●●●●●●	Maul, plastic transit sheet; "Una Verdad, Un Odio"
	TPM	1999	47 × 68.5	●●●●●●●	Amidala, plastic transit sheet; "Un Amor, Una Búsqueda"
	AOTC	2001	26.5 × 39	●●●●	Advance teaser; two-sided
	AOTC	2002	26.5 × 39	●●●●	Drew Struzan art; two-sided "El Ataque de los Clones"
	AOTC	2002	47 × 68	●●●●●	Mace and Obi-Wan; "Episodio II: El Ataque de los Clones"
	AOTC	2002	47 × 68	●●●●●	Jango; "Episodio II: El Ataque de los Clones"
	AOTC	2002	47 × 68	●●●●●	Anakin and Padmé; "Episodio II: El Ataque de los Clones"
	AOTC	2002	47 × 68	●●●●●	Dooku and troopers; "Episodio II: El Ataque de los Clones"
SPANISH LANGUAGE					
	SW	1978	27 × 41	●●●●●●●●	Advance with title in Spanish, white on blue
	SW	1978	27 × 41	●●●●●●●●	Hildebrandt art, mostly Spanish
	SW	1978	27 × 40	●●●●●●●	Hildebrandt art, mostly Spanish; bottom inch trimmed off at press
	SW	1978	27 × 40	●●●●●●●●●	Hildebrandt art, first Spanish dubbed version: "Ahora Por Primera Vez Totalmente Hablanda En Español!"
	SW	1978	27 × 41	●●●●●●●●●●	Like US "C" sheet with title in Spanish
	ESB	1980	27 × 41	●●●●●●●	US Vader Advance: "Estará muy pronto en su galaxia"
	ESB	1980	27 × 41	●●●●●●●●	Ohrai art; Mexico "B" sheet with text "La Saga de la Guerra de las Galaxias Continua" at top
	ESB	1980	27 × 41	●●●●●●●●	Ohrai art; Mexico "B" sheet with text "La Epopeya de la Guerra de las Galaxias Continua" at top
	ROTJ	1983	27 × 41	●●●●●●●	Advance like US *Revenge* art with Spanish title
	ROTJ	1983	27 × 41	●●●●●●●	US "A" sheet in Spanish
	ROTJ	1983	27 × 41	●●●●●●●	US "B" sheet in Spanish
	EWOK1	1985	27 × 41	●●●●●●	Spanish International "A" sheet
	EWOK1	1985	27 × 41	●●●●●●	Spanish International "B" sheet
	TRILSE	1997	27 × 40	●●●●	Two-sided Ingot art
	SWSE	1997	27 × 40	●●●●	Two-sided Drew Struzan art
	ESBSE	1997	27 × 40	●●●●	Two-sided Drew Struzan art
	ROTJSE	1997	27 × 40	●●●●	Two-sided Drew Struzan art
	TPM	1998	27 × 40	●●●●	Two-sided Advance; "International Span. One Sheet Camp. A"
	TPM	1999	27 × 40	●●●●	International Spanish one-sheet Campaign "B"; two-sided; Drew Struzan art
	AOTC	2001	27 × 40	●●●●	Advance; two-sided
	AOTC	2002	27 × 40	●●●●	Two-sided Drew Struzan art
SWEDEN					
	SW	1978	27.5 × 39	●●●●●●●	Uses some of US "A" sheet art plus photo of Han/Chewie
	SW	1978	13 × 27.5	●●●●●●	Uses some of US "A" sheet art plus photo of Han/Chewie
	ESB	1980	27.5 × 39	●●●●●●●	US "B" sheet art (bleed border)
	ESB	1980	13 × 27.5	●●●●●●	US "B" sheet art with thin black border
	ROTJ	1983	27.5 × 39	●●●●●●	US "B" sheet art (bleed border)
	ROTJ	1983	13 × 27.5	●●●●●	US "B" sheet art with wide borders at top and bottom for theater info
	TRILSE	1997	27.5 × 39	●●●●	One-sided Ingot art
	TRILSE	1997	27.5 × 39	●●●●	Two-sided Ingot art
	SWSE	1997	27.5 × 39	●●●	One-sided Drew Struzan art
	SWSE	1997	12.5 × 27.5	●●●	Drew Struzan art with photo of R2-D2/C-3PO and crew in cockpit below
	ESBSE	1997	27 × 39	●●●●	Two-sided Drew Struzan art
	ESBSE	1997	12.5 × 27.5	●●●	Drew Struzan art with photo of Vader and Yoda and Luke below
	ROTJSE	1997	27 × 39	●●●●	One-sided Drew Struzan art
	TPM	1999	27 × 39	●●●●	Drew Struzan art; "Episod I: Det Morka Hotet"; two-sided
	TPM	1999	12.5 × 27.5	●●●	Drew Struzan art with photo of duel and group below
	TPM	1999	46.5 × 69	●●●●●●●	Obi-Wan "One" subway poster; "En Kraft, Ett Val"
	TPM	1999	46.5 × 69	●●●●●●●	Qui-Gon "One" subway poster; "En Rebell, En Larare"
	TPM	1999	46.5 × 69	●●●●●●●	Anakin "One" subway poster; "En Hjalte, Ett Ode"
	TPM	1999	46.5 × 69	●●●●●●●	Darth Maul "One" subway poster; "En Sanning, Ett Hat"
	TPM	1999	46.5 × 69	●●●●●●●	Amidala "One" subway poster; "En Karlek, Ett Uppdrag"
	AOTC	2002	27 × 39	●●●●	Drew Struzan art; "Episod II: Klonerna Anfaller"
SWITZERLAND					
	SWSE	1997	35 × 50	●●●●	Drew Struzan art; German language; Swiss Fox logo
	SWSE	1997	23 × 31	●●●	Drew Struzan art; French language; Swiss Fox logo
	ESBSE	1997	35 × 50	●●●●	Drew Struzan art; German language; Swiss Fox logo
	ESBSE	1997	23 × 31	●●●	Drew Struzan art; French language; Swiss Fox logo
	ROTJSE	1997	35 × 50	●●●●	Drew Struzan art; German language; Swiss Fox logo
	ROTJSE	1997	23 × 31	●●●	Drew Struzan art; French language; Swiss Fox logo

THEATRICAL POSTERS

	Film	Year	Size	Rating	Description
TAIWAN					
	TPM	1999	20 × 30	•••	Drew Struzan art
	AOTC	2001	20 × 30	•••	Teaser with Anakin and Padmé
THAILAND					
	SW	1977	22 × 31	••••	Style "C" art with "The War of the World" in English
	ROTJ	1983	21 × 29	••••	Reprints US Style "B" but with Thai language overlay
	SWSE	1997	21 × 31	•••	Drew Struzan art
	ESBSE	1997	21 × 31	•••	Drew Struzan art
	ROTJSE	1997	21 × 31	•••	Drew Struzan art
	TPM	1998	24 × 35	•••	Advance art
	TPM	1999	24 × 35	•••	Drew Struzan art
	AOTC	2002	27 × 40	••••	Drew Struzan art
	AOTC	2002	48 × 72	••••••	Anakin and Padmé; Thai language
	AOTC	2002	48 × 72	••••••	Obi-Wan and Mace; Thai language
	AOTC	2002	48 × 72	••••••	Jango; Thai language
TURKEY					
	SW	1978	27 × 39	•••••••	Hildebrandt art with some minor changes including MPC model X-wing image
	ESB	1980	27 × 39	••••••	US "B" art; "Imparator . . ."
	ROTJ	1983	26.5 × 38.5	••••••	US "B" sheet art with two fuzzy photos on either side of title block; coated stock
	ROTJ	1983	26.5 × 38.5	••••••	US "B" sheet art with two fuzzy photos on either side of title block; flat stock
	TRILSE	1997	27 × 39	•••	Ingot art
	TPM	1999	27 × 39	••••	Drew Struzan art; two-sided; "Bolum I: Gizli Tehlike" (Ozenfilm)
	AOTC	2002	27 × 39	••••	Drew Struzan art; "Bolum II: Klonlar 'in Saldirisi" (Ozenfilm)
UNITED KINGDOM					
	SW	1977	30 × 40	••••••••••	Quad with Hildebrandt art
	SW	1977	30 × 40	•••••••••	Quad with Leia in center; middle piece for Heroes/Villains ensemble
	SW	1977	20 × 30	•••••••••	"Double Crown" Heroes
	SW	1977	20 × 30	•••••••••	"Double Crown" Villains
	SW	1977	20 × 30	•••••••••	"Double Crown" Excitement
	SW	1977	20 × 30	•••••••••	"Double Crown" Adventure
	SW	1978	30 × 40	•••••••••	Like US "C" sheet art by Chantrell (no Academy Awards)
	SW	1978	30 × 40	•••••••••	Like US "C" sheet art by Chantrell but with Oscar logo and "7 Academy Awards"
	ESB	1980	30 × 40	•••••••••	"BEWARE!" Red, white on black Advance
	ESB	1980	30 × 40	••••••••••	US "A" sheet artwork but by a different artist
	ESB	1980	30 × 40	•••••••••	Like US "B" sheet with black and silver logo
	ESB	1980	30 × 40	•••••••••	Like US "B" sheet with black-and-white logo
	ESB	1980	20 × 30	•••••••••	A. "Fun for everyone with . . ." Five-poster set like early serial posters, in red, white, and blue with black-and-white photos
	ESB	1980	20 × 30	•••••••••	B. ". . . space for a little romance"
	ESB	1980	20 × 30	•••••••••	C. "The heroes return . . ."
	ESB	1980	20 × 30	•••••••••	D. ". . . but so do the villains"
	ESB	1980	30 × 40	•••••••••	E. "Thrills . . . Excitement"
	SW/ESB	1982	30 × 40	•••••••	Double bill with elements of Star Wars and Empire posters
	SW/ESB	1982	20 × 30	•••••••••	Red, white, and blue "double crown" with R2-D2 and C-3PO with space for tipped-in photo of Luke and C-3PO
	ROTJ	1982	30 × 40	•••••••••	Struzan Revenge art with Return logo; coated stock
	ROTJ	1982	30 × 40	•••••••••	Struzan Revenge art with Return logo; flat stock
	ROTJ	1983	20 × 30	••••••	Advance, like US Style "A"; "From June 2"
	ROTJ	1983	60 × 120	••••••••••	Kirby montage art in three sheets
	ROTJ	1983	30 × 40	••••••••	Kirby montage art, coated stock
	ROTJ	1983	30 × 40	•••••••	Kirby montage art, flat stock
	ROTJ	1983	30 × 40	•••••••	Kirby montage art with Ewoks and other elements added
	ROTJ	1983	20 × 30	••••••	A. Robots in forest; Vader reviews troops–Double Crowns, vertical with two photos, flat stock
	ROTJ	1983	20 × 30	••••••	A. Robots in forest; Vader reviews troops–Double Crowns, vertical with two photos, coated stock
	ROTJ	1983	20 × 30	••••••	B. Luke, Leia at Jabba's; Imperial cruiser; flat stock
	ROTJ	1983	20 × 30	••••••	B. Luke, Leia at Jabba's; Imperial cruiser; coated stock
	ROTJ	1983	20 × 30	••••••	C. Han in carbonite; Han, Chewie captured; flat stock
	ROTJ	1983	20 × 30	••••••	C. Han in carbonite; Han, Chewie captured; coated stock
	ROTJ	1983	20 × 30	••••••	D. Bibb Fortuna; Forest battle; flat stock
	ROTJ	1983	20 × 30	••••••	D. Bibb Fortuna; Forest battle; coated stock
	TRIL	1983	30 × 40	•••••••	"3 in One Programme" with art from all three films
	EWOK1	1984	30 × 40	••••••	Like US "B" sheet
	EWOK1	1984	10 × 15	•••••	Like US "B" sheet; "At a Cinema Near You From Dec. 14"
	TRILSE	1997	30 × 40	••••	Two-sided Ingot art
	TRILSE	1997	24 × 36	••••	Three Drew Struzan artworks with "Three Reasons Why They Build Theatres"
	SWSE	1997	30 × 40	••••	Two-sided Drew Struzan art
	ESBSE	1997	30 × 40	••••	Two-sided Drew Struzan art
	ROTJSE	1997	30 × 40	••••	Two-sided Drew Struzan art
	TPM	1998	30 × 40	••••	Two-sided advance quad
	TPM	1999	30 × 40	••••••	Quad for Virgin Cinemas, Episode I logo on black: "The Saga Begins Here July 15"
	TPM	1999	30 × 40	••••	Two-sided Drew Struzan art
	TPM	1999	46 × 60	•••••••	Maul: "One Truth, One Hate"
	TPM	1999	46 × 60	•••••••	Amidala: "One Love, One Quest"
	TPM	1999	46 × 60	•••••••	Anakin: "One Hero, One Destiny"
	TPM	1999	46 × 60	•••••••	Battle Droid: "One Mind, One Mission"
	TPM	1999	46 × 60	•••••••	Obi-Wan: "One Force, One Choice"
	TPM	1999	46 × 60	•••••••	Qui-Gon: "One Rebel, One Teacher"
	TPM	1999	46 × 60	•••••••	Watto: "One Businessman, One Gambler"
	AOTC	2001	30 × 40	••••	Two-sided Advance with Anakin and Padmé
	AOTC	2002	30 × 40	••••	Drew Struzan artwork quad; two-sided
	AOTC	2002	48 × 96	•••••••••	Anakin and Obi-Wan "Force-Force-Two" horizontal
	AOTC	2002	48 × 60	•••••••••	Anakin and Obi-Wan "Force-Force-Two"
	AOTC	2002	48 × 96	•••••••••	Mace "Our Goalie Uses the Force" horizontal
	AOTC	2002	48 × 60	•••••••••	Mace "Our Goalie Uses the Force"
	AOTC	2002	48 × 96	•••••••••	Padmé and heroes "Girls Play on Our Team" horizontal
	AOTC	2002	48 × 60	•••••••••	Padmé and heroes "Girls Play on Our Team"
	AOTC	2002	48 × 96	•••••••••	Bad guys "The Other 'Group of Death'" horizontal
	AOTC	2002	48 × 60	•••••••••	Bad guys "The Other 'Group of Death'"
	AOTC	2002	48 × 96	•••••••••	Yoda "On Our Pitch, Size Matters Not" horizontal
	AOTC	2002	47 × 71	••••••	Mace and Obi-Wan; "May 16"; two-sided
	AOTC	2002	47 × 71	••••••	Dooku and troopers; "May 16"; two-sided
	AOTC	2002	47 × 71	••••••	Anakin and Padmé; "May 16"; two-sided
	AOTC	2002	47 × 71	••••••	Jango; "May 16"; two-sided

THEATRICAL POSTERS

Film	Year	Size	Rating	Description
UNITED STATES				
SW	1976	27 × 41	••••••••••	Mylar Advance
SW	1976	27 × 41	•••••••••	Silver/gray Advance
SW	1977	7.5 × 9.5	•••••••	Wild post handbill; "An Entertainment Odyssey…" with white space below
SW	1977	8 × 10	•••••••	Wild post handbill; like teaser "B" with white space below
SW	1977	6.75 × 7.5	•••••••	Wild post handbill; silver *Star Wars* logo on blue with white space below
SW	1977	84 × 91	••••••••••	Teaser "B" seven-sheet "STARTS MAY 25TH"
SW	1977	27 × 41	•••••••••	Teaser "B" one-sheet white on blue
SW	1977	billboard	••••••••••	Style "A" twenty-four-sheet with half-sheet artwork
SW	1977	84 × 91	••••••••••	Style "A" art seven-sheet
SW	1977	77 × 80	•••••••••	Style "A" art six-sheet
SW	1977	41 × 81	•••••••	Style "A" art three-sheet
SW	1977	40 × 60	•••••••••	Style "A" art on heavy stock
SW	1977	40 × 60	•••••••	Style "A" art standee
SW	1977	30 × 40	•••••••••	Style "A" art on heavy stock
SW	1977	27 × 41	•••••••	Style "A" one-sheet
SW	1977	27 × 41	••••••••••	Style "A" one-sheet but *Star Wars* logo in black and large 20th Century Records logo
SW	1977	22 × 28	•••••••••	Style "A" half-sheet with different artwork than one sheet
SW	1977	14 × 36	•••••••	Style "A" insert
SW	1977	27 × 41	•••••••••	Style "C" Chantrell artwork; international with no rating box
SW	1977	27 × 41	••••••••••	Style "C" Chantrell artwork; PG rating for possible use on military bases, etc.
SW	1978	84 × 91	••••••••••	Style "D" "Circus" seven-sheet poster
SW	1978	40 × 60	•••••••••	Style "D" "Circus" poster
SW	1978	40 × 60	•••••••••	Style "D" standee
SW	1978	30 × 40	•••••••••	Style "D" "Circus" poster
SW	1978	27 × 41	•••••••••	Style "D" one-sheet "Circus" poster
SW	1978	27 × 41	••••••	Style "D" one-sheet but with blue oval in lower left corner: "Original Soundtrack on 20th Century Fox Records"
SW	1978	27 × 41	••••••••••	Happy Birthday one-sheet
SW	1979	27 × 41	•••••••	Rerelease one-sheet; silver and blue with red snipe
ESB	1979	billboard	••••••••••	Advance with Vader head twenty-four-sheet
ESB	1979	60 × 129	••••••••••	Advance with Vader head eight-sheet
ESB	1979	81 × 91	•••••••••	Advance with Vader head six-sheet
ESB	1979	41 × 81	•••••••••	Advance with Vader head three-sheet
ESB	1979	27 × 41	•••••••	Advance one-sheet with Vader head
ESB	1980	45 × 58	•••••••••	Advance with Vader head NYC subway
ESB	1980	60 × 129	••••••••••	Style "A" "*Gone with the Wind*" eight-sheet; horizontal with blue credit field at right; in three parts
ESB	1980	45 × 58	•••••••••	Style "A" "*Gone with the Wind*" NYC subway "Opens Wednesday May 21"
ESB	1980	40 × 60	••••••••••	Style "A" "*Gone with the Wind*"
ESB	1980	40 × 60	•••••••	Style "A" "*Gone with the Wind*" standee
ESB	1980	30 × 40	•••••••••	Style "A" "*Gone with the Wind*"
ESB	1980	27 × 41	•••••••••	Style "A" "*Gone with the Wind*" one-sheet
ESB	1980	22 × 28	••••••	Style "A" "*Gone with the Wind*" half-sheet
ESB	1980	14 × 36	••••••	Style "A" "*Gone with the Wind*" insert
ESB	1980	17.5 × 23	•••••••	Phoenix premiere, uses duo-tone "A" artwork
ESB	1980	40 × 60	•••••••	Style "B"
ESB	1980	30 × 40	••••••	Style "B"
ESB	1980	27 × 41	••••••	Style "B" one-sheet; NSS version with light blue tones
ESB	1980	27 × 41	•••••••	Style "B" one-sheet; studio version with darker tones
ESB	1980	22 × 28	••••••	Style "B" half-sheet
ESB	1980	14 × 36	••••••	Style "B" insert
SW	1981	27 × 41	••••••	Rerelease one-sheet with yellow snipe
SW	1981	22 × 28	••••••	Rerelease half-sheet with yellow snipe
SW	1981	14 × 36	••••••	Rerelease insert with yellow snipe
ESB	1981	40 × 60	•••••••	Rerelease Jung art including Yoda
ESB	1981	40 × 60	••••••	Rerelease standee of Jung art including Yoda
ESB	1981	30 × 40	•••••••	Rerelease with Jung art including Yoda
ESB	1981	27 × 41	••••••	Rerelease one-sheet with Jung art including Yoda
ESB	1981	22 × 28	••••••	Rerelease half-sheet with Jung art including Yoda
ESB	1981	14 × 36	••••••	Rerelease insert with Jung art including Yoda
SW	1982	40 × 60	•••••••	Rerelease with *Revenge* snipe
SW	1982	40 × 60	••••••	Rerelease with *Revenge* snipe standee
SW	1982	30 × 40	•••••••	Rerelease with *Revenge* snipe
SW	1982	27 × 41	•••••	Rerelease one-sheet with *Revenge* snipe
SW	1982	22 × 28	•••••	Rerelease half-sheet with *Revenge* snipe
SW	1982	14 × 36	•••••	Rerelease insert with *Revenge* snipe
ESB	1982	40 × 60	•••••••	Rerelease with Jung art; larger Han Solo
ESB	1982	40 × 60	•••••••	Rerelease standee with Jung art; larger Han Solo
ESB	1982	30 × 40	•••••••	Rerelease with Jung art; larger Han Solo
ESB	1982	27 × 41	••••••	Rerelease one-sheet with Jung art; larger Han Solo
ESB	1982	27 × 41	••••••••••	Rerelease one-sheet variation with light blue background, NSS # and print block, union bug
ESB	1982	24.5 × 38.5	•••••••••	Rerelease mini-standee with Jung art; larger Han Solo
ESB	1982	22 × 28	••••••	Rerelease half-sheet with Jung art; larger Han Solo
ESB	1982	14 × 36	••••••	Rerelease insert with Jung art; larger Han Solo
ROTJ	1982	27 × 41	•••••••••	*Revenge* Advance one-sheet with May 25th opening date
ROTJ	1982	27 × 41	••••••••••	*Revenge* Advance one-sheet without opening date
ROTJ	1983	40 × 60	•••••••	Style "A" lightsaber art
ROTJ	1983	40 × 60	•••••••	Style "A" lightsaber art standee
ROTJ	1983	30 × 40	•••••••	Style "A" lightsaber art
ROTJ	1983	27 × 41	••••••	Style "A" one-sheet lightsaber art
ROTJ	1983	22 × 28	••••••	Style "A" half-sheet lightsaber art
ROTJ	1983	14 × 36	••••••	Style "A" insert lightsaber art
ROTJ	1983	82 × 84	•••••••••	Style "B" six-sheet (in four parts); montage art
ROTJ	1983	41.5 × 84	•••••••••	Style "B" three-sheet montage art
ROTJ	1983	40 × 60	•••••••	Style "B" montage art
ROTJ	1983	40 × 60	•••••••	Style "B" standee montage art
ROTJ	1983	30 × 40	•••••••	Style "B" montage art
ROTJ	1983	27 × 41	••••••	Style "B" one-sheet montage art
ROTJ	1983	27 × 41	•••••••••	Style "B" International one-sheet; has white border like domestic version, but no rating box
ROTJ	1983	24.5 × 38.5	•••••••••	Style "B" mini-standee
ROTJ	1983	22 × 28	••••••	Style "B" half-sheet montage art
ROTJ	1983	14 × 36	••••••	Style "B" insert montage art
EWOK1	1984	27 × 41	••••••	*Caravan of Courage* "A" one-sheet International
EWOK1	1984	27 × 41	••••••	*Caravan of Courage* "B" one-sheet International

THEATRICAL POSTERS

Film	Year	Size	Rating	Description
UNITED STATES, CONT.				
EWOK1	1984	25.5 × 33	•••••••••	"Opens Nov. 25 on ABC"; Like "A" sheet with yellow border
ROTJ	1985	27 × 41	••••••	Rerelease one-sheet with exploding Death Star and characters below
ROTJ	1985	22 × 28	••••••	Rerelease half-sheet with exploding Death Star and characters below
ROTJ	1985	14 × 36	••••••	Rerelease insert with exploding Death Star and characters below
TRIL	1985	27 × 41	••••••••••+	Triple-bill one-sheet; Egyptian Theater, Hollywood, CA; two printed on photographic paper
TRIL	1985	27 × 41	••••••••••+	Triple-bill one-sheet; Avco Theater, Westwood, CA; two printed on photographic paper
TRIL	1985	27 × 41	••••••••••+	Triple-bill one-sheet; Galaxy Theater, San Francisco, CA; two printed on photographic paper
TRIL	1985	27 × 41	••••••••••+	Triple-bill one-sheet; Continental Theater, Denver, CO; two printed on photographic paper
TRIL	1985	27 × 41	••••••••••+	Triple-bill one-sheet; Carnegie Theater, Chicago, IL; two printed on photographic paper
TRIL	1985	27 × 41	••••••••••+	Triple-bill one-sheet; Warner #1, New York, NY; two printed on photographic paper
TRIL	1985	27 × 41	••••••••••+	Triple-bill one-sheet; North Park #1, Dallas, TX; two printed on photographic paper
TRIL	1985	27 × 41	••••••••••+	Triple-bill one-sheet; UA 150, Seattle, WA; two printed on photographic paper
TRILSE	1997	27 × 40	••••	One-sided Ingot art; no version designation; March 7 for ROTJ
TRILSE	1997	27 × 40	•••••	Two-sided Ingot art; no version designation; March 7 for ROTJ
TRILSE	1997	27 × 40	•••••	One-sided version "F"; March 14 for ROTJ
TRILSE	1997	27 × 40	••••	International one-sided Version "A"; Ingot art
TRILSE	1997	27 × 40	•••••	International two-sided Version "A"; Ingot art
SWSE	1997	27 × 40	••••	One-sided; Version "B"
SWSE	1997	27 × 40	•••••	Two-sided Drew Struzan art version "B"
SWSE	1997	27 × 40	•••••	International two-sided version "B"; Drew Struzan art
ESBSE	1997	27 × 40	••••	One-sided Drew Struzan art version "C"
ESBSE	1997	27 × 40	•••••	Two-sided Drew Struzan art version "C"
ESBSE	1997	27 × 40	•••••	International two-sided version "C"; Drew Struzan art
ROTJSE	1997	27 × 40	••••	One-sided Drew Struzan art version "D"; March 7
ROTJSE	1997	27 × 40	•••••	Two-sided Drew Struzan art version "D"; March 7
ROTJSE	1997	27 × 40	•••••	International two-sided version "D"; Drew Struzan art
ROTJSE	1997	27 × 40	•••••	One-sided; Version "E"; March 14; Drew Struzan art
ROTJSE	1997	27 × 40	••••••	Two-sided Drew Struzan art version "E"; March 14
TRILSE	1997	16 × 26	••••••	Triptych of Drew Struzan art for three posters; horizontal
TPM	1998	48 × 96	•••••••	Advance horizontal banner with Anakin casting shadow of Vader
TPM	1998	47 × 69	••••••	Advance two-sided
TPM	1998	27 × 40	•••••	Two-sided Advance; Version "A"
TPM	1998	27 × 40	••••	One-sided Advance; Version "A"
TPM	1999	47 × 69	••••••	Drew Struzan artwork two-sided
TPM	1999	27 × 40	••••	One-sided International; Drew Struzan art version "B"
TPM	1999	27 × 40	•••••	Two-sided International; Drew Struzan art version "B"
TPM	1999	27 × 40	•••••	One-sided Drew Struzan art one-sheet "C" with PG rating
TPM	1999	27 × 40	••••••	Two-sided Drew Struzan art one-sheet "C" with PG rating
AOTC	2001	60 × 108	•••••••	Advance banner of Anakin and Padmé
AOTC	2001	27 × 40	••••	One-sided Advance; Anakin and Padmé one sheet "A"
AOTC	2001	27 × 40	•••••	Two-sided Advance one sheet "A"
AOTC	2002	47 × 69	••••••	Two-sided bus stop poster; Drew Struzan art
AOTC	2002	27 × 40	••••	One-sided International; Drew Struzan art one sheet "B"
AOTC	2002	27 × 40	•••••	Two-sided International; Drew Struzan art one sheet "B"
AOTC	2002	27 × 40	•••••	Two-sided; Drew Struzan art one sheet "C"
AOTC	2002	48 × 60	•••••••	IMAX banner with Yoda: "Size Matters Not . . ."
AOTC	2002	27 × 40	•••••	Two-sided IMAX one sheet of Yoda: "Size Matters Not . . ."
ROTS	2004	120 × 180	•••••••	Horizontal banner of Anakin with Vader image in cape
ROTS	2004	60 × 96	•••••••	Banner of Anakin with Vader image in cape
ROTS	2004	27 × 40	••••	Two-sided Advance one sheet of Anakin with Vader image in cape
ROTS	2005	27 × 40	••••	Two-sided Drew artwork one sheet
YUGOSLAVIA				
SW	1977	19 × 27	•••••••	Hildebrandt art; from Sarajevo, "Ratovi Zvijezda"
SW	1977	19 × 27	•••••••	US "C" art; from Sarajevo, "Ratovi Zvijezda"
ESB	1982	19 × 27	••••••	US Style "B" art; "Imperija Uzvraca Udarac"
ROTJ	1983	19 × 27	•••••••	Jouin art; "Povratak Dzedaja"
ESB	1991	13 × 27	••••••••	Artwork of Yoda; printed in Zagreb for the Filmoteka 16
ROTJ	1991	13 × 27	••••••••	Neon magenta on navy with tricked images of *Falcon*, Luke, Han and rear of C-3PO
TRILSE	1996	16.5 × 25	•••	Ingot art; "Rat Zvesda Trilogija"
ROTJSE	1997	16.5 × 25	•••	Drew Struzan art; "Povratak Jedija"
AOTC	2002	19 × 27	•••	Drew Struzan art; "Napad Klonova"

EVENTS POSTERS

	Title	Year	Size	Rating	Description
AUSTRALIA					
	Starwalking	1990	12 × 14.5	•••	Second Convention; Indy and Luke, mauve on gray
	Starwalking	1995	12 × 14.5	••••	Luke on Tatooine, Hugh Fleming art for Star Force One convention
	Force Two Con	1997	12 × 17	•	For Force Two convention
	Star Wars Convention	2002	23 × 33	••	Australia; The Kessel Run
BELGIUM					
	50 Films in 50 Days	1985	14.5 × 21.5	••••	Horizontal Struzan artwork for Twentieth Century Fox 50th anniversary, including *Star Wars* characters
FINLAND					
	Art of *Star Wars*	2002	27 × 39	•••••••	Headshot of C-3PO
	Art of *Star Wars*	2002	27 × 39	•••••••	Darth Maul art head
FRANCE					
	Comics Sci-fi Horror con	1999	16 × 24	•	Arkham presente...
	Generations *Star Wars* and SF	2001	16 × 24	•••	At La Ville de Cusset; Massoneau art
	Collectors Rendezvo	2002	24 × 31	••	Comic characters including Vader, R2, etc.
	Collectors Rendezvo	2003	16 × 24	•	Convention guest list including Ray Park, Peter Mayhew, and David Prowse
GERMANY					
	Star Wars Festival	1983	12 × 17	•••••	*Return of the Jedi* festival; orange and white with lots of text
	Star Wars Night	1987	12 × 17	•••••	Unifilm; triple-bill on green paper
	Star Wars German Con	1998	16 × 23	••	Krieg der Nikolause convention
	Star Wars German Con	1998	12 × 16	••	Krieg der Nikolause convention
	Power of Myth	1999	23 × 33	•••••	For canceled exhibit in Frankfurt; montage with Maul in middle
	Power of Myth	1999	23 × 33	•••••	For canceled exhibit in Berlin; montage with Maul in middle
	Adventures of Film	2001	23 × 33	•••••	Concert with photo of half Vader helmet
	Jedi-Con	2001	23 × 33	•••••	Sanda artwork
	Star Wars Convention	2002	11 × 16.5	•••	In Hamburg September 6–8; several characters depicted
HUNGARY					
	Sci-Fi Con	2001	16 × 23	•••	Budapest
IRELAND					
	Power of Myth	1999	40 × 60	•••••	For exhibit in Dublin RDS; June 17–20; montage with Maul in middle
ITALY					
	Guerre Stellari a Venezia	1997	27 × 38	•••••	Illustration of C-3PO in *Falcon* cockpit with Venice scene in background
JAPAN					
	Great Robot exhibit	1983	20 × 28.5	•••••••	R2-D2 and C-3PO with Robby, King Kong, etc.
	SF Music	1993	29 × 40	•••••••	Cartoon C-3PO leading orchestra with E.T., Yoda, etc.; for Orchestra in Screen CD and tour; Japan Railway
	George Lucas exhibit	1993	29 × 40	•••••••	Sezon Museum; CGI lightsaber blade with wire-frame X-wing, TIE, and R2-D2
	George Lucas exhibit	1993	29 × 40	•••••••	Sezon Museum; film scenes inside letters of Lucas' name; photo at bottom of special phone card
	George Lucas exhibit	1993	23 × 33	•••••	Sezon Museum; *Jedi* "B" art with pre-printed Lucas signature
	George Lucas exhibit	1993	23 × 33	•••••	Sezon Museum; *Jedi* dogfight with pre-printed Lucas signature
	George Lucas exhibit	1993	23 × 33	••••••	Sezon Museum; Lucas among props with pre-printed signature
	George Lucas exhibit	1993	14 × 20	••••••	Sezon Museum; film scenes inside letters of Lucas' name; July 30–Sept. 27
	George Lucas exhibit	1994	20 × 29	••••••	Hiroshima City Museum of Contemporary Art; Lucas with props; April 16–June 19
	George Lucas exhibit	1994	14 × 20	•••••	Daimaru; Lucas with props
	Star Wars exhibition	1997	29 × 40	•••••••	Space World; Vader full figure; July 5–Nov. 3
	Star Wars exhibition	1997	20 × 29	••••••	Space World; Vader full figure; July 5–Nov. 3
	Star Wars exhibition	1997	29 × 40	•••••••	Space World; Vader full figure; black strip at bottom: Space World Presents
	Star Wars exhibition	1997	20 × 29	••••••	Space World; Vader full figure; black strip at bottom: Space World Presents
	Star Wars exhibition	1997	12 × 33	•••••	Vader left, text right
	Star Wars exhibition	1997	29 × 40	•••••••	Space World; C-3PO full figure; black band at bottom
	Star Wars exhibition	1997	29 × 40	•••••••	Space World; C-3PO full figure; no black band at bottom
	Star Wars exhibition	1997	20 × 29	••••••	Space World; C-3PO full figure
	Star Wars exhibition	1997	29 × 40	••••••	Space World; *Star Wars* Special Edition artwork with white border
	Tokyo Special Concert	1997	20 × 29	••••	Tokyo New Philharmonic Orchestra Special Concert; Utah Symphony album cover and *Jedi* "B" art
	Fan Event	2001	16 × 23	••	In Yokohama; July 24
	Shannon Baksa Tour	2001	11 × 15	•	Mara Jade tour poster
	Tokyo Toy Festival	2002	12 × 16	•	On photo paper
	Art of *Star Wars*	2003	29 × 40	••••••	Photo of C-3PO among *Star Wars* props; Kyoto National Museum; June 24–Aug. 31
	Art of *Star Wars*	2003	20 × 29	•••••	Photo of C-3PO among *Star Wars* props; Kyoto National Museum; June 24–Aug. 31
	Art of *Star Wars*	2003	20 × 29	•••••	Photo of C-3PO among *Star Wars* props; Kyoto National Museum; "US/Japan" in upper right corner
	Star Wars Science and Art	2004	20 × 29	•••••	Headshot of Amidala from Episode I; Kyoto National Museum
	Star Wars Science and Art	2004	14 × 20	••••	Horizontal, image of Amidala and C-3PO from Episode I; Kyoto National Museum
	Star Wars Science and Art	2004	20 × 29	•••••	C-3PO and Amidala from Episode I; March 20–June 20
	Star Wars Science and Art	2004	29 × 40	••••••	C-3PO and Amidala from Episode I; white band at bottom with text
MEXICO					
	Conque	1997	21 × 32.5	••	Mexican convention
	Star Wars Mexican Convention	2000	21 × 33	•••	Primera *Star Wars* Convencion; March 17–19
	Star Wars Mexican Convention	2000	17 × 22	••	Primera *Star Wars* Convencion; March 17–19
	Star Wars Mexican Convention	2001	22 × 34	•••	Second con; Obi-Wan, droids, Naboo fighters, etc.
	Star Wars Connections	2002	16 × 21	••	Mexican con event; two-sided with program on reverse
	Tercera Convencion	2002	22 × 34	•••	Anakin and Clones
	Star Wars Mexican Convention	2003	22 × 31	••	Primera Convencion de Coleccionistas; Vader action figure image; July 12–13
	Star Wars en Concierto	2004	25.5 × 36	••••	Mexican *Star Wars* concert, July 13–14, 2004; image of Bith musician
	Star Wars en Concierto	2004	13 × 19	•••	Mexican *Star Wars* concert, July 13–14, 2004; image of Bith musician
	Star Wars Encuentros	2004	25.5 × 36	•••	Mexican *Star Wars* Convention; Obi-Wan and Anakin above, classic duel below
	Star Wars Encuentros/Park	2004	15 × 24	•••••	Mexican *Star Wars* Convention Ray Park appearance poster
NETHERLANDS					
	Star Wars: The Party	1999	16.5 × 23	••••	Amsterdam; black-and-white illustration of Podrace behind text; at dance club
	Echo Base Con	2001	12 × 16	••	Dutch Fan Club con; Maul
	Echo Base Charity	2002	16 × 23	••••••	Charity con put on by Dutch fan club; Matt Busch art
	Echo Base Charity	2003	19 × 28	••••	Charity con put on by Dutch fan club; artwork of Obi-Wan, Anakin, and Vader
	Echo Base Charity	2003	12 × 18	••••	Artwork print of charity con put on by Dutch fan club; artwork of Obi-Wan, Anakin, and Vader
SCOTLAND					
	Art of *Star Wars*	2002	17 × 23	••••	At City Art Centre, Edinburgh; C-3PO waist high against black
SPAIN					
	Star Wars Saga	1985	27.5 × 39	••••••	"20th Fantasy Fox"; B. de Pedro art with montage of character film festival, including Yoda, R2, C-3PO, etc.
	Star Wars Party	1999	27 × 38	••	For Episode I; pink and white, image of Anakin in racer; Sept. 24
	Power of Myth	1999	35 × 51	•••••	For canceled exhibit in Barcelona; montage with Maul in middle
	Star Wars BarnaCon	2000	19 × 27	•••	Spanish Fan Club first con
UNITED KINGDOM					
	Imperial Invasion	1995	16.5 × 23	••••	Tour poster for video release; stormtrooper with venue information
	LSO	1998	31 × 47	•••••••	Photo of C-3PO conducting the London Symphony Orchestra
	Power of Myth	1999	25 × 35	••••••	For canceled European Tour; summer 1999
	Power of Myth	1999	40 × 60	•••••	Canceled exhibit at Wembly exhibition Hall; July 1–11; montage
	Art of *Star Wars*	2000	48 × 72	••••••	Exhibit at Barbican Gallery; Maul with Portrait; April 13–Sept. 3

EVENTS POSTERS

Title	Year	Size	Rating	Description
UNITED KINGDOM, CONT.				
Art of *Star Wars*	2000	20 × 30	••••	Exhibit at Barbican Gallery; Maul with Portrait; April 13–Sept. 3
Art of *Star Wars*	2000	11 × 16	•••	Exhibit at Barbican Gallery; Maul with Portrait; April 13–Sept. 3
Art of *Star Wars*	2000	48 × 72	••••••	Exhibit at Barbican Gallery; C-3PO looking through frame; April 13–Sept. 3
Art of *Star Wars*	2000	20 × 30	••••	Exhibit at Barbican Gallery; C-3PO looking through frame; April 13–Sept. 3
Art of *Star Wars*	2000	11 × 16	•••	Exhibit at Barbican Gallery; C-3PO looking through frame; April 13–Sept. 3
Art of *Star Wars*	2000	11 × 16	•••	Exhibit at Barbican Gallery; C-3PO looking through frame; October 13–April 29
UNITED STATES				
American Marketing Assn.	1977	18 × 23	••••••••••	Artwork poster by Bob Watts for San Diego meeting on Sept. 22
Memorial Hospital	1978	8.5 × 14	•••••••	Brown on yellow; photo of George, Chewie, and cameraman for Premiere by Memorial Hospital Foundation
Supersnipe	1978	11 × 17	••••••••••	B&W window poster for The Designing of *Star Wars* exhibit for Supersnipe Comic Art Gallery, NYC
Music From Outer Space	1978	14 × 21	••••	B&W on cardstock; Zubin Mehta conducts April 1 at Anaheim Stadium
Sounds of Space	1978	20 × 48	••••••••••	Laser concert in San Francisco Bay Area; uncut proof of three posters, two by McQuarrie, one by Johnson
Star Wars Concert	1978	24 × 37	••••••••••	Alvin art of R2-D2 and C-3PO as two-man band; for canceled concert series
Music From Outer Space	1978	17 × 22	••••••••••	Illustration of yellow C-3PO in tuxedo conducting
Yoda Mardi Gras	1981	22 × 29	•••••••	Yoda sitting on street lamp during Mardi Gras in New Orleans
Cincinnati Pops	1982	18 × 28	•••••••••	John Williams *Star Wars* Festival May 31; Vader conducts with saber
Creation Con	1983	20 × 24	••••	Kid in *Jedi* shirt opening bedroom door
America's Movies for the World Athletes	1984	22 × 36	•••••••	American Film Institute poster for 23rd Olympiad; Drew art includes Vader
Northridge	1985	12 × 16	•••	Northridge Student Union screening; B&W with three films' poster art
Palomar	1985	12 × 18	•••••	Palomar College exhibit of Phil Tippett models for movies
Marin County Fair	1988	9 × 23	••••••••	Vertical red, white, and black for Fair includes "Magic of Lucasfilm" with art of droids
Art of *Star Wars*	1994	26 × 60	••••••••	Yerba Buena Gardens Dec. 27–March 12; laminated banner of Cloud City chasm (McQuarrie)
Art of *Star Wars*	1994	47 × 68	•••••••	Yerba Buena Gardens (laminated): Yoda, Death Star, droids
Art of *Star Wars*	1994	14 × 24	•••••	Yerba Buena Gardens: Yoda, Death Star, droids
Children's Museum	1995	12.5 × 36	••••	For Indianapolis flight exhibit; artwork includes *Millennium Falcon*
Houston Film Festival	1995	21.5 × 32	•••••	Photo of C-3PO in color and shadowy Chaplin in black-and-white
Arizona *Star Wars* Con	1997	16 × 20	•	For Arizona con in black, white, and green
Magic of Myth	1997	36 × 53	••••••••	Large Advance poster with Yoda; laminated
Magic of Myth	1997	23 × 35	•••••••	Smithsonian; Gala opening night; C-3PO with black band across top; Oct. 29
Magic of Myth	1997	23 × 35	••••	Smithsonian; C-3PO photo; Oct. 1997–Oct. 1998
Magic of Myth	1997	23 × 35	•••••	Smithsonian; Vader photo; Oct. 1997–Oct. 1998
Star Wars Celebration I	1999	24 × 36	••••	Alvin art of Darth Maul looming above young Anakin
Magic of Myth	1999	24 × 36	••••	San Diego Museum; C-3PO photo
Magic of Myth	1999	10 × 21	•••	San Diego Museum; Vader costume photo on heavy stock
Magic of Myth	2000	24 × 36	••••	Field Museum; C-3PO photo
Magic of Myth	2000	11 × 28	•••••	Field Museum; translite of Yoda
Roleplaying Event	2000	22 × 28	•••••	Game event at San Diego Comic-Con; photo of Vader's helmet
Roleplaying Event	2000	22 × 28	•••••	Game event at Wizard World; photo of Vader's helmet
Star Wars Weekends	2000	24 × 36	•••••	Randy Noble art of Lightsaber cutting Mickey silhouette
Magic of Myth	2001	24 × 36	••••	Houston; C-3PO photo
Magic of Myth	2001	20 × 28	••••	Toledo; C-3PO photo
Magic of Myth	2001	17 × 24	••••	Toledo; C-3PO photo
Star Wars Weekends	2001	24 × 32	••••	Randy Noble art of Mickey projected as hologram from R2-D2
Star Wars Weekends	2001	18 × 24	•••••	Randy Noble art of Mickey and R2-D2; edition size of 1000
Star Wars Celebration II	2002	22 × 28	•••••	Anakin and Vader image
Star Wars Weekends	2003	24 × 32	•••••	Randy Noble art of Mickey and Yoda as Jedi with lightsabers flashing
Star Wars Weekends	2004	24 × 32	•••••	Randy Noble art of Mickey and Minnie as Luke and Leia

ADVERTISING & PROMOTIONAL POSTERS

	Film	Year	Size	Licensee	Rating	Description
AUSTRALIA						
	ESB	1980	16.5 × 24	Irvine's Twinkies	••••••••	Photo of box of Twinkies plus six premium stickers available
	SW	1982	9 × 24	GE	•••••••	GE banner for *Star Wars* release on TV; "Win trip to USA" snipe
	SW	1982	18 × 36	GE	•••••••	GE presents *Star Wars*, sponsored by Kenner; photo of Vader in carbon freeze chamber
	ROTJ	1983	6 × 24	Bing Harris Sargood	•••	Black-and-white poster with "Posters, Badges, Erasers, Available Here"
	ROTJ	1983	6 × 24	Bing Harris Sargood	•••	*Return of the Jedi* logo in black-and-white
	SW	1983	18 × 24	CBS Fox	••••	Vader against pink; "Star Wars: Where the Saga Began . . . at the Video Cross Roads Store In Your Galaxy"
	ROTJ	1983	16.5 × 24	Crystal Craft Gifts	•••••	Vader photo with four images below of various collectibles: stationery, banks, rubber stamps, stickers, etc.
	ROTJ	1983	40 × 59	Immunization	•••••••	For immunization, photo of droids on Endor; for subway use (heavy stock)
	ROTJ	1983	15 × 20	Immunization	••••••	For immunization, photo of droids on Endor; glossy stock
	ROTJ	1983	16 × 23	n/a	•••	Vader photo with "Challenge" and "A force to be reckoned with"; educational
	ROTJ	1983	13 × 19	NSW Building Society	•••••••	ROTJ "B" artwork with parts missing for stickers (promo with account)
	ROTJ	1983	9 × 14	Peters	•••••••	For popsicles; *Revenge* and "B" artwork, *Jedi* Competition snipe; "With Jedi Jelly"
	ROTJ	1983	16.5 × 22.5	Peters	•••••••	For popsicles—"Peters with Jedi Jelly"; Toltoys Competition with photos of toys
	ESB	1984	27 × 40	CBS Fox	••••••	For video; like US Advance with Vader helmet
	ESB	1984	27 × 40	CBS Fox	•••••••	For video; Ohrai art with blue *Empire* logo
	ESB	1984	16.5 × 33	CBS Fox	••••••	For video; McQuarrie art of Cloud City with "Coming Soon to Your Galaxy"
	EWOK	1985	10.5 × 11	Break	•••••••	Window sheet for *Ewok Adventure* poster and stickers offer
	ROTJ	1986	28 × 39	CBS Fox	•••••	For video; "B" artwork with "Now Available" sticker across credits
	TRIL	1988	27 × 36	CBS Fox	•••••	For video trilogy; *Star Wars* Style "A" artwork with three covers at left
	n/a	1993	28 × 39	LucasArts	••••	For "TIE Fighter" video game; "Coming Soon" text at top above perforation for removal; Metro Games
	n/a	1994	26.5 × 38	LucasArts	••••	For "X-Wing," "Imperial Pursuit," and "B-Wing" video games; star field with three games and "CD-ROM" and Metro Games
	TRIL	1995	28 × 39	20th C Fox Home Ent.	••••••	For video trilogy; "Give the Power of the Force This Christmas"; Vader helmet, factory laminated
	TRIL	1995	28 × 39	20th C Fox Home Ent.	••••••	For video trilogy; "The Original One Last Time" with artwork of Vader, Luke, Leia, Han, etc.
	n/a	1995	22 × 24	Bantam	•••••	One square from long plastic banner roll, *Star Wars* logo and MTFBWY, Bantam logo, blue/white
	n/a	1995	28 × 39	LucasArts	••••••	"Rebel Assault II" distributed by Metro Games; pilot running toward X-wing in hangar
	TRILSE	1996	27 × 38	KFC	•••••	Boba Fett; "Free Action Toy with Kids Meal"
	TRILSE	1996	27 × 38	KFC	•••••	Stormtrooper "Family Feast" chicken in a bucket
	TRIL	1997	12 × 17	Panini	••••	For sticker collection
	n/a	1998	28 × 39	LucasArts	•••••	"*Star Wars* Rogue Squadron" for Nintendo 64; art of X-wings and other ships; two-sided
	TPM	1999	21 × 29	Dorling Kindersley	••••	Episode I Incredible Cross Sections book cover image
	TPM	1999	21 × 29	Dorling Kindersley	••••	Episode I Visual Dictionary book cover image
	TPM	1999	27 × 38	KFC	•••••	For "Mega Feast" meal with image of Amidala
	TPM	1999	27 × 38	KFC	•••••	For "Twister Combo" meal with image of Qui-Gon
	TPM	1999	27 × 38	KFC	•••••	For *Star Wars* charity auction with image of Darth Maul; KFC logo at bottom
	TPM	1999	14 × 23	TV Guide	••	Australian *TV Guide* poster showing Obi-Wan and battle droid, McGregor interview blurb
	TPM	1999	16 × 21.5	Who Weekly Magazine	•••••	For June 7 issue, with cover of Portman, Lloyd, McGregor, and Neeson
	TPM	2001	30 × 40	Showtime	••••••	Episode I premiere on Australian Showtime; Maul face
	AOTC	2002	16.5 × 23.5	n/a	•••••	Sweepstakes to win various *Star Wars* prizes; cast photos and dairy products
	AOTC	2002	12 × 16	Australia Post	••••	Promo for Episode II stamp sheet souvenir
	AOTC	2002	25 × 27.5	Hungry Jacks	•••••	Promo for mini frames; "Get One With Every Kids Meal"
BRAZIL						
	SW	1980	21.5 × 30	Savory Derechos	••••••••	For "Centella" popsicle; art of *Star Wars* and *Empire* characters and vehicles around title
	ESB	1982	14 × 31	Savory Derechos	••••••••	For the "Laser" popsicle; art of popsicle with *Empire* "B" art in background
	TPM	1999	16 × 23.5	LucasArts	••	Drew art with "Ameaca Fantasma" and video game scenes below
	TPM	1999	16 × 23.5	LucasArts	••••••	For "Racer" video game; Podrace with insets of Anakin and Sebulba
	TPM	1999	15 × 24	Pepsi	•••	For Pepsi/Pizza Hut pitcher premiums; photo of Anakin and three pitchers
CANADA						
	SW	1978	16 × 27	Coca-Cola	••••••••	Coke contest: Match the liners on C-3PO bottle caps
	SW	1979	15.5 × 22.5	Ottawa Journal	•••••••	For newspaper comic strip; artwork of droids with "exclusively in the *Ottawa Journal*"
	ROTJ	1983	25 × 38	Coca-Cola	•••••••	Slurpee poster for Jedi Collector Cups; crude artwork of Vader/Luke; red, white, blue, and black
	ESB	1984	22 × 34	Super Channel	•••••	Pay channel poster for February; uses *Empire* rerelease '82 artwork
	ROTJ	1984	22 × 34	Super Channel	•••••	Pay channel poster for March; photo of Luke and Leia on sail barge
	TRILSE	1997	19 × 25	Guide magazine	•	Sci Fi Invasion—includes C-3PO; for *Guide* magazine
	n/a	1997	18 × 23	Mutual Group	••••	"Transplantation—A New Hope;" artwork of droids in rebel hangar
	n/a	1997	9 × 11	Mutual Group	••	"Transplantation—A New Hope;" artwork of droids in rebel hangar
	n/a	1999	15 × 40	Dark Horse	••	"Vader's Quest" artwork poster
	TPM	1999	21 × 33	Unisource Papers	••••••	Image of Maul's face
	AOTC	2002	27 × 40	20th C Fox Home Ent.	•••••	Yoda "Unlock the Saga on Video and DVD November 12"
	TRILSE	2004	27 × 40	20th C Fox Home Ent.	••••	Trilogy on DVD; black-and-white ingot art
	n/a	2004	22 × 28	LucasArts	•••	"Battlefront" game for Future Shop; shows games for X-box and PlayStation 2
	n/a	2004	14 × 43.5	LucasArts	•••	"Battlefront" game for Future Shop; full figure stormtrooper
FRANCE						
	n/a	1980	23 × 30.5	n/a	•••••••	"Muppets in Space"; Style "A" artwork with Kermit, Piggy, and Darth Gonzo
	ESB	1981	21 × 30	Glaces Motta	••••••••	*Empire* "B" artwork with white boxes around border for stickers
	SW	1982	23.5 × 33	n/a	••••	Like US "A" sheet in French; no white border, small *Star Wars* title below in black; for video release
	TRIL	1995	24 × 33	20th C Fox Home Ent.	•••••	International art of Luke, Leia, Han, droids, and Vader for "original" trilogy's last release
	TRIL	1995	31.5 × 47	Quick	•••••	Vertical poster for trilogy on video; Han, Chewie, droids at bottom with three cassettes
	n/a	1996	16 × 24	IMAX Film	•••••••	"Special Effects" presentation, Paris
	TRILSE	1997	12 × 17	Pizza Hut	•••••	For premiums: C-3PO in pieces, *Falcon* in asteroids, Han in carbonite, and Death Star
	n/a	1997	12 × 16	Star Wars Magazine	•	For issue #10: orange cover
	n/a	1997	12 × 16	Star Wars Magazine	•	Green "Nouvelle Trilogie" cover
	TPM	1998	12 × 16	Star Wars Magazine	•	For issue #13: C-3PO cover
	TPM	1998	12 × 16	Star Wars Magazine	•	For issue #14: Vader and Young Anakin cover
	TPM	1999	16 × 24	Bouygues Telecom	••••	Episode I cell phones by Nokia
	TPM	1999	59 × 22	Francaise des Jeux	•••••	Vertical poster for *Star Wars* Saga lottery tickets
	TPM	1999	9 × 21	Francaise des Jeux	•••	"Saga *Star Wars*" with Jar Jar on right
	TPM	1999	14 × 21	Francaise des Jeux	•••	*Star Wars* Saga stickers or game pieces
	TPM	1999	9 × 21	Francoise de Jeux	•••	Lotto tickets "Saga *Star Wars*" with Jar Jar
	TPM	1999	14 × 21	Francoise de Jeux	•••	Episode I lotto with several game tickets
	TPM	1999	12 × 31	Francoise de Jeux	•••	Episode I lotto with Amidala and game tickets
	TPM	1999	11 × 12	Francoise de Jeux	•••	Episode I lotto with several game tickets
	TPM	1999	16.5 × 23	Kertel	•••••	For phone cards; Maul on right, duel on left
	TPM	1999	12 × 16	Star Wars Magazine	••	For "Official Guide to Episode I" issue
	AOTC	2002	20 × 30	Hollywood Chewing Gum	•••	Heroes and villains; horizontal
	AOTC	2002	20 × 23	Hollywood Chewing Gum	•••	Heroes and villains
	AOTC	2002	16 × 39	Hollywood Chewing Gum	•••	Heroes and villains
	AOTC	2002	14 × 22	Hollywood Chewing Gum	•••	Promo for cards
	AOTC	2002	12 × 25	Hollywood Chewing Gum	•••	Promo for cards
	AOTC	2002	12.5 × 51.5	Hollywood Chewing Gum	•••	Promoting premium cards, stickers plus contest to win home cinema or watch *L'Attaque des Clones*
	AOTC	2002	10 × 20	Hollywood Chewing Gum	•••	Promo for cards
	AOTC	2002	19 × 26	LEGO	•••	LEGO Republic gunship; on reverse is what appears to be half of a larger gunship poster in French

ADVERTISING & PROMOTIONAL POSTERS

	Film	Year	Size	Licensee	Rating	Description
FRANCE, CONT.						
	AOTC	2002	17 × 23	LucasArts	•••••	Teaser for "Star Wars: Bounty Hunter" (November 2002); head shot of Jango against black
	CW	2003	47 × 69	Cartoon Network	••••••	Large poster with Clone Wars artwork and black stripe at bottom; halftone reverse
	CW	2003	23.5 × 31.5	Cartoon Network	••••••	Clone Wars artwork like US version but French
GERMANY						
	ESB	1982	23 × 33	CBS Fox	••••••	Luke in flight outfit with Yoda on shoulder; logo in white on blue background; square 20th Century Fox logo
	ESB	1982	23 × 33	CBS Fox	••••••	Luke in flight outfit with Yoda on shoulder; snipe for CBS/Fox video and mention of book and soundtrack
	TRIL	1986	23.5 × 33	CBS Fox	••••••	For videos, shows cassettes of SW, ESB, ROTJ, and EWOKS flying like ships toward "Krieg der Sterne"; Silver Screen Collection
	EWOK2	1988	33 × 47	n/a	••••••	Battle for Endor (R. Casaro art); "George Lucas Film" at top; for video release
	n/a	1993	23 × 33	LucasArts	•••••	"TIE Fighter" video game; dogfight imagery with various games along right border
	TRIL	1994	17 × 25	Modern Graphics	•••••	Star Wars/Indiana Jones Archive book
	TRIL	1995	27 × 38	20th C Fox Home Ent.	•	Blue star field with absolutely no copy at all
	TRIL	1995	23.5 × 33	20th C Fox Home Ent.	••••••	For video trilogy; artwork of Vader, Luke, Han, Leia, etc. with inset photos to compare quality of new THX version
	TRIL	1995	16.5 × 23	20th C Fox Home Ent.	••••	For video trilogy; space battle from Return of the Jedi
	TRIL	1995	15 × 54	20th C Fox Home Ent.	•••••••••	For video trilogy; horizontal "Star Wars Trilogy" text
	TRIL	1995	15 × 54	20th C Fox Home Ent.	•••••••••	For video trilogy; vertical blue lightsaber art by Alvin
	TRIL	1995	15 × 54	20th C Fox Home Ent.	•••••••••	For video trilogy; vertical green lightsaber art by Alvin
	TRIL	1995	15 × 54	20th C Fox Home Ent.	•••••••••	For video trilogy; vertical red lightsaber art by Alvin
	n/a	1996	33 × 47	Feest Comics	•••••••	Star Wars comics; "Die Erben des Imperiums"
	TRILSE	1997	23 × 33	20th C Fox Home Ent.	••••	Trilogy SE on video—Droids
	TRILSE	1997	23 × 33	20th C Fox Home Ent.	••••	Trilogy SE on video—Vader
	TRILSE	1997	23 × 33	20th C Fox Home Ent.	••••	Trilogy SE on video—Yoda
	n/a	1997	21 × 31	VGS	••••	Vader image with novels, Chronicles, etc. below
	TPM	1999	17 × 23	Blanvalet	••••	Poster for novelization
	TPM	1999	23 × 33	Klax Max	••••	Episode I cell phone covers for Nokia
	n/a	1999	19 × 27	Lego	•••	Vader holding "infinity symbol" with Vader's TIE
	TPM	1999	16 × 23	LucasBooks	•••	German "Making of" book poster; Burgschmiet Verlag
	TPM	1999	23 × 33	n/a	•••	For soundtrack; Drew Struzan art
	TPM	1999	23 × 33	Pizza Hut	•••	Pizza Hut/Pepsi for collector cards
	TPM	1999	23 × 33	VGS	•••	Episode I "Cross Sections" and "Illustrated Universe" books
	TPM	2000	23 × 33	20th C Fox Home Ent.	•••	Horizontal video poster: Amidala
	TPM	2000	23 × 33	20th C Fox Home Ent.	•••	Horizontal video poster: Anakin
	TPM	2000	23 × 33	20th C Fox Home Ent.	•••	Horizontal video poster: Maul
	TPM	2000	23 × 33	20th C Fox Home Ent.	•••	Horizontal video poster: Obi-Wan
	TPM	2000	23 × 33	20th C Fox Home Ent.	•••	Video release poster including Episode I
	TPM	2000	23 × 33	20th C Fox Home Ent.	•••	Video release poster-characters above, Podrace below
	TPM	2000	47 × 69	Hente kommt	•••••••••	Lenticular poster for Episode I on TV: Darth Maul and Yoda
	TPM	2000	47 × 69	Hente kommt	•••••••	Two-sided poster for Episode I on TV: Amidala
	TPM	2000	47 × 69	Hente kommt	•••••••	Two-sided poster for Episode I on TV: Darth Maul
	TPM	2000	47 × 69	Hente kommt	•••••••	Two-sided poster for Episode I on TV: Yoda
	TPM	2000	11 × 16	Modern Graphics Comics	•	Art of kid in Maul make-up
	TPM	2001	16 × 23	Dino Comics	••••	Darth Maul comic; Drew Struzan cover artwork
	AOTC	2002	23 × 31	Cinema Magazine	••••	For 5/02 issue; blowup of cover showing Obi-Wan, Padmé, and Anakin
	n/a	2002	23 × 33	Das Hipperium	••••	Promo for hippo toys in Star Wars outfits
	n/a	2002	23 × 33	Das Hipperium	••••	Promo for hippo toys with Vader hippo
	AOTC	2002	23 × 33	Hasbro	•••	Hasbro figures, vehicles, games, etc.
	DROID	1985–86	23 × 33	CBS Fox	••••••	For four Droids cartoon video cassettes
	n/a	n/a	16 × 23	Lucas Learning	••••••	Droids video game (not animated characters); R2 and C-3PO
	n/a	n/a	17 × 23	Nautilus	•••••	Michael Whelan art of Yoda with "Nautilus" above
	n/a	n/a	23 × 33	VGS	•	Image of a book in asteroids, includes Star Wars among other titles at bottom
HONG KONG						
	TRILSE	2000	16 × 24	n/a	••••	Vader-SW Trilogy available on VCD (in English)
	TRILSE	2000	16 × 24	n/a	••••	Yoda-SW Trilogy available on VCD (in English)
HUNGARY						
	TPM	2000	18 × 26	Continental Film	•••	Episode I on video and DVD
	AOTC	2002	16.5 × 23.5	LucasArts	•••	Two-sided poster for LucasArts; "Jedi Outcast" backed with "Racer Revenge"; Activision
	AOTC	2002	16.5 × 23.5	LucasArts	•••	Two-sided poster for LucasArts; "Jedi Outcast" backed with "Starfighter"; Activision
	AOTC	2002	16.5 × 23.5	Sony	•••	Soundtrack poster for AOTC; Drew Struzan art
ITALY						
	TRIL	1995	11 × 27	20th C Fox Home Ent.	•••	For trilogy on video; shows Panasonic TV/VCR and three videos with Alvin art covers
	TPM	1999	16 × 23	DK/LucasBooks	••••	Battle droids poster for DK/LucasBooks (in English)
	AOTC	2002	27 × 38	Hasbro	••••	Attacco dei Cloni figures and vehicles
	n/a	n/a	18 × 27	Profondo Rosso	••••••	Artwork of R2 and C-3PO in storefront; for toy stores in Rome and Milan
JAPAN						
	SW	1977–78	29 × 40	Coca-Cola	••••••••••	"Drink Coca-Cola STAR WARS"; battle scene illustrated by Shimaoka
	SW	1977–78	20 × 28.5	Coca-Cola	••••••••••	Drink Coca-Cola with illustration of thirteen bottle caps with Luke and droids, photos of four sodas, R2-D2 at bottom
	SW	1977–78	12 × 16	Coca-Cola	••••••••••	Horizontal poster for Coke caps, R2-D2 radio, and T-shirt
	SW	1977–78	7 × 20	Coca-Cola	••••••••••	Small window poster for Coca-Cola R2-D2 AM radio premium
	SW	1978	14 × 20	Bandai Books	••••••••	Horizontal photo X-wing and TIE fighter; photo album and story book below
	SW	1978	11 × 24	Bandai Books	••••••••	Vertical poster for novelization; Death Star, X-wing, Vader TIE, and Y-wing at top, silver background, Star Wars title in yellow/red
	SW	1978	10 × 28.5	Bandai Books	••••••••	Vertical photo X-wing and TIE fighter above, photo album and story book below
	SW	1978	14 × 20	Factors	••••••••••	For Japanese Factors ten badge set
	SW	1978	8 × 23	Fuji	••••••••	Star Wars on Fuji (16mm) film
	SW	1978	20 × 29	King Records	••••••••	For soundtrack, photo of droids in ship corridor
	SW	1978	20 × 29	King Records	••••••••	For soundtrack, photo X-wing and TIE fighter
	SW	1978	20 × 29	Meiji	••••••••••	For candy, droids above with candy and premiums below
	SW	1978	20 × 28.5	Morinaga	••••••••••	Candy poster with Hildebrandt art above and three candy boxes below
	SW	1978	20 × 28.5	Morinaga	••••••••••	For candy; Vader, X-wing art, and logo above, three Morinaga products below
	SW	1978	14 × 20	Morinaga	••••••••••	Candy poster with Hildebrandt art above and three candy boxes below
	SW	1978	14.5 × 14.5	n/a	•••••••	Unknown promotion, uses Seito poster art; transit
	SW	1978	23 × 33	Pioneer	•••••••	Pioneer Synthesizer record poster, art of X-wing/TIE by Osamu Shouji; "Star Wars Collector's Disk!"
	ESB	1980	21 × 30	Boy's Photo News	•••••••	Transit ad showing Falcon landing on Cloud City (No. 853)
	ESB	1980	21 × 30	Boy's Photo News	•••••••	Transit ad showing Star Destroyer (No. 850)
	ESB	1980	23.5 × 33	RSO	••••••••	Ohrai artwork with RSO label and title in English
	ROTJ	1983	11 × 24	n/a	••••••	Horizontal poster for novel; Star Destroyer with photos above, photo of book below
	ROTJ	1983	11 × 24	n/a	••••••	Vertical poster for novel; Falcon/TIEs in Death Star tunnel, photo of book below
	ROTJ	1983	14.5 × 20	PNN News	••••	Cover cartoon with Jedi and other film characters
	ROTJ	1986	20 × 29	CBS Fox	••••	For video, Jedi "A" artwork and "Best Library"; dated 1983, but probably 1986
	ROTJ	1986	14.5 × 20	CBS Fox	••••	For video; Jedi "A" artwork
	ROTJ	1986	14.5 × 20	CBS Fox	••••	For video; Jedi "A" artwork and "A Chorus Line" on lower half

ADVERTISING & PROMOTIONAL POSTERS

	Film	Year	Size	Licensee	Rating	Description
JAPAN, CONT.						
	n/a	1987	14 × 20	Mitsutoshi Ishigami	•••••	ILM—Art of Special Effects; Japanese book cover art
	n/a	1987	20 × 28.5	Panasonic	•••••••••	Panasonic Rally: R2-D2, C-3PO, map of Shibuya; neon yellow and pink
	n/a	1987	29 × 40	*TOB Magazine*	••••••••	Illustrated poster of Hollywood icons with Lucas at top center
	n/a	1987	14.5 × 20	*TOB Magazine*	••••••	Illustrated poster of Hollywood icons with Lucas at top center
	n/a	1987–88	7 × 20	Panasonic	•••••••••	*Millennium Falcon* (vertical)
	n/a	1987–88	7 × 20	Panasonic	•••••••••	Two Ewoks (vertical)
	n/a	1987–88	7 × 20	Panasonic	•••••••••	Yoda with earphones (vertical)
	n/a	1987–88	41 × 57	Panasonic	••••••••••	Chewbacca, Lucas with pocket TV
	n/a	1987–88	41 × 57	Panasonic	••••••••••	Darth Vader
	n/a	1987–88	41 × 57	Panasonic	••••••••	Lucas balancing TIE Interceptor on finger
	n/a	1987–88	41 × 57	Panasonic	••••••••••	Lucas with camcorder, C-3PO with butterfly net
	n/a	1987–88	41 × 57	Panasonic	••••••••••	Lucas with lightsaber
	n/a	1987–88	41 × 57	Panasonic	••••••••••	Two Ewoks
	n/a	1987–88	41 × 57	Panasonic	••••••••••	Yoda with earphones
	n/a	1987–88	29 × 40	Panasonic	•••••••••	Lucas balancing TIE Interceptor on finger
	n/a	1987–88	29 × 40	Panasonic	••••••••••	Lucas with camcorder, C-3PO with butterfly net
	n/a	1987–88	20 × 29	Panasonic	•••••••	Lucas with camcorder, C-3PO with butterfly net; reverse shows ad for movie "Big Town"
	n/a	1987–88	14 × 40.5	Panasonic	••••••••	Jabba (PIA Intermedia Theater plug)
	n/a	1987–88	14 × 40.5	Panasonic	••••••••	Lucas, C-3PO with net; tenth anniversary logo
	n/a	1987–88	14 × 40.5	Panasonic	••••••••	R2, C-3PO with umbrella and portable computer
	n/a	1987–88	14 × 40.5	Panasonic	••••••••	Two Ewoks with Japanese boy
	n/a	1987–88	14 × 20	Panasonic	••••••••	Lucas balancing TIE Interceptor on finger
	n/a	1987–88	14 × 20	Panasonic	••••••••	Yoda with earphones
	n/a	1988	35.5 × 56	Panasonic	••••••••••	Plastic-coated outdoor banner; photo of Lucas and *Jedi* characters in tall grass
	n/a	1988	28.5 × 40.5	Panasonic	••••••••••	Fair in Akihabara; hot pink background with circular photo of Lucas and *Jedi* characters
	n/a	1988	21 × 70	Panasonic	•••••••••	Silk-like cloth banner, green top, photo of C-3PO with laptop and R2-D2
	n/a	1988	21 × 70	Panasonic	•••••••••	Silk-like cloth banner, pink top, photo of Lucas and C-3PO with butterfly net
	n/a	1988	19.5 × 35.5	Panasonic	••••••••••	Silk-like cloth banner, photo of C-3PO and red stripe at bottom with "Maclord"
	n/a	1988	14 × 40.5	Panasonic	••••••••••	Horizontal; Fair in Akihabara; hot pink background with circular photo of Lucas and *Jedi* characters
	n/a	1988–89	41 × 57	Panasonic	••••••••	Lucas talks to illuminated Sparky robot
	n/a	1988–89	41 × 57	Panasonic	•••••••••	Lucas, Chewie, and Wicket on metal pole for satellite dish
	n/a	1988–89	41 × 57	Panasonic	••••••••••	Movie theater with Lucas, Sparky robot, and many *Star Wars* characters seated
	n/a	1988–89	41 × 57	Panasonic	••••••••	Sparky robot plays flute, Lucas on porch
	n/a	1988–89	41 × 57	Panasonic	•••	Sparky robot with kite and small girl
	n/a	1988–89	41 × 57	Panasonic	•••••••	Sparky, Lucas, and dog
	n/a	1988–89	41 × 57	Panasonic	•••••••	Wicket and Sparky skateboarding
	n/a	1988–89	29 × 40	Panasonic	••••••••••	Lucas and Yoda, legs crossed, both floating
	n/a	1988–89	21 × 70	Panasonic	•••	Silk-like cloth banner with Sparky robot
	n/a	1988–89	21 × 70	Panasonic	•••••••	Silk-like cloth banner with Sparky robot and Lucas
	n/a	1988–89	21 × 70	Panasonic	••••••••	Silk-like cloth banner with Yoda and Lucas
	n/a	1988–89	20 × 28.5	Panasonic	••••••••••	Lucas and Yoda, legs crossed, both floating
	n/a	1988–89	14 × 42	Panasonic	•••••••	Lucas scratching beard, small Sparky robot as rocket
	n/a	1988–89	14 × 42	Panasonic	•••••••	Profile of Lucas with eyes closed
	n/a	1988–89	14 × 42	Panasonic	•••	Sparky robot with kite and small girl
	n/a	1988–89	14 × 42	Panasonic	•••	Sparky robot with digital clock in stomach
	n/a	1988–89	14 × 42	Panasonic	•••••••	Three kids with Chewie, R2-D2, and two Ewoks
	n/a	1988–89	14 × 40	Panasonic	••••••••••	Lucas and Yoda, legs crossed, both floating
	n/a	1988–89	14 × 20	Panasonic	••••••••	Lucas, Chewie and Wicket on metal pole for satellite dish
	n/a	1988–89	14 × 20	Panasonic	••••••••	R2-D2 and C-3PO with laptop computer
	n/a	1988–89	14 × 20	Panasonic	•••••••	Sparky robot plays flute, Lucas on porch
	n/a	1988–89	14 × 20	Panasonic	•••••••	Wicket and another Ewok with large leaf
	n/a	1989	41 × 57	Panasonic	••••••••	"Red is the most difficult"; black and white photo of Lucas with red flower
	n/a	1989	41 × 114	Panasonic	•••	Sparky robot on rocky desert for Hi-Bit digital component system; Japan Railways two-sheet
	n/a	1989	29 × 40	Panasonic	•••	July Panasonic Fair in Akihabara with Sparky
	n/a	1989	14.5 × 40.5	Panasonic	••••••	"Pure Red"; black and white photo of Lucas with red flower; ad for Video FS90
	n/a	1989	14.5 × 40.5	Panasonic	••••••	Black and white photo of Lucas with red apple suspended above palm; for audio/video VHS player
	n/a	1989	14.5 × 40.5	Panasonic	••••••••	Lucas in white on high director's chair surrounded by characters from SW, Indy, *Tucker, American Graffiti*; for Maclord laptop video player
	n/a	1989	14.5 × 20	Panasonic	••••••	"Pure Red"; black and white photo of Lucas with red flower; ad for Video FS90
	n/a	1989	14.5 × 20	Panasonic	•••	Sparky: Super Festival in Dome
	n/a	1989	41 × 114	Star Tours	••••••••••	Japan Railways two-sheet for Star Tours Tokyo Disneyland opening July 12; large star speeder, one smaller flying over metropolis with lighted Cinderella castle; "Space Open!"
	n/a	1989	33 × 47	Star Tours	••••••••••	Original silk-screened Tokyo Disneyland entrance poster for Star Tours, with printer's color blocks in margin; edition size of 100
	n/a	1989	29 × 40	Star Tours	•••••••	JR Eastern Japan division, with photo of R2-D2 and C-3PO in lower left; "Space Open!"
	n/a	1989	29 × 40	Star Tours	•••••••	JR Eastern Japan division, with photo of R2-D2 and C-3PO in lower left; all Japanese except for Star Tours logo; white border at bottom for writing; "Space Open!"
	n/a	1989	29 × 40	Star Tours	•••••••	Mickey's Space Fantasy: Mickey in silver space suit floating between R2-D2 and C-3PO with dancers
	n/a	1989	29 × 40	Star Tours	•••••••	Mickey's Space Fantasy: Mickey in silver space suit floating between R2-D2 and C-3PO with dancers; yellow band at top for Prefecture Day visit
	n/a	1989	23.5 × 33	Star Tours	•••••••	Similar to Mickey's Space Fantasy, but with Mickey & Minnie in front of Star Tours building; "National/Panasonic" in white bottom strip
	n/a	1989	14 × 41	Star Tours	••••••••	Poster showing two star speeders over Magic Kingdom; July 12 date, in two sheets
	n/a	1989	14.5 × 20	Star Tours	••••••	Mickey's Space Fantasy: Mickey in silver space suit floating between R2-D2 and C-3PO with dancers in front; horizontal transit ad
	n/a	1989	14.5 × 20	Star Tours	•••••••	Two star speeders over lighted city and castle
	n/a	1989	29 × 40.5	Star Tours/Panasonic	•••••••	Panasonic Fair; mostly pink with speeder and space mice art in lower right
	n/a	1989	23 × 33	Star Tours/Panasonic	•••••••	Photo of boy holding Star Tours/Panasonic inflatable "beach shuttle" next to photo of castle, art of star speeder
	n/a	1989	14.5 × 40.5	Star Tours/Panasonic	•••••••	Invitation Sale; speeder, castle, Space Fantasy Mickey & Minnie
	n/a	1989	14.5 × 40.5	Star Tours/Panasonic	•••••••	Panasonic Fair; December 1–31, with art of speeders and Space Fantasy mice in lower right
	TRIL	1989	20 × 29	CBS Fox	••••••	Video poster for Japanese dubbed original trilogy and animated series
	SW	1990	14.5 × 20	CBS Fox	•••••	"Best Library" release of *Star Wars* and *Sound of Music*
	n/a	1990	14.5 × 40.5	Panasonic	••••••••	Lucas in field of floating red roses for VCRFS700 EP Power
	n/a	1990	14.5 × 40.5	Panasonic	•••••••	Lucas with young girl dressed as angel for Maclord video camera
	n/a	1990	29 × 40	Star Tours	••••	Donald Duck's American Oldies with inset of star speeder; Chiba Prefecture week 6/10/90
	n/a	1990	29 × 40	Star Tours	••••	Japan Rail "Disney Vacation" promo with small Star Tours poster in lower right and star speeders
	n/a	1990	29 × 40	Star Tours	••••	Mickey Mouse Sports Festival with small Star Tours logo lower right; for Saitama Prefecture 11/14/90
	n/a	1990	29 × 40	Star Tours	••••	Travel agency poster: The Kingdom of Dreams & Magic; photo of Japanese family, Mickey & Minnie, C-3PO, balloons
	n/a	1990	23.5 × 33	Star Tours	•••	Tokyo Disneyland 1990 calendar with small photo of Star Tours waiting area and star speeder
	n/a	1990	14.5 × 20	Star Tours	•••	Transit ad poster for *Nikkei Trendy* magazine 6/4/90 with photo story on opening of Star Tours Disney World

ADVERTISING & PROMOTIONAL POSTERS

	Film	Year	Size	Licensee	Rating	Description
JAPAN, CONT.						
	n/a	1990	14.5 × 20	*TV Week*	•	Silvery transit ad with R2-D2 and C-3PO as part of cover
	TRIL	1991	29 × 40	CBS Fox	••••	Photo collage for "Best Library" release of trilogy in Japanese dubbed and subtitled versions
	SW	1991	20 × 29	Fox Video	•	Laserdisc low price release of *Star Wars*, other films with photo of Han Solo aiming pistol
	n/a	1991	14 × 20	JVC	••••	"Attack on the Death Star" MNM software
	n/a	1991	29 × 40	Star Tours	•••	Campus Day with small Star Tours logo from Tobu Travel
	n/a	1991	29 × 40	Star Tours	•••	Campus Day with small Star Tours logo from Tokyo Travel
	n/a	1991	29 × 40	Star Tours	••••	Disney Vacation with Star Tours art included
	n/a	1991	29 × 40	Star Tours	•••	Party Gras for Chiba citizens with inset of star speeder
	n/a	1991	29 × 40	Star Tours	•••	Party Gras for Chiba citizens with inset of star speeder; travel agency name at bottom
	TRIL	1991	14 × 20	Victor	•••••	"Attack on the Death Star" video game; dogfight photo from *Jedi*
	n/a	1992	29 × 40.5	GLSLA	••••••••••	George Lucas Super Live Adventure: Black with white and gold words; Lucas visage in red (1 of 28)
	n/a	1992	29 × 40.5	GLSLA	•••••••	Hiro montage of Lucas films including *Tucker, American Graffiti*, etc.
	n/a	1992	29 × 40.5	GLSLA	•••••••	Hiro montage of Lucas films including *Tucker, American Graffiti*, etc.; different text at bottom
	n/a	1992	20 × 29	GLSLA	••••••	Hiro montage of Lucas films including *Tucker, American Graffiti*, etc.
	n/a	1992	20 × 28.5	PIA	•	"Special Line-Up" with one photo of Chewie and Han along with race cars and MC Hammer
	TRIL	1992	7 × 20	Victor	•••	"Attack on the Death Star" video game; dogfight photo from *Jedi*
	TRIL	1992	14.5 × 40.5	WOWOW	••••	Home Theater Channel *Star Wars* triple-bill for March '92
	n/a	1993	14.5 × 20.5	n/a	••••	Cartoon of Lucas' head springing out of C-3PO's body with Luke on his shoulder fighting Vader; for GLSLA
	n/a	1993	29 × 40.5	GLSLA	•••••••	Different Hiro montage art, *Star Wars* with large Indy face, *Willow*, etc.; running April 27–July 4
	n/a	1993	29 × 40.5	GLSLA	•••••••	Different Hiro montage art, *Star Wars* with large Indy face, *Willow*, etc.; running April 27–July 4; bottom TCF band
	n/a	1993	29 × 40.5	GLSLA	•••••••	Different Hiro montage art, *Star Wars* with large Indy face, *Willow*, etc.; running September 15–26 (sticker)
	n/a	1993	25 × 36	GLSLA	••••••	Reddish brown photo of Lucas in sunglasses with pre-printed signature; available for purchase at show
	n/a	1993	20.5 × 29	GLSLA	••••••	Different Hiro montage art, *Star Wars* with large Indy face, *Willow*, etc.; running April 27–July 4
	n/a	1993	20.5 × 29	GLSLA	••••••	Different Hiro montage art, *Star Wars* with large Indy face, *Willow*, etc.; running September 15–26 (sticker)
	n/a	1993	14.5 × 20	GLSLA	••••••	Hiro art (horizontal) transit ad; schedule and ticket phone numbers
	SW	1993	20 × 28.5	Shinseido	•	Shinseido video chain with lots of small video cases including *Star Wars*
	n/a	1993	20 × 29	Victor	•••••	"*Star Wars* Rebel Assault" video game; horizontal
	n/a	1994	20 × 29	Sega	••	Sega 32x with small blurb for "*Star Wars* Arcade"; yellow/red
	n/a	1994	20 × 29	Sega	••	Sega 32x; pink/white
	TRIL	1995	8 × 23	Aeon Inc.	•••••	*Star Wars* Chronicles (book) poster
	SW	1995	20 × 29	20th C Fox Home Ent.	••••	For *Star Wars*, art of hands holding up saber, "A long time ago . . ."; logo and THX in gold, all English
	TRIL	1995	20 × 29	20th C Fox Home Ent.	•••	For videos; half Vader helmet with three cassettes below (Alvin art covers)
	TRIL	1995	14 × 20	20th C Fox Home Ent.	•••	Classic video trilogy
	TRIL	1995	10 × 29	20th C Fox Home Ent.	•••	Vertical; THX Mastered Trilogy; Vader head above, three cassettes below (Alvin covers)
	TRIL	1995	8 × 23	Dark Horse	•••	Japanese three-pack comic in slipcase poster
	TRIL	1995	14 × 20	Dark Horse	••••	Comics three-pack in slipcase poster; horizontal
	n/a	1995	58 × 40	LucasArts	••••••	Two-piece poster with two 29 × 40 halves of Vader helmet which combine to make single image; "Rebel Assault II" and "Dark Forces;" mostly red
	TRIL	1996	7 × 20	Hasbro	•••	Hasbro vehicles above, Leia figure below; vertical
	TRIL	1996	7 × 20	Hasbro	•••	*Star Wars* video board game
	SWSE	1996	23 × 33	KFC	••••	Toys available with meals below
	n/a	1996	29 × 40	Mitsubishi	•••••••	"Star Cars" Japanese campaign; glossy, droids against star field; white area in center with cars
	n/a	1996	29 × 40	Mitsubishi	•••••••	"Star Cars" Japanese campaign; glossy, droids against star field; white area in center with minis
	n/a	1996	29 × 40	Mitsubishi	•••••••	"Star Cars" Japanese campaign; glossy, droids against star field; white area in center with RVs
	n/a	1996	29 × 40	Mitsubishi	•••••••	"Star Cars" Japanese campaign; R2 above, C-3PO below, car in pasture; April 6–7, 1996
	n/a	1996	29 × 40	Mitsubishi	•••••••	"Star Cars" Japanese campaign; R2 above, C-3PO below, car in pasture; April 6–7, 1996; different cars featured
	n/a	1996	29 × 40	Mitsubishi	•••••••	"Star Cars" Japanese campaign; stars above, R2 and C-3PO; March 2–3, 1996
	n/a	1996	29 × 40	Mitsubishi	•••••••	"Star Cars" campaign; R2 in upper right with flowers, C-3PO in lower left on field, cars middle/right
	n/a	1996	29 × 40	Mitsubishi	•••••••	"Star Cars" campaign; white band through center of star field, R2 and 3PO at upper right; glossy stock
	n/a	1996	17 × 22	Mitsubishi	•••••	"Star Cars" Japanese campaign; droids against purple background with car models below
	TRILSE	1997	29 × 40	n/a	•••••	For phone cards, SWSE artwork with three phone cards at right
	SWSE	1997	29 × 40	n/a	•••••	SWSE Drew art with three phone cards featuring Trilogy SE poster artwork at right
	TRILSE	1997	24 × 40	n/a	••••	Two-sided banner of six characters; for video trilogy
	n/a	1997	11 × 29	n/a	•••	For *Star Wars* Technical Journal; full shot of Star Destroyer with annotations and photo of book cover
	TRILSE	1997	8 × 23	20th C Fox Home Ent.	•••	SWSE art above with several novel covers below, including Chronicles snipe
	TRILSE	1997	29 × 40	20th C Fox Home Ent.	••••	Case of videos, cast above
	TRILSE	1997	23 × 33	20th C Fox Home Ent.	•••	Ingot art with three cassettes below
	TRILSE	1997	20 × 29	20th C Fox Home Ent.	•••	Case of videos, cast above
	TRILSE	1997	20 × 29	20th C Fox Home Ent.	•••	Ingot art with videos below
	TRILSE	1997	14 × 20	20th C Fox Home Ent.	•••	For videos, cast on left, cassettes on right, blurb about spirit Obi-Wan figure and Micro-Machines at bottom
	n/a	1997	20 × 29	Dark Horse	••••	Images of *Star Wars* comics covers
	SOTE	1997	20 × 29	LucasArts	•••••	For Nintendo 64, stormtrooper surrounded by game scenes
	n/a	1997	17 × 23	LucasArts	••••	"Jedi Knight: Dark Forces II" promo poster
	n/a	1997	17 × 23	LucasArts	••••	"X-Wing vs. TIE Fighter" promo poster
	TRIL	1997	29 × 38	Aeon Inc.	•••••••	Capital Ships Comparison Chart—Death Star, Star Destroyer, Executor, etc.
	TRILSE	1998	10 × 29	20th C Fox Home Ent.	•••	Video case above, various *Star Wars* videos below
	TRILSE	1998	10 × 28	20th C Fox Home Ent.	•••	SE video collectors set (including pewter medallion)
	n/a	1998	16 × 24	Drew Struzan	•••	Drew Struzan exhibit; Struzan with artworks including TRILSE surrounding him
	TRIL	1998	29 × 40	Sega	•••••••	For "*Star Wars* Trilogy Arcade" game, speeder bikes, X-wing, and AT-AT
	TRIL	1998	29 × 40	Sega	•••••••	For "*Star Wars* Trilogy Arcade" game, X-wings and Death Star
	n/a	1998	29 × 39	Sega	••••••	C-3PO photo (same as Magic of Myth poster) with three cards in lower right; glossy, rounded corners
	n/a	1998	12 × 33	Sony	••••••	Vertical poster for "Masters of Terās Kāsi;" Arlen Lyn
	n/a	1998	12 × 33	Sony	••••••	Vertical poster for "Masters of Terās Kāsi;" Arlen, Luke, Fett
	n/a	1998	12 × 33	Sony	••••••	Vertical poster for "Masters of Terās Kāsi;" Boba
	n/a	1998	12 × 33	Sony	••••••	Vertical poster for "Masters of Terās Kāsi;" Luke
	TPM	1999	28 × 40	Nagatanien	•••••	Curry powder with collector discs and stickers
	TPM	1999	25 × 37	n/a	••••	Sewing Kits; cases with images on them
	TPM	1999	14 × 20	Tentomushi Comics	••••••	Episode I Manga art poster
	TPM	1999	14 × 20	PIA	••••	Japanese weekly magazine ad poster featuring Lucas with Yoda ears and scenes from Episode I
	TPM	1999	20 × 29	Dark Horse	••••	Comic poster with artwork (like US version)
	TPM	1999	16.5 × 20.5	Decipher	•••	Young Jedi CCG laminated play mat; various card images and playfields
	TPM	1999	24 × 34	KFC	••••	Anakin face with six premiums
	TPM	1999	20 × 29	LucasArts	•••	Episode I Jedi Knights
	TPM	1999	20 × 29	LucasArts	•••	Episode I Racer; Jedis above, Podracers below
	TPM	1999	20 × 28	LucasArts	•••	Episode I video game photomontage
	TPM	1999	20 × 28	LucasArts	•••	Episode I video game; photo montage, available December 9, 1999
	TPM	1999	9.5 × 20	Meiji	•••	Episode I cast above, case and keychain-type items below
	TPM	1999	24 × 36	Meiji	••	Horizontal; Photo of cast over scenes
	TPM	1999	40.5 × 57	Pepsi	•••••••	Cap topper left half: Amidala
	TPM	1999	40.5 × 57	Pepsi	•••••••	Cap topper left half: Anakin

ADVERTISING & PROMOTIONAL POSTERS

	Film	Year	Size	Licensee	Rating	Description
JAPAN, CONT.						
	TPM	1999	40.5 × 57	Pepsi	•••••••	Cap topper left half: Darth Maul
	TPM	1999	40.5 × 57	Pepsi	•••••••	Cap toppers poster, right half; combines with three different left halves to make three different posters with a combined dimension of 40.5 × 114 (horizontal)
	TPM	1999	20 × 29	Pizza Hut	••	"Get Into It"; cast above, pizza below
	TPM	1999	20 × 29	Tomy	••••	Glossy, Amidala with scene below
	TPM	1999	20 × 29	Tomy	••••	Glossy, Anakin with scene below
	TPM	1999	20 × 29	Tomy	••••	Glossy, battle droid with scene below
	TPM	1999	20 × 29	Tomy	••••	Glossy, Darth Maul with scene below
	TPM	1999	29 × 40	Toys 'R' Us	••••	Naboo fighter contest from Toys 'R' Us Japan
	TPM	2000	20 × 29	20th C Fox Home Ent.	•••	Episode I available on laserdisc; cast above, Podrace below; April 7 release date
	TPM	2000	20 × 29	20th C Fox Home Ent.	•••	Episode I available on laserdisc; cast above, Podrace below; snipe for four posters
	TPM	2000	20 × 28	20th C Fox Home Ent.	•••	Episode I on DVD and laserdisc
	TPM	2000	14 × 40	20th C Fox Home Ent.	••	For video; horizontal with cast on left, three cassettes on right
	TPM	2000	14 × 20	20th C Fox Home Ent.	••	Cast photo with April 7 release date for video; two-sided and tapered bottom arrow
	TPM	2000	13 × 41	20th C Fox Home Ent.	•••••	Two-sided vertical video poster with Podracers; glossy
	SAGA	2000	13 × 28	20th C Fox Home Ent.	••••••	*Star Wars* saga on DVD; C-3PO above, characters on Endor below; vertical
	SAGA	2000	13 × 28	20th C Fox Home Ent.	••••	*Star Wars* saga on DVD; characters on left, Vader center, X-wing/TIE on right; horizontal.
	SAGA	2000	13 × 28	20th C Fox Home Ent.	••••	*Star Wars* saga on DVD; Yoda above, duel below; vertical
	TPM	2000	20 × 29	Tomy	•••••	CCG-Young Jedi; numerous cards on poster
	TPM	2000	20 × 28	Tomy	•••••	Young Jedi cards (Decipher); shows many cards
	TPM	2001	29 × 40	20th C Fox Home Ent.	•••	DVD/Video; four characters above, Podrace below; July 4 release
	TPM	2001	20 × 29	20th C Fox Home Ent.	•••	DVD/Video; cassette cover art montage
	TPM	2001	20 × 29	20th C Fox Home Ent.	•••	DVD/Video; four characters above, Podrace below
	TPM	2001	20 × 29	20th C Fox Home Ent.	•••	DVD/Video; four characters above, Podrace below; ad for four premium posters
	SAGA	2001	20 × 29	WOWOW	••••	Shows classic trilogy and Episode I posters (not framed); "*Star Wars* Saga"
	SAGA	2001	14 × 40	WOWOW	••••	Horizontal image of classic trilogy and Episode I posters framed on wall; for videos
	AOTC	2002	20 × 29	20th C Fox Home Ent.	•••	Episode II on DVD; Image of Yoda, Obi-Wan, and Anakin, clones below
	AOTC	2002	20 × 29	20th C Fox Home Ent.	•••	Episode II on DVD; Yoda image, pictures of DVDs below
	AOTC	2002	23 × 33	7-11	••••	Promo for phone card, R2-D2 refrigerator
	AOTC	2002	16 × 23	7-11	••••	Promo for phone card, R2-D2 refrigerator
	AOTC	2002	29 × 40	*Crea*	••••••	For *Crea* magazine; image of Anakin and Padmé embracing
	AOTC	2002	12 × 16.5	Fine Molds	•••	Jedi starfighter art above with various *Star Wars* models below
	n/a	2002	29 × 20	Kotobukia	•••	Poster for vinyl models of Vader, clone trooper, Anakin, Mace, Obi-Wan, Jango, and Yoda
	n/a	2002	23 × 16	Kotobukia	•••	Poster for vinyl models of Vader, clone trooper, and Anakin
	n/a	2002	14 × 20	Loft Shibuya	••••	Promo for Kotobukiya models, Pepsi caps, pens, Fact Files
	n/a	2002	20 × 29	LucasArts	•••	"Rogue Squadron II": Vader/ X-wings
	AOTC	2002	20 × 29	Pepsi	••••	Pepsi caps poster "Get SW Bottle Caps"
	AOTC	2002	14 × 20	*Premiere Magazine*	••••••	Magazine cover photo of Anakin/Padmé against blue on left, text on right
	AOTC	2002	14 × 20	*Premiere Magazine*	•••••	Portman posed on left, scenes from Episode II on right; "*Star Wars* A to Z"
	AOTC	2002	20 × 29	Wizards/Coast	•••	*Star Wars*: Trading Card Game: hands holding lightsaber up
	AOTC	2002	20 × 29	Wizards/Coast	•••	*Star Wars*: Trading Card Game: shows cards for Attack of the Clones
	AOTC	2002	14 × 20	Loft Shibuya	•••	Horizontal, various toys and collectibles pictured
	AOTC	2002	16 × 35	*Sony Magazine*	••••	Vertical, high gloss, nine pictures of cast
MEXICO						
	TRIL	1995	12 × 35	20th C Fox Home Ent.	•••••	For video trilogy; raised blue lightsaber
	TRIL	1996	23 × 31	Chupa Chups	••••	Poster with twenty-four spaces to affix stickers
	TRILSE	1997	26 × 37	20th C Fox Home Ent.	••••	For video SE Trilogy; Luke/Leia on barge
	TRILSE	1997	26 × 37	20th C Fox Home Ent.	••••	For video SE Trilogy; Yoda on Dagobah
	TRILSE	1997	26 × 37	20th C Fox Home Ent.	••••••	TRILSE on video-bronze-tone poster with image of half Vader helmet
	TRILSE	1997	13 × 37	20th C Fox Home Ent.	••••	For video SE Trilogy; Chewbacca and Yoda
	TRILSE	1997	13 × 37	20th C Fox Home Ent.	••••	For video SE Trilogy; head shot of C-3PO and R2
	TRILSE	1997	13 × 37	20th C Fox Home Ent.	••••	For video SE Trilogy; Vader and stormtrooper
	n/a	1997	15 × 23	Kenner	•••••	Boba with Toys; Power of the Force Collection
	SWSE	1997	16 × 23	Pepsi	••••	Vader helmet, X-wing and TIE; Spanish
	n/a	1997	12 × 16	Universo *Star Wars*	••	Promo for SW Official Magazine
	n/a	1999	24 × 36	20th C Fox Home Ent.	••••••	"Bart Wars" and "The Simpsons Strike Back" video poster; Bart and Homer dressed as Vader
	TPM	1999	8 × 12	Agfa	••	For camera film with Jar Jar
	TPM	1999	19 × 27	Agfa	••	For Frisbee premium; Jar Jar
	TPM	1999	9.5 × 13.5	KFC	••••	Horizontal image of Maul, Qui-Gon, Amidala, and Obi-Wan; *La Amenaza Fantasma*
	TPM	1999	19 × 28	KFC	••••	KFC meals and cups with Obi-Wan pictured; *La Amenaza Fantasma*
	TPM	1999	16 × 16	KFC	•••	Promo for four free cards with purchase from KFC
	n/a	1999	19 × 27	Lego	•••	Vader holding "infinity" symbol
	TPM	1999	47 × 69	Pepsi	••••••	Plastic material, large Amidala
	TPM	1999	47 × 69	Pepsi	••••••	Plastic material, large Anakin
	TPM	1999	47 × 69	Pepsi	••••••	Plastic material, large Darth Maul
	TPM	1999	47 × 69	Pepsi	••••••	Plastic material, large Jar Jar
	TPM	1999	16 × 23	Pepsi	•••	Pide mas "Llevate La Cubeta Galactica *Star Wars*"
	TPM	1999	16 × 24	Sabritas	•••	Jar Jar on right, '99 Tigra car, collector stamps
	TPM	1999	16 × 24	Lays	••••	*La Amenaza Fantasma*—Maul image; promo to win Episode I binoculars and communicators
	TPM	1999	12 × 16	Lays	••••	*La Amenaza Fantasma*—Jar Jar long tongue toy promo
	TPM	1999	12 × 16	Lays	••••	*La Amenaza Fantasma*—Obi-Wan image; promo to win Episode I binoculars and communicators; die-cut top
	TPM	2000	24 × 36	20th C Fox Home Ent.	•••	For video, cast above, Podrace below
	TRILSE	2000	24 × 35	20th C Fox Home Ent.	••••	Video trilogy, photo of droids
	SAGA	2001	27 × 37	Movie City	••••	SW Saga, March 2001 at Movie City; Drew art for Episode I
	SAGA	2001	27 × 37	Movie City	••••	SW Saga, March 2001 at Movie City; photo of droids
	SAGA	2001	27 × 37	Movie City	••••	SW Saga, March 2001 at Movie City; photo of Vader
	n/a	2002	18 × 26	De' Agostini	•••	*Star Wars* Fact File promo poster; to be released Oct. 15
	AOTC	2002	10 × 29.5	Bimbo	••••	For Star Cards: collectible punch-out cards that make 3D ships and figures
	AOTC	2002	21 × 63	Dark Horse	••••	Horizontal poster promoting an exclusive associated with Dark Horse and "Vid"
	AOTC	2002	19 × 26	Universo *Star Wars*	•••	Portraits of Episode II characters in tinted monotones for fan club magazine
	AOTC	2003	27 × 37	Movie City	••••	For Episode II; Anakin
NETHERLANDS						
	SW	1978	19.5 × 32	Musiek Expres	••••••	Style "C" art in English with logo at lower right: maandblad Musiek Expres
	TPM	2000	27 × 39	Canal +	••••	Dutch pay TV sign up poster; Drew artwork with "May the Force . . ." below and free double CD
NEW ZEALAND						
	ESB	1980	14 × 19	Tip Top	•••••••	For popsicles; photo of Vader, "Free mask while supplies last"
	ROTJ	1983	33 × 29	Macleans	•••••••	Promo to win ROTJ tickets and posters; red, white, and blue
	ROTJ	1983	12 × 19.5	Tip Top	•••••••	Tip Top with Jedi Jelly popsicles; "Free Ewok Stickers—Collect All 4"
	TPM	1999	17 × 24	Telecom	••••	Heroes collage for prepaid mobile phone packs and free Episode I soundtrack snipe
	TPM	1999	16.5 × 23	Telecom	••••	Photo collage of villains; for phones, SW phone cards, soundtrack snipe
	TPM	1999	12 × 16.5	Telecom	••••	Heroes collage for prepaid mobile phone packs and free Episode I soundtrack snipe

ADVERTISING & PROMOTIONAL POSTERS

	Film	Year	Size	Licensee	Rating	Description
PHILIPPINES						
	AOTC	2002	27 × 38	Jollibee	•••••	Jollibee kids meal poster for five desktop accessories
POLAND						
	AOTC	2002	19 × 27	Chio	••••	Chio Chips promo poster; Anakin and Padmé
	AOTC	2002	19 × 27	Chio	••••	Chio Chips promo poster; Anakin, Padmé, and Obi-Wan
	AOTC	2002	19 × 27	Chio	••••	Chio Chips promo poster for premium paper mini-standees
SINGAPORE						
	AOTC	2002	30 × 43	SingTel	••••	Photo collage of characters with "pod" written in lower left corner
SPAIN						
	ESB	1980	39 × 59	Yoplait	••••••••••	Artwork of Vader and characters, for free posters and stickers
	ESB	1980	24 × 34	Yoplait	••••••••	Four montages from *Empire* with spaces for stickers
	ESB	1980	13 × 19	Yoplait	••••••••	Artwork of Vader and characters, for free posters and stickers
	DROIDS/ EWOKS	1986	9 × 13	Crecs	••••••••	Crecs chips promo for collecting twenty "tiras" (stickers)
SWEDEN						
	TRIL	1983	18 × 25	Select Video	••••••••	For original trilogy story cassettes; art of Luke, droids, Yoda, etc.; *Starjornas Krig*
THAILAND						
	TRIL	1995	22 × 34	20th C Fox Home Ent.	••••	For SW trilogy on video/VCD; artwork of Vader, Luke, Han, Leia, etc.
UNITED KINGDOM						
	SW	1977	15 × 20	Heinz	••••••••	Spectacular *Star Wars* School Set Offer; art of X-wing, Helix School Set, Heinz pork and beans cans
	SW	1977	10 × 12	Heinz	•••••••	Spectacular *Star Wars* School Set Offer; art of X-wing, Heinz pork and beans cans
	SW	1977	14 × 20	Mountain Films	•••••••	Black-and-white image of droids; for *Star Wars* super-eight movies
	SW	1977	19 × 29	W. H. Smith	•••••••	Toned down Hildebrandt art for bookstore chain
	SW	1978	20 × 30	Sphere	••••••••••	For Sphere Books paperback version of novel; shows book cover
	SW	1978	11 × 19	Sphere	••••••••	For Sphere Books paperback version of novel; store window poster with Hildebrandt art and three photos
	ESB	1980	9.5 × 39	Express Dairy	••••••••	Black, orange, and white promo poster for free poster; *Empire* logo and snipe for drink flavors; horizontal
	ESB	1980	10 × 15	Express Dairy	•••••••	Black, orange, and white promo poster for free poster; *Empire* logo and snipe for drink flavors
	ESB	1980	10 × 14	Vymura	•••••••	In store poster for wallpaper, says "Available Here" at lower left, photo of bedroom
	ESB	1982	17 × 23	Airfix	••••••••	*Star Wars* Competition; photo of toy AT-AT
	ROTJ	1983	16.5 × 23.5	Bridge Farm Dairies	••••••••	*Star Wars* Yogurts; SW "A" artwork with five yogurt containers, ROTJ logo
	ROTJ	1983	12 × 16.5	Bridge Farm Dairies	••••••••	*Star Wars* Yogurts; SW "A" artwork with five yogurt containers
	ROTJ	1983	30 × 40	Bridge Farm Dairies	•••••••••	*Jedi* Advance artwork with "*Star Wars* Yogurts Available Here" snipe
	ROTJ	1983	30 × 40	Palitoy	•••••••••	*Jedi* Advance artwork with "Toys Available Here" snipe
	ROTJ	1983	30 × 40	Parker	•••••••••	*Jedi* Advance artwork with "Parker Video Games Available Here" snipe
	ESB	1984	15.5 × 22	CBS Fox	•••••	For video; *Empire* "B" sheet art with CBS Fox logo lower left
	ROTJ	1984	16.5 × 23	Domark	••••••	For ROTJ video game; artwork of Luke, Vader, speeder bike, AT-ST, etc.
	n/a	1984	25 × 38	Digital	••••••	Image of Star Destroyer model with Digital logo and astronaut with Digital computer
	TRIL	1994	19 × 84	20th C Fox Home Ent.	••••••	Tall banner of Jung's Luke/Leia artwork with "*Star Wars* Trilogy" at top; for digitally remastered edition
	TRIL	1995	n/a	20th C Fox Home Ent.	•••••	Artwork of Luke, Leia, and Han in front of Vader; for classic trilogy release
	TRIL	1995	19 × 36	20th C Fox Home Ent.	••••••	"One Last Time . . ." poster of Alvin video artwork on chrome paper
	TRIL	1995	16.5 × 33	20th C Fox Home Ent.	•••••	Alvin artwork of blue lightsaber for classic video release
	n/a	1995	14 × 21	Bantam	•••••	Leia aiming blaster: "Read This Or I Shoot" with Crystal Star and Darksaber novels
	n/a	1995	14 × 21	Bantam	•••	"Truce at Bakura" with photo of Solo and small book cover inset
	TRILSE	1996	16.5 × 23	Pepsi	••••	"Defeat the Empire" with Vader's head/ X-wing vs. TIE against star field; "Win a Holiday to Florida"
	n/a	1997	24 × 33	LucasArts	••••	"X-wing vs. TIE Fighter" game for PC; art of X-wing and pilot, TIE fighter and pilot
	SOTE	1997	16.5 × 23.5	LucasArts	•••	Shadows video game for Nintendo 64; artwork of AT-AT and snowspeeder, two-sided
	n/a	1998	16.5 × 23.5	LucasArts	••••	For Rogue Squadron on Nintendo 64; X-wing and TIE against "wire-frame" space-scape
	TPM	1999	40 × 60	ASDA	••••	"News of the World" in lower left corner, ASDA in right; large Maul head on one side, full body Obi-Wan on reverse for use with 3-D glasses
	TPM	1999	47 × 70	Kellogg's	••••••	"Enter the Star Wars Zone" two-sided bus shelter poster; cereal box with Maul face
	TPM	1999	23 × 33	LucasArts	••••	Episode I "Racer" for Nintendo; "HMV"
	TPM	1999	23 × 33	LucasArts	•••••	For Episode I "Racer" video game; shows two Podracers with large rock in background
	TPM	1999	20 × 27	The Face Magazine	•••••	Newsstand poster for The Face magazine with Amidala cover
	TPM	1999	20 × 27.5	Time Out Magazine	•••••	For 5/12/99 issue, blowup of cover showing Obi-Wan with lightsaber
	TPM	1999	23 × 33	Pepsi	•••	Anakin: "He gives without . . ."
	TPM	1999	23 × 33	Pepsi	•••	Maul: "He uses fear . . ."
	TPM	1999	23 × 33	Pepsi	•••	Obi-Wan: "No one was more devoted . . ."
	TPM	1999	23 × 33	Pepsi	•••	Queen Amidala: "She gave more . . ."
	TPM	1999	23 × 33	Pepsi	•••	Qui-Gon: "He sees the worth . . ."
	TPM	1999	17 × 23	Pepsi	•••	"Win a Nintendo 64 Console at this Outlet"; including Pepsi Max
	TPM	1999	16.5 × 20.5	Pepsi	•••	Anakin head shot/Podracer; "Ask for More"
	TPM	2000	20 × 60	20th C Fox Home Ent.	•••••	Tall Maul with saber poster promoting DVD or video; added text for midnight opening
	TPM	2000	20 × 60	20th C Fox Home Ent.	•••••	Tall Maul with saber poster promoting DVD or video; reverse side has Obi-Wan
	TPM	2000	12 × 24	Pepsi	•••	"Exclusive SW Prizes"—Amidala
	TPM	2000	12 × 24	Pepsi	•••	"Exclusive SW Prizes"—Anakin/ Podrace
	TPM	2000	12 × 24	Pepsi	•••	"Exclusive SW Prizes"—Maul/ duel
	TPM	2000	12 × 24	Pepsi	•••	"Exclusive SW Prizes"—Obi-Wan
	AOTC	2002	16.5 × 23	LucasArts	•••	"Galactic Battlegrounds: Clone Campaign Expansion Pack;" Clone helmet with battle in background
	AOTC	2002	16.5 × 23	LucasArts	••••••	"Jedi Starfighter:" "Out Soon;" image of landed starfighter bathed in green light
	AOTC	2002	16 × 22	Daily Telegraph	•	*Star Wars*—A Love Story poster for Daily Telegraph newspaper (May 11, 2002)
	n/a	2003	16.5 × 23	LucasArts	•••••	"Rebel Strike;" Luke on Snowspeeder with AT-AT approaching
	TRILSE	2004	16.5 × 23	20th C Fox Home Ent.	•••	For trilogy on DVD; Vader with saber
UNITED STATES						
	SW	1976	40 × 60	20th Century Fox	••••••••••	"26 for 76" poster used at early Fox event to promote *Star Wars* and other films to theater owners
	SW	1976	20 × 29	20th Century Fox	••••••••••••	"*Star Wars* Poster 1" by Howard Chaykin; sold at 1976 conventions
	SW	1977	22 × 33	20th Century Records	•••••••	Foil record promo, black and silver; head of Darth Vader with words "*Star Wars*"
	SW	1977	22 × 33	20th Century Records	••••••	Story of *Star Wars* soundtrack poster with C-3PO and R2-D2
	SW	1977	12 × 16	Braun's Town Talk Bread	•••••••	Poster for *Star Wars* cards available in Braun's
	SW	1977	22 × 33	Burger Chef	••••••••••	For free *Star Wars* posters; large "*Star Wars* Posters" logo with X-wing
	SW	1977	23 × 35	Casablanca Records	••••••••	For Meco album "*Star Wars* and Other Galactic Funk"; album cover art
	SW	1977	22 × 44	Clarks	••••••••	"*Star Wars* by Clarks" transparent banner; Hildebrandt-like artwork
	SW	1977	18 × 25	Don Post	••••••••	For first four SW masks; heavy stock
	SW	1977	18 × 27	General Mills	••••••••	Cheerios poster offer; "Save up to $45 on Kenner toys"
	SW	1977	14 × 17	Pictorial News of the Day	••••••	Black-and-white photo of SW cast—June 29, 1977; "For Best Results, List with Us"
	SW	1977	20 × 28	Thermos	•••••••	Art from front of first metal lunch box : TIE fighter vs. X-wing battle
	SW	1977	23 × 35	Weingeroff Ent.	••••••	All print (red and black) window poster for R2-D2, C-3PO, and "Lord Darth Vader" jewelry
	SW	1977	12 × 24	Wonder Bread	••••••	Pole sign for *Star Wars* cards available in Wonder Bread
	SW	1977	12 × 16	Wonder Bread	••••••	Poster for *Star Wars* cards available in Wonder Bread
	SW	1977	30 × 40	Coca-Cola	••••••••••	Photo of premium cup with Vader art; for "Snow Biz" frozen Coke
	SW	1977	24 × 36	Coca-Cola	••••••••••	Koolee Corp.; *Star Wars* Cups promo with frozen Coke; 19 of 20 pictured on yellow background
	SW	1977	14 × 22	Coca-Cola	••••••••••	7-Eleven store poster to collect set of eight SW cups
	SW	1977	22 × 35	Coca-Cola/Mr. Pibb	••••••••••	Store poster for eight 20-oz cups with photo of X-wing fighter
	SW	1977	18 × 30	Coca-Cola/Mr. Pibb	••••••••••	Store poster for eight 20-oz cups with photos of all cups

ADVERTISING & PROMOTIONAL POSTERS

Film	Year	Size	Licensee	Rating	Description
UNITED STATES, CONT.					
SW	1978	14 × 36	20th Century Fox	•••••••••	Two-part paper insert, blue on white with Hildebrandt art and touting Oscars (taped together)
SW	1978	29 × 29	Burger Chef	••••••••••	Fun Meal promo poster (translite)
SW	1978	23 × 35	Burger Chef	•••••••••	Fun Meal promo poster (glossy)
SW	1978	13.5 × 56	Burger Chef	•••••••••	"Collect all 7 Action Trays" (FunMeals); split in two sections (translite)
SW	1978	18 × 30	Coca-Cola/Mr. Pibb	••••••••••	Collect set of eight 16-oz cups
SW	1978	17 × 24	Drawing Board	•••••••	"The Force Is With Us"; photo of R2 and C-3PO
SW	1978	15 × 24	Estes	•••••••	For flying model rockets
SW	1978	17 × 22	Lionel	••••••••••	Store poster for Duel at Death Star Racing Set
ESB	1978	14 × 18	Lucasfilm	••••••••••	Suite of eleven lithos of Boba Fett by Joe Johnston, some with slight coloring
SW	1978	11 × 17	Pendulum Press	••••••	Classroom poster by Charles Nicholas to accompany Contemporary Motivators reading program
SW	1978	25 × 38	Vymura	•••••••••	Store poster for wall vinyl; like US "C" sheet
SW	1978	27 × 41	Warner Bros	••••••	Mylar *THX 1138* rerelease poster with top line: Before George Lucas explored the outer regions of space in *STAR WARS* he explored the inner regions of society
SW	1979	14 × 22	Health	••••••	Immunization poster with R2 and C-3PO; bottom text starts "Do Your Records . . ."
SW	1979	14 × 22	Health	••••••	Immunization poster with R2 and C-3PO; bottom text starts "Make Sure . . ."
SW	1980	16.5 × 25.5	Don Post	•••••••	"Men of a Thousand Faces"; promo with masks of Vader, C-3PO, Stormtrooper, etc.; mail-in
ESB	1980	22 × 28	B Dalton Books	•••••••••	Black-and-white sketch of Vader and *Empire* logo on card
ESB	1980	11 × 17	Ballantine	•••••••	McQuarrie Cloud City illustration; for books and calendars
ESB	1980	15 × 42	Dixie/Lipton	•••••••	Double poster, in-store with Vader, droids, Leia, and Luke in front of Dixie logo and *Empire* logo
ESB	1980	10 × 16	Dixie/Lipton	•••••••	For *Empire* Collectors Kit; shows two *Empire* premium posters and eight 5 × 7 cards
ESB	1980	17.5 × 24	Drawing Board	•••••••	Greeting cards in-store promo; art like "B" sheet
ESB	1980	18 × 18	Factors	•••••••	Silver on blue star field: "The Saga of *Star Wars* Continues With *The Empire Strikes Back*"
ESB	1980	21.5 × 27	MPC	•••••••••	For *Empire* model kits; various images of ships with logo
ESB	1980	36 × 36	RSO Records	•••••••	Soundtrack poster with Vader head and small red inset of album
n/a	1980	24 × 36	RSO Records	•••••••	Christmas in the Stars with McQuarrie art
ESB	1980	24 × 36	RSO Records	•••••••	For soundtrack, photo of album against maroon background
ESB	1980	24 × 36	RSO Records	•••••••	Promo poster for four different *Empire* records
ESB	1980	24 × 36	RSO Records	••••••	Soundtrack poster with Vader head and small red inset of album
ESB	1980	17 × 22	Noble	•••••••	Empire concept art pencil signed by Lawrence Noble; later used as basis of *Empire* tenth anniversary poster
SW	1981	17 × 29	National Public Radio	•••••••••	Artwork of C-3PO with microphone by Celia Strain; blank space at bottom for station info
SW	1981	17 × 29	National Public Radio	••••••••	Artwork of C-3PO with microphone by Celia Strain; station info listed at bottom
SW	1982	6 × 23	CBS Fox	••••••	Mini-banner for *Star Wars* video release
SW	1982	20 × 28	CBS Fox	••••••	Small version of *Star Wars* "A" sheet
SW	1982	11 × 47	CBS Fox	•••••••	Banner for *Star Wars* video release
SW	1982	27 × 41	CBS/Fox	•••••••	Style "A" sheet on heavy stock; Lucasfilm copyright below artwork, dated 1977; for the 1982 video release
SW	1982	14 × 36	CBS/Fox	•••••	Style "A" insert on heavy stock; Lucasfilm copyright below artwork, dated 1977; for the 1982 video release
ESB	1982	17 × 28	National Public Radio	••••••••••	Artwork of Yoda on Dagobah by McQuarrie; blank space at bottom for station info at bottom
ESB	1982	10 × 22	National Public Radio	•••••••••	Black-and-white artwork of Yoda by Celia Strain with blank box for information
ESB	1982	24 × 36	Parker Bros	•••••••••	*Empire* video game cartridge for Atari system
SW	1982	28 × 40	RCA	•••••••••	RCA videodisc promo to take home *Star Wars* free
SW	1982	26 × 80	RCA	•••••••••	RCA videodisc promo to take home *Star Wars* free
SW	1983	20 × 30	Atari	•••••••••	For "*Star Wars* Arcade" game
ROTJ	1983	13 × 22	Ballantine	•••••••	Art of ROTJ promo; photo of Imperial Shuttle model
ROTJ	1983	15 × 26	Buena Vista Records	••••••	For ROTJ story records
ROTJ	1983	13 × 13	Buena Vista Records	•••••	For ROTJ story records
ROTJ	1983	8 × 48	Burger King	•••••••	"They're Here! ROTJ Glasses" banner
ROTJ	1983	21.5 × 29	Burger King	•••••••	Blue and white crew-room poster for ROTJ glasses promotion
ROTJ	1983	21.5 × 29	Burger King	•••••••	"COMING TO A THEATER IN YOUR GALAXY MAY 25"
ROTJ	1983	22 × 28	Coca-Cola	•••••••	For free 50-oz collector pitcher
ROTJ	1983	14 × 22	Del Rey	••••••	For paperback book
ROTJ	1983	20.5 × 30	Drawing Board	••••••	For greeting cards; "The excitement starts here"
ROTJ	1983	16 × 20	Kenner	•••••••	For sweepstakes; Darth, Nien Numb, Admiral Ackbar
n/a	1983	22 × 34	Library Council	•••••	Yoda "READ" poster showing Yoda with book
ROTJ	1983	22 × 28	Mall	••••••	"Welcome to the Jedi Adventure Center" poster with Style "A" artwork in lower right corner
SW	1983	23 × 36	Parker Bros	•••••••••	For "Death Star Battle" game cartridge for Atari
SW	1983	23 × 36	Parker Bros	•••••••••	For "Jedi Arena" game cartridge for Atari
SW	1983	23 × 36	Parker Bros	•••••••••	For "*Star Wars* Arcade" game cartridge for Atari
SW	1983	17 × 22	Parker Bros	•••••••	"Jedi Arena" Honor Roll; game artwork with spaces for names in yellow box
TRIL	1983	18 × 27	Pepperidge Farm	•••••••	In-store poster for cookies
ROTJ	1983	9 × 22	RSO Records	••••••	ROTJ logo for soundtrack "Now Available"
ROTJ	1983	22 × 33	RSO Records	•••••	For ROTJ soundtrack; droids approaching Jabba's palace with other soundtracks above
ROTJ	1983	11.5 × 23.5	Sales Corp of America	••••••	Ad poster for Darth Vader door poster
ROTJ	1983	10 × 12	Sales Corp of America	••••••	For ROTJ mini-posters
TRIL	1983	22 × 28	Stride Rite	•••••••••	Illustration of Vader head, droids, and battle scene with shoes: "Shoes that are out of this world"
ROTJ	1983	16 × 20	Thermos	•••••••••	For ROTJ lunch kit; artwork of lunch box lid
ROTJ	1983	9 × 13	Topps	•••••	For ROTJ stickers and albums
n/a	1983	13 × 39	Tower Records	••	KDKB radio promo calendar poster; pop icons including R2-D2
n/a	1984	22 × 36	AFI	•••••••	America's Movies for the World's Athletes; Drew Struzan art including Vader
ESB	1984	23 × 58	CBS Fox	••••••	For video; "Coming Soon" over *Empire* logo and "B" sheet
ESB	1984	23 × 24	CBS Fox	••••••	For video; "Coming Soon" and *Empire* logo
ESB	1984	14.5 × 24.5	CBS Fox	••••••	For video; "Don't be struck Empireless;" two-sided poster sent to dealers with *Empire* key art
n/a	1984	16 × 39	Struzan	•••••••	Poster for Drew Struzan Illustration Inc. that includes *Star Wars* "D" and *Revenge* Advance
ROTJ	1985	18 × 24	Coca-Cola	••••••••••	In-theater peel-sticker-from-cup promo with Kenner toys; enhanced battle scene and toy images
DROID	1985	17 × 22	Sales Corp. of American	•••••••	Artwork of animated Droids; on card stock
EWOK	1985	17 × 22	Sales Corp. of American	••••••	Artwork of animated Ewoks—"Friends Come in all Shapes and Sizes"; on card stock
ROTJ	1986	24 × 34.5	CBS Fox	••••••	For video; Endor speeder bike scene: "The movie everyone's been waiting for"
TRIL	1986	20 × 30	Del Rey	••••••	For ILM special effects book; book cover image
SW	1987	22 × 28	Broderbund	•••••••••	*Star Wars* video game for home PC; McQuarrie art of battle over Death Star with Luke inset
SW	1987	18 × 24	Kilian Ent	••••••••••	Poster promoting *Star Wars* tenth anniversary Mylar posters; hand drawn lettering on Mylar, 1 of 2
n/a	1987	33 × 47	Star Tours	••••••••••	Original silk-screened Disneyland Star Tours attraction poster; edition size of 100
n/a	1987	20 × 30	Star Tours	•••••••	PSA/Walt Disney Travel Co. "Magical Smiles" Tours to Disneyland promo
n/a	1987	17 × 24	Star Tours	•••••••	Black-and-white poster for cast premiere party; star speeder orbiting planet
n/a	1987	17 × 24	Star Tours	•••••••	Black-and-white poster for Imagineering Inaugural Flight (January 5); star speeder orbiting planet
TRIL	1987	17 × 22	West End Games	•••••	"Fulfill Your Destiny"; departing X-wing and pictures of first three games
n/a	1988	22 × 27	Abrams Book	••	"Films of Science Fiction and Fantasy" book poster with several films including Vader
TRIL	1988	25.5 × 38	CBS Fox	••••	Video poster for Trilogy; shows all three cassettes
SW	1988	18 × 24	Rarities Mint	••••	For silver, gold coins; *Star Wars* "A" artwork
n/a	1988	20 × 30	Star Tours	••••	Oldsmobile promo, celebrating first anniversary of Star Tours; art by Kriegler
n/a	1989	18 × 28	Star Tours	••••	Disney/MGM; photo of model star speeder and TIE in trench; glossy
TRIL	1990	25.5 × 38	CBS Fox	••••	Video poster for Trilogy; merges elements of SW "A", ESB "A" plus Yoda and ROTJ "B" against stars
n/a	1990	27 × 39	ILM	•••••••	ILM—1975–1990; posters of all films involving ILM
EWOK1	1990	24 × 36	MGM/UA Home Video	•••••	*The Ewok Adventure* home video; Sano art

ADVERTISING & PROMOTIONAL POSTERS

Film	Year	Size	Licensee	Rating	Description
UNITED STATES, CONT.					
EWOK2	1990	24 × 36	MGM/UA Home Video	•••••	*Ewoks: Battle for Endor* home video; Berrett art
n/a	1990	24 × 36	Star Tours	•••	Grand Opening Jan. 13 at Disney-MGM Studios in FL; two M&M candies below saucer
n/a	1991	17 × 22	Bantam Books	••••	In-store poster for "Heir to the Empire;" book cover art by Tom Jung
n/a	1991	23 × 33	Nintendo/Lucas Games	••••••	Store display for premium poster; photo of Vader with red band at top for free offer
n/a	1991	17 × 22	Walden Books	•	In store "Hailing Frequencies" sign for Tim Zahn (Heir to the Empire)
n/a	1992	22 × 28	B Dalton	••	"The Force is Back"; for "Dark Force Rising" book and tape
n/a	1992	17 × 22	Bantam Books	•••••	In-store poster for "The Glove of Darth Vader" to announce entire children's line; Struzan art
SW	1993	22 × 32	Highbridge Audio	••••	Larger version of original Celia Strain art for *Star Wars* radio show on NPR
ESB	1993	23.5 × 37	JVC	••••	For Super Nintendo Empire game, collage art by Winters
n/a	1993	16.5 × 23.5	LucasArts	••••	CG cover art for "X-Wing" PC game; glossy stock
n/a	1993	17 × 22	Topps	•••	"*Star Wars* Galaxy On Sale Here"; Steacy art
n/a	1994	10 × 19	Dark Horse	•••	For Dark Empire II, art by Dorman
SW	1994	20 × 29	Fox Video	•••	Small reproduction of Style "A" poster, marked 1994 Fox Video
n/a	1994	17 × 22	Topps	••••	"*Star Wars* Galaxy On Sale Here"; McQuarrie bounty hunters artwork
n/a	1994	17 × 20	Topps	•••	For *Star Wars* Galaxy II; Boris art of R2 and C-3PO
TRIL	1995	31.5 × 54	20 C Fox Home Ent.	••••	Vader helmet and X-wing/TIE dogfight; "The Original. One Last Time"
TRIL	1995	31.5 × 54	20 C Fox Home Ent.	•••••	Last video release of original trilogy; shows three cassette covers above with Lucas letter below
TRIL	1995	36 × 48	20 C Fox Home Ent.	••••	Vader helmet and X-wing/TIE dogfight; "The Original. One Last Time"; horizontal from Suncoast
TRIL	1995	27 × 40	20 C Fox Home Ent.	••••	For video trilogy ". . . One last time;" high-gloss with image of Vader and X-wing/TIE
n/a	1995	11 × 17	Dark Horse	•••	"No Greater Force in the Galaxy" and "*Star Wars* Comics On Sale Here"; Dorman art
n/a	1995	16.5 × 22	Fan Magazine	•••	Cover for Fan #5; Dark Horse "Heir to the Empire" adaptation
n/a	1995	24 × 30	Hallmark	•	In-store poster for *Star Wars* Shoebox card line with one *Star Wars* image on each side
n/a	1995	27 × 36	LucasArts	••••••	"Rebel Assault II"; art of Rebel pilot on heavy stock with credit block
n/a	1995	17 × 20	Topps	•••	For *Star Wars* Galaxy 3; Jabba's Palace scene
n/a	1995	24 × 31	LucasArts	•••	"Dark Forces" game; computer graphics art of stormtroopers
SOTE	1996	22 × 34	Bantam Books	•••••	*Shadows of the Empire;* cover art by Drew Struzan
n/a	1996	20.5 × 27	Decipher	••••	CCG "Expand the Empire" game card image of two Star Destroyers and star field background
SW	1996	10 × 33	Decipher	•••	CCG "A New Hope" card set poster
ESB	1996	10 × 33	Decipher	•••	CCG cards—Dagobah; checklist on back
ESB	1996	10 × 33	Decipher	•••	CCG cards—Hoth; checklist on back
n/a	1996	48 × 68	IMAX	••••••••	"Special Effects" presentation at Balboa Park
n/a	1996	27 × 39	IMAX	•••••••	"Special Effects"; includes images of X-wings, TIE fighter, droids, Chewbacca, Jawa, troopers
n/a	1996	18 × 24	IMAX	•••••••	"Special Effects"; for Cincinnati Museum Center
SOTE	1996	16 × 22	LucasArts	•••	Insert poster for Electronic Gaming Monthly; image of AT-AT and snowspeeder
n/a	1997	26 × 66	Bantam Books	•••••••	Full body C-3PO artwork poster
n/a	1997	24 × 36	Dark Horse	•••	For comics; "New Adventures On Sale Here;" Dorman art
SOTE	1997	11 × 17	Dark Horse	•••	Hugh Fleming art for Shadows of the Empire comic series
ESB	1997	25 × 33	Decipher	••••	CCG cards—Fett: "As You Wish"
ESB	1997	25 × 33	Decipher	••••	CCG cards—Yoda: "Do or Do Not"
TRILSE	1997	24 × 36	Frito Lay	••••	Yoda illustration—"Experience the Adventure"
SWSE	1997	21 × 32	Frito Lay	•••	"Message to Luke Skywalker Competition Sweepstakes;" Drew art
n/a	1997	22 × 34	Library Association	•••	C-3PO: "Information Overload?"
n/a	1997	22 × 34	Library Association	•••	Chewbacca: "Navigate the next Millennium: READ"
n/a	1997	22 × 34	Library Association	•••	Droids: "Download and Learn"
n/a	1997	22 × 34	Library Association	•••	Vader: "Use the Power of the Force: READ"
n/a	1997	16 × 21	LucasArts	••••	For "Masters of Teräs Käsi;" Fett and Luke below, Arlen Lyn above
n/a	1997	15 × 20	LucasArts	••••	For "Masters of Teräs Käsi"; Fett and Luke, two-sided
n/a	1997	17 × 22	MAD Magazine	••	"50 Years of Stupidity" 1997 calendar poster; including 1981 Yoda cover
TRILSE	1997	27 × 37.5	Pepsi	••••	For *Star Wars* Super Big Gulp cups; shows three cups with different characters
TRILSE	1997	11 × 22	Pepsi	••••	Two-sided Pepsi/General Cinema poster for glow-in-the-dark cup
TRILSE	1997	24 × 36	RCA Victor	•••	Ingot art and three CDs; "Three Reasons Why They Make Stereos"
TRILSE	1997	14.5 × 24	Scholastic	•••	Jabba reading book with several Scholastic books below; "Coming January 1997"
TRILSE	1997	54 × 24	Taco Bell	•••••	Horizontal "Collect All 7" premiums
SWSE	1997	23 × 34	Taco Bell	•••	Drew artwork with purple banner across lower half
ESBSE	1997	23 × 34	Taco Bell	•••	Drew artwork with purple banner across lower half
ROTJSE	1997	23 × 34	Taco Bell	•••	Drew artwork with purple banner across lower half
TRILSE	1997	18 × 24	Taco Bell	••••	Drive-thru sign: "Get Your Limited Edition *Star Wars* Collectibles Now"
TRILSE	1997	18 × 24	Taco Bell	••••	Intergalactic Draw promo poster; shows all prizes
TRILSE	1997	22 × 28	The For All Kids Fndn.	•••••	*Millennium Falcon* Sweepstakes; contest to win large *Falcon* display; inset of Rosie O'Donnell
SWSE	1997	19 × 25	Wizard Press	•	"Sci-Fi Invasion" magazine promo; includes photo of stormtroopers
n/a	1997	19 × 25	Wizard Press	•	For Toyfare magazine #1; "On Sale in July!" with toy AT-AT
n/a	1997	19 × 25	Wizard Press	•	Toy Boba Fett against "Wanted" posters
TRILSE	1997	16 × 24	Pepsi	••	Pepsi alien mascot (Marfalump) used during *Star Wars* campaign
SWSE	1998	22 × 28	Decipher	•••	CCG Vader head shot
TRILSE	1998	10 × 33	Decipher	•••	CCG "SW: Special Editions" card set poster
SWSE	1998	10 × 33	Decipher	•••	CCG Jabba's Palace card set poster
n/a	1998	22 × 34	LucasArts	••••	For "Rogue Squadron" on Nintendo 64; X-wing flying over village, two-sided
SWSE	1998	27 × 39.5	Showtime	••••••	For *Star Wars* on Showtime: "This time, root for the man in black."
TPM	1999	23 × 71	At-A-Glance	•••••	Horizontal poster of Episode I characters over desert landscape; also used as bin wrap-around
TPM	1999	24 × 36	Dark Horse	••••	Comic display artwork poster with text on reverse
TPM	1999	24 × 36	Dark Horse	••••	US Manga artwork poster for Episode I
TPM	1999	22 × 28	Decipher	••••	CCG Endor; speeder bikes
TPM	1999	22 × 28	Decipher	•••	CCG Young Jedi; Maul and Obi-Wan
ROTJ	1999	10 × 33	Decipher	•••	CCG Endor expansion set
TPM	1999	8 × 22	DK Books	•	Promo of books and standees available
TPM	1999	14 × 23	DK Books	•••	N-1 Naboo starfighter cross-section art for Visual Dictionaries and Incredible Cross-sections books
n/a	1999	37 × 48	LEGO	••••••	LEGO Mindstorm R2-D2 Droid Developer Kit
TPM	1999	24 × 36	LEGO	•••••	Galactic Challenge with Naboo fighters
TPM	1999	24 × 36	LEGO	•••••	Image of LEGO Naboo starfighter
TPM	1999	22 × 28	LEGO	••••	LEGO Jedi Lightsaber Building Contest; Wal-Mart, two-sided
n/a	1999	19 × 27	LEGO	•••	Darth Vader holding "infinity" symbol
TPM	1999	11 × 17	LEGO	••••	LEGO Jedi Lightsaber Building Contest; Wal-Mart
TPM	1999	23 × 33	LucasArts	•••	*The Phantom Menace* game, Qui-Gon on left, Obi-Wan on right
TPM	1999	23 × 33	LucasArts	•••	*The Phantom Menace* game, Qui-Gon on right, Obi-Wan on left
TPM	1999	22 × 28	LucasArts	••••	Episode I "Racer"—Jedi above, Podracers below, Maul face
TPM	1999	22 × 28	LucasArts	••••	"Racer" for Nintendo 64; Watto above, Podrace below
TPM	1999	18 × 24	LucasArts	•••••	Episode I "Racer"—Anakin and Sebulba artwork from retail poster with Podracers
TPM	1999	16 × 21	Newsweek	••••	Newsweek cover poster for May 17, 1999, issue; "Hyping of SW"; international prices at bottom
TPM	1999	25 × 38	Pepsi	•••	"Collect all 24 Cans;" four characters surrounded by 24 cans
TPM	1999	25 × 38	Pepsi	•••	"Find Yoda and Win Cash;" Qui-Gon and Maul above, Yoda below, blank white center
TPM	1999	18 × 27	Pepsi	••	Pole sign; alien mascot (Marfalump) holding color Anakin can
TPM	1999	17 × 21	Pepsi	••	Anakin image; "He gives without . . ."

ADVERTISING & PROMOTIONAL POSTERS

Film	Year	Size	Licensee	Rating	Description
UNITED STATES, CONT.					
TPM	1999	12 × 24	Pepsi	••	Anakin image; "Exclusive *Star Wars* Prizes"
TPM	1999	20 × 24	Premiere Magazine	••••	For 5/99 issue, blowup of cover of Amidala with three other covers shown below
TPM	1999	24 × 36	RCA Victor	•••	For soundtrack, Drew Struzan art
TPM	1999	12 × 24	RCA Victor	•••	For soundtrack, two-sided, photo art perforated in center
TPM	1999	24 × 54	Taco Bell	••••	Large Jar Jar on left; "Get All 9 *Star Wars* Episode I Collectibles $1.49 Each"
TPM	1999	72 × 47	Things/Another World	••••••	Two piece horizontal "20% Off All *Star Wars* Comics . . ." "Things From Another World"
TPM	1999	14.5 × 21	Time Out NY Magazine	•••••	For 5/13/99 issue, blowup of cover of Darth Maul with "Summer Movie Preview"
TPM	1999	11 × 17	Topps	••	For card set; Qui-Gon and Obi-Wan, Celebration I premium
TPM	1999	17 × 22	Toys 'R' Us	••••	"Win Big Naboo Sweepstakes;" large Naboo fighter above boy
TPM	1999	22 × 34	Williams	••••••	For pinball machine; Maul face in ball; "Don't panic, you've got flippers"
TPM	1999	18 × 24	Library Association	•••	"Get Caught Reading;" Jake Lloyd reading in rowboat
TPM	2000	27 × 40	20 C Fox Home Ent.	••	For video—cast above, Podrace below; "Reserve Your Copy Today"
TPM	2000	27 × 40	20 C Fox Home Ent.	••	For video—cast above, Podrace below; April 4
TRILSE	2000	27 × 40	20 C Fox Home Ent.	••••	*Star Wars* Trilogy: "Continue the Adventure on Video"; left half Yoda and duel, right is black with text
TPM	2000	47 × 72	20 C Fox Home Ent.	•••	Video banner—"Reserve Your Copy Today"; two-sided with "It's Here" attached over "Arriving 4-4" on back
TPM	2000	54 × 39	Decipher	•••••	Two-piece poster that will work independently, Obi-Wan and Qui-Gon on left, Maul on right
n/a	2000	19 × 27	Decipher	•••	Jedi Knights TCG; Vader head–half is vector wireframe graphics
TPM	2000	19 × 27	Decipher	•••	Young Jedi CCG—Maul and Trade Fed ship; glossy image of emperor on matte poster
TPM	2000	19 × 27	Decipher	•••	Young Jedi CCG—Obi-Wan and Qui-Gon; glossy image of Amidala on matte poster
ROTJ	2000	10 × 33	Decipher	•••	CCG Death Star II card set
TPM	2000	19 × 27	LucasArts	•••••	"Starfighter" game for PlayStation 2; artwork of Naboo starfighter, pilots, etc.; two-sided
n/a	2000	13 × 22	LucasArts	•••	Propaganda-style poster "Endurance, Strength, Energy"—stormtrooper; two-sided promo for Force Commander
n/a	2000	13 × 22	LucasArts	••••	Propaganda-style poster "Forward to Victory"—line of AT-ATs; two-sided promo for "Force Commander"
n/a	2000	13 × 22	LucasArts	•••	Propaganda-style poster Vader: "You Will Join Us"; two-sided promo for "Force Commander"
n/a	2000	10 × 18	LucasArts	•••	Propaganda-style poster "Are You Ready"—Luke; for "Force Commander"
n/a	2000	10 × 18	LucasArts	•••	Propaganda-style poster "Endurance, Strength, Energy"—stormtrooper; for "Force Commander"
n/a	2000	10 × 18	LucasArts	••••	Propaganda-style poster "Forward to Victory"—line of AT-ATs; for "Force Commander"
n/a	2000	10 × 18	LucasArts	•••	Propaganda-style poster "I Want YOU to Join the Rebellion"—Leia; for "Force Commander"
n/a	2000	10 × 18	LucasArts	•••	Propaganda-style poster "Join the Fight Against the Empire"; soldier in tank; premium for "Force Commander"
TPM	2000	22 × 28	Nintendo	••••	Two-sided "Battle for Naboo" poster
TPM	2000	12 × 12	RCA Victor	•••	Record flat: Episode I Ultimate Edition soundtrack; two-sided Maul in blue
ROTJ	2000	22 × 34	Scorpio Posters	•••	Tenchi Muyo satire poster using ROTJ Style "B" composition
TPM	2000	18 × 25	Siggraph	•••••	Recruitment poster for ILM at Siggraph; Naboo starfighter N-1
TPM	2000	16 × 28	Wizards of the Coast	••••••	For role-playing game; Struzan art mixing classic trilogy with Episode I characters
n/a	2001	17 × 22	Dark Horse	•••	*Star Wars* Tales poster; info on reverse
n/a	2001	13 × 36	Dark Horse	•••	Two-sided graphic novel chronology
n/a	2001	26 × 30	Decipher	•••	Jedi Knights TCG; stormtroopers with Solo reflected in visors; two-sided
n/a	2001	24 × 36	LucasArts	•••	"SW: Galactic Battlegrounds"—bird's-eye view of different *Star Wars* settings combined
TPM	2001	22 × 28	LucasArts	••••	"Super Bombad Racing;" caricature images of Maul, Yoda, etc.; two-sided
n/a	2001	22 × 28	Wizards of the Coast	••••	For role-playing game; McQuarrie art of duel in Cloud City, "Control Your Destiny"
AOTC	2002	18 × 59	20 C Fox Home Ent.	•••••	For DVD/video release, heavy card stock image of Jango
AOTC	2002	18 × 59	20 C Fox Home Ent.	•••••	For DVD/video release, heavy card stock image of Yoda
AOTC	2002	40 × 189	Blockbuster	••••••	Seven-piece horizontal display (each 27 × 40) for video release; character photo montage
AOTC	2002	24 × 36	Dark Horse	•••	Sanda AOTC artwork; reverse has info on Dark Horse series
AOTC	2002	18 × 23	Hasbro	•••••	Episode II saga figure poster
n/a	2002	24 × 36	"Industrial Automaton"	•••••	Hasbro Interactive R2-D2 poster
AOTC	2002	35 × 64	LEGO	••••••	Two-sided, Jango full figure with LEGO logo at bottom
AOTC	2002	19 × 26	LEGO	•••	Obi-Wan and Anakin figures, asteroid chase below
AOTC	2002	19 × 26	LEGO	•••	Two-sided with Coruscant speeders on one side, Republic gunships on the other
AOTC	2002	19 × 26	LEGO	•••	Two-sided with Jedi starfighter and *Slave I* on one side, Obi-Wan and Republic gunship on other
AOTC	2002	24 × 29	LucasArts	••••	For "Jedi Starfighter" video game; cloaked Jedi standing before a Jedi starfighter; perforated edge
AOTC	2002	22 × 28	LucasArts	•••	Two-sided for "Bounty Hunter"
AOTC	2002	22 × 28	LucasArts	•••	Two-sided for "Clone Wars" video game; ship over troopers
AOTC	2002	15 × 21	LucasArts	•••	Two-sided for "Clone Wars" and "Bounty Hunter"
n/a	2002	10 × 14	Scholastic	•••	Jedi Quest: growth of Anakin in five figures; Boba and Jango on reverse
AOTC	2002	24 × 36	Sony	•••	Yoda with three album cover variations below
AOTC	2002	12 × 24	Sony	•••	Yoda above, poster art below, perforated in middle
CW	2003	48 × 69	Cartoon Network	••••••••	Large poster with *Clone Wars* artwork, no black at bottom
CW	2003	24 × 36	Cartoon Network	•••••••	Artwork from *Clone Wars* series: "Begun the Micro-Series Has."
CW	2003	18 × 24	Cartoon Network	•••••••	*Clone Wars* Hyperspace/Comic-Con exclusive
CW	2003	11 × 46	Cartoon Network	•••••••	*Clone Wars* two-sided banner; "Begun the Micro-Series Has."
n/a	2003	12 × 36	Dark Horse	•••	"*Star Wars* Jedi" comic poster
n/a	2003	12 × 36	Dark Horse	•••	"*Star Wars* Tales" comic poster
n/a	2003	17 × 23	Hasbro	•••	Boba Fett Unleashed
n/a	2003	22 × 28	LucasArts	•••	Two-sided "*Star Wars* Galaxies: An Empire Divided"
n/a	2003	15.5 × 22.5	LucasArts	••	"Rebel Strike" video game; magazine insert, AT-AT approaching crashed snowspeeder
ROTS	2003	22 × 33	Lucasfilm	••••••••••	Cast and crew poster—Episode III Sydney 2003; numerous photos of cast and crew
AOTC	2003	18 × 23	Siggraph	••••••	Siggraph ILM poster of Yoda and Hulk
TRILSE	2004	27 × 40	20 C Fox Home Ent.	•••	DVD package cover art
SWSE	2004	27 × 40	20 C Fox Home Ent.	•••	DVD cover art photo-collage
ESBSE	2004	27 × 40	20 C Fox Home Ent.	•••	DVD cover art photo-collage
ROTJSE	2004	27 × 40	20 C Fox Home Ent.	•••	DVD cover art photo-collage
CW	2004	24 × 36	Cartoon Network	•••••••	*Clone Wars: The Microseries Continues*; Grievous, Anakin, Mace, Obi-Wan, and Asajj
n/a	2004	20 × 30.5	Hasbro	•••	Action figures arranged into *Star Wars* Style "C" composition
n/a	2004	15 × 21	LucasArts	•••	"KOTOR: The Sith Lords" fold-out artwork from Electronic Gaming Monthly
TRILSE	2004	24 × 30	Sony Classical	•••	For trilogy CDs with the 2004 DVD release artwork on each
AOTC	2004	21 × 30	Wizards of the Coast	•••	*Star Wars* Miniatures: Rebel Storm; Vader/Luke duel
ROTS	2005	15 × 34	Kellogg's	••••	"Kellogg's Celebrates the Saga"; saga character photos

COMMERCIAL POSTERS

Film	Year	Size	Publisher	Rating	Description
AUSTRALIA					
ESB	1980	17 × 25	Golden Fleece	●●●●●●●●	Golden Fleece gas stations premium; art with five circles for stickers
ESB	1980	23 × 35	Valentine Greetings	●●●●●●●	Droids on Hoth and on *Falcon*; *Empire* logo in blue/green
ESB	1980	23 × 35	Valentine Greetings	●●●●●●●	Vader on Cloud City and duel; *Empire* logo in blue/green
ESB	1980	23 × 35	Valentine Greetings	●●●●●●●	Luke/Yoda on Dagobah and on Luke's back
ROTJ	1983	19 × 25.5	Crystal Craft	●●●●●●	Highly shellacked poster—Style "B" artwork
ROTJ	1983	19 × 25.5	Crystal Craft	●●●●●●	Highly shellacked poster—Luke & Leia
ROTJ	1983	19 × 25.5	Crystal Craft	●●●●●●	Highly shellacked poster—battle in front of Death Star
ROTJ	1983	19 × 25.5	Crystal Craft	●●●●●●	Highly shellacked poster—Jabba the Hutt
ROTJ	1983	19 × 25.5	Crystal Craft	●●●●●●	Highly shellacked poster—Wicket
ROTJ	1983	19 × 25.5	Crystal Craft	●●●●●●	Highly shellacked poster—Darth Vader
ROTJ	1983	19 × 25.5	Crystal Craft	●●●●●●	Highly shellacked poster—R2 & C-3PO
EWOK1	1985	26 × 39.5	Break Fruit Drinks	●●●●●●●●	"Build an Ewok Adventure with Break" fruit drinks; needs 28 stickers to complete image
SW	1995	23 × 35	Impact Posters	●●●	Black-and-white photo of Han and Chewbacca from *Star Wars*
ESB	1996	23 × 35	Impact Posters	●●●●	McQuarrie art of *Falcon*/TIEs over asteroid
ROTJ	1996	23 × 35	Impact Posters	●●●●	McQuarrie art of B-wings
TPM	1999	24 × 36	Impact Posters	●●	Advance poster image
TPM	1999	24 × 36	Impact Posters	●●●	Dogfight in space with credits
TPM	1999	24 × 36	Impact Posters	●●●	Heroes collage
TPM	1999	24 × 36	Impact Posters	●●●●●	Podracing
TPM	1999	24 × 36	Impact Posters	●●●	Villains collage
TPM	1999	24 × 36	Impact Posters	●●	Darth Maul in three poses
TPM	1999	24 × 36	Impact Posters	●●	Jedi vs. Sith artwork
TPM	1999	16 × 20	Impact Posters	●	Advance poster image
TPM	1999	16 × 20	Impact Posters	●	Dogfight in space with credits
TPM	1999	16 × 20	Impact Posters	●	Heroes collage
TPM	1999	16 × 20	Impact Posters	●	Podracing
AOTC	2002	24 × 36	Impact Posters	●●	Advance poster image
AOTC	2002	24 × 36	Impact Posters	●●	Drew Struzan art release poster
CANADA					
ROTJ	1983	24 × 36	General Mills	●●●●●●●	Mail-in premium; English/French Vader
ROTJ	1983	24 × 36	General Mills	●●●●●●●	Mail-in premium; English/French *Revenge* artwork with cast
ROTJ	1983	24 × 36	General Mills	●●●●●●●	Mail-in premium; English/French Star Destroyer and TIEs
ROTJ	1984	20 × 30	Kellogg's	●●●●●●●	C-3PO's cereal premium poster; English and French below
ROTJ	1986	23 × 35	CBS Fox	●●●●●	For video; "Coming soon from CBS Fox Video;" perforated top with ROTJ logo
n/a	1995	23 × 32	Draconis	●●●●●	Incom T-65 X-wing Starfighter; art above, front and side elevations below
n/a	1995	24 × 36	Draconis	●●●●	Vehicles of the Rebel Alliance; art and blueprints of 10 ships
SW	1995	23.5 × 32	Draconis	●●●●●	Battle of Yavin litho on heavy stock
ESB	1996	22 × 34	Trends International	●●●●	*The Empire Strikes Back* Collectors Edition; Style "A" artwork
n/a	1996	24 × 36	Draconis	●●●●	Vehicles of the Galactic Empire
ROTJ	1996	22 × 34	Trends International	●●●	*Return of the Jedi* Collectors Edition; Style "B" artwork
SW	1996	22 × 35	Trends International	●●●●●	*Star Wars* Collectors Edition; Berkey art from book cover
TPM	1999	22 × 34	Trends International	●●	Drew Struzan artwork
TPM	1999	22 × 34	Trends International	●●	Heroes collage
TPM	1999	22 × 34	Trends International	●●	Villains collage
TPM	1999	22 × 34	Trends International	●●	Jedi vs. Sith saber battle; horizontal
TPM	1999	22 × 34	Trends International	●●	Jar Jar; head shot and name above
TPM	1999	22 × 34	Trends International	●●	Advance poster image of Anakin/shadow
AOTC	2002	11 × 17	Lucasfilm	●	Skywalker family tree in English and French
FRANCE					
SW	1978	23.5 × 34	F. Nugeron	●●●●●	Style "A" artwork in French; commercial sales
ESB	1980	24 × 34	Yoplait	●●●●●●●●	Four Yoplait posters on one sheet with blank space for stickers
ESB	1981	21 × 29	Glaces Motta	●●●●●●●●	Style "B" artwork surrounded by spaces for thirty stickers
ROTJ	1983	27 × 38.5	Ed. du Weekend	●●●●●●●	Editions du Weekend #1 print of Jouin art without credits and red logo
ROTJ	1983	27 × 38.5	Ed. du Weekend	●●●●●	Editions du Weekend #2 print of cast in Endor forest
ROTJ	1983	27 × 38.5	Ed. du Weekend	●●●●●	Editions du Weekend #3 print of Logray
ROTJ	1983	27 × 38.5	Ed. du Weekend	●●●●●	Editions du Weekend #4 print of *Revenge* art with red "Retour" logo
ROTJ	1984	12 × 25	General Mills	●●●●●	Artwork of Kenner vehicles in space; store premium
TPM	2000	16 × 23	OSWFCFR	●●●●●	Fan Club poster of Podrace artwork by Alvin
AOTC	2002	16 × 23	OSWFCFR	●●●	Fold out poster of Geonosis battle scene
ROTS	2003	16 × 23	Lucasfilm Magazine	●●	Fold out poster of Obi-Wan posed for Episode III
GERMANY					
SW	1977	7 × 22.5	Das Freizeit	●	Das Freizeit-Magazin insert poster; black-and-white photo of droids backed with Dead End Kids
SW	1978	47 × 66	Kenner	●●●●●●●	*Star Wars* "Super-Poster" artwork collage; two sheets with flyer
ROTJ	1983	23 × 33	Kenner	●●●●●	Two-sided; AT-AT, snowspeeder, *Falcon*, AT-ST vehicles on one side, other SW toys on other
EWOKS	1985	16.5 × 23	Scandecor	●●●●●	Cartoon Wicket/Princess Kneesa swinging on vine #6988
ESB	1993	26 × 40	Zig Zag	●●●	Reprint of *Empire* Style "A"
ESB	1993	26 × 40	Zig Zag	●●●	Reprint of *Empire* Style "B"
ROTJ	1993	26 × 40	Zig Zag	●●●	Reprint of *Return of the Jedi* Style "B"
ROTJ	1993	27 × 40	Zig Zag	●●●	Revenge art with *Return of the Jedi* logo
SW	1993	26 × 40	Zig Zag	●●●	Reprint of SW Style "A"
SW	1993	26 × 40	Zig Zag	●●●	Reprint of SW Style "C"
TRIL	1993	26 × 40	Zig Zag	●●●	Reprint of British triple-bill quad
SW	1995	23.5 × 33	Zig Zag	●●●	Reprint enlargement of *Star Wars* Style "A" half-sheet poster
ESB	1996	27 × 40	Zig Zag	●●●	*Empire* Japanese Ohrai art with US copy block
ESB	1996	10.5 × 15	OSWFC	●●	Montage artwork from *Empire*; "MTFBWY" from Official Fan Club
ROTJ	1996	27 × 40	Zig Zag	●●●	Space battle before second Death Star fan club reprint with *Star Wars* logo
SW	1996	22 × 40	Zig Zag	●●●●●	Horizontal spaceship and characters art by Noriyoshi Ohrai
SW	1996	27 × 40	Zig Zag	●●●	McQuarrie fan club art reprint with *Star Wars* logo
ESB	1997	25 × 36.5	Filmwelt Berlin	●●●●●	*Empire* artwork by Alvin; used for international video campaign
ESB	1997	27 × 39	Zig Zag	●●●	*Empire* radio show poster reprint
ESBSE	1997	27 × 40	Zig Zag	●●	Drew Struzan art
ROTJ	1997	25 × 36.5	Filmwelt Berlin	●●●●●	*Jedi* artwork by Alvin; used for international video campaign
ROTJSE	1997	27 × 40	Zig Zag	●●	Drew Struzan art
SW	1997	25 × 36.5	Filmwelt Berlin	●●●●●	*Star Wars* artwork by Alvin; used for international video campaign
SW	1997	27 × 39	Zig Zag	●●●	1978 *Star Wars* Concert poster reprint
SWSE	1997	27 × 40	Zig Zag	●●	Drew Struzan art
TRILSE	1997	27 × 39	Zig Zag	●●●●	Poster checklist (like Kilian version) but includes Special Edition one-sheets
TRILSE	1997	27 × 40	Zig Zag	●●	Ingot artwork
ESB	2003	27 × 40	Zig Zag	●●●●●	Chantrell artwork for unused *Empire* poster
TRILSE	2004	27 × 40	Zig Zag	●●●●	Black-and-white image of Vader's helmet with "*Star Wars* Trilogy"

COMMERCIAL POSTERS

	Film	Year	Size	Publisher	Rating	Description
HONG KONG						
	n/a	1997	16.5 × 23.5	n/a	••	Photo of Leia on left with calendar months on right
	n/a	1997	16.5 × 23.5	n/a	••	Photo of droids on left with calendar months on right
JAPAN						
	SW	1977	24 × 34	Factors	••••••••	Droids with X-wing/TIE in background; distributed by Toho
	SW	1978	20.5 × 29	Roadshow	•	Magazine insert of droids in desert on one side, black-and-white of Luke at homestead on other
	ESB	1980	21 × 30	n/a	•	Ohrai art; black-and-white photo of Tatum O'Neil & Kristy McNichol
	ESB	1980	20.5 × 30	Screen Magazine	•	Magazine insert with *Empire* Advance art on one side, photo of Leia, Han, Luke and Chewie on the other
	ESB	1980	24 × 34	Toho	••••••	*Empire* photo montage, title in copper
	ESB	1980	21 × 29	Toho	•••••	Star Destroyer and *Falcon,* logo in copper
	ROTJ	1983	21 × 30.5	Yamakatsu	••••••••••	Ohrai art of R2-D2 and C-3PO on orange-red star field; "Starfall"
	ROTJ	1983	21 × 30.5	Yamakatsu	••••••••	Artwork collage of scenes and characters; large Vader and *Millennium Falcon*
	EWOK1	1984	20 × 29	n/a	••••	Photo montage on red background
	EWOK2	1987	14.5 × 20	n/a	••	Magazine insert poster of girl in center twinned with Japanimation film by Bandai
	n/a	1989	20 × 30	Star Tours	•••••••	Silver Mylar poster of star speeder pursued by TIE fighters with Tokyo Disneyland below
	TRIL	1994	12 × 16	n/a	••••••	Combination of artwork from classic trilogy posters; for 1994 video release
	ESB	1997	16.5 × 23.5	Sony Magazine	••••••	AT-AT, AT-ST, Snowspeeder, etc.; art by Yoshiyuki Takani
	AOTC	2002	24 × 35	Heart	•••	Anakin and Padmé; vertical
	AOTC	2002	24 × 35	Heart	•••	Heroes with Mace, Yoda, clone troopers, etc.; horizontal
	AOTC	2002	24 × 35	Heart	•••	Release poster art; "Heart" not printed below
	AOTC	2002	16 × 19.5	Heart	•••	Jango and clone troopers; glossy
	AOTC	2002	16 × 19.5	Heart	•••	Anakin, Obi-Wan, Vader above; glossy
	AOTC	2002	16 × 19.5	Heart	•••	"Faces" character collage; glossy
	AOTC	2002	16 × 19.5	Heart	•••	Villains horizontal collage; glossy
	AOTC	2002	16 × 19.5	Heart	•••	Luke/Leia above, Anakin/Padmé below; glossy
	AOTC	2002	24 × 35	Heart	•••	Advance poster art; "Heart" not printed below
	n/a	2002	20 × 26	Tomy	••••	Tomy figures (in Japanese)
MEXICO						
	ESBSE	1997	18 × 27	Pepsi	•••	Premium poster of C-3PO (like US mail-away in Spanish)
	ROTJSE	1997	18 × 27	Pepsi	•••	Premium poster of Yoda (like US mail-away in Spanish)
	SWSE	1997	18 × 27	Pepsi	•••	Premium poster of Vader (like US mail-away in Spanish)
	TPM	1999	19 × 27	Kellogg's	•••	Heroes montage "*La Amenaza Fantasma*"
	TPM	1999	19 × 27	Kellogg's	•••	Villains montage "*La Amenaza Fantasma*"
	TPM	1999	23 × 35	Pepsi	••	Game field poster for Pepsi promotion
	TPM	1999	17 × 24	Pepsi	••	Premium Qui-Gon "*La Amenaza Fantasma*"
	TPM	1999	17 × 24	Pepsi	••	Premium Anakin "*La Amenaza Fantasma*"
	TPM	1999	17 × 24	Pepsi	••	Premium Jar Jar "*La Amenaza Fantasma*"
	TPM	1999	17 × 24	Pepsi	••	Premium Obi-Wan "*La Amenaza Fantasma*"
	TPM	1999	23 × 17	Spanish FC	••	Spanish fan magazine fold out montage
	TPM	1999	16 × 22	Spanish FC	•	Spanish fan magazine fold out of Maul
	n/a	2001	26 × 36	n/a	•	Filmoteca calendar poster; several sci-fi icons including Vader, R2, C-3PO
	ROTJ	2003	25 × 36	Spanish FC	••••	*Return of the Jedi* 20th Anniversary; montage of Vader, Han, Leia, Fett, and Luke before funeral pyre
NEW ZEALAND						
	ESB	1980	23 × 35	JD Enterprise	•••••••	Photo collage with *Empire* logo at bottom center
	ESB	1980	23 × 35	JD Enterprises	•••••••	Luke on Tauntaun with three photos above and three below
	ESB	1980	23 × 35	JD Enterprises	•••••••	Luke pilot uniform portrait from *Empire*
POLAND						
	ESB	1983	26 × 38	n/a	••••••••	Artwork of *Empire* characters and scenes below, *Star Trek Enterprise* above; created for tourist trade
	AOTC	2002	17 × 24	Chio	•••	Anakin and Obi-Wan on front, spaces for premium cards #1–10 on back
	AOTC	2002	17 × 24	Chio	•••	Anakin and Yoda on front, spaces for premium cards #11–15 on back
	AOTC	2002	17 × 24	Chio	•••	Yoda, Mace, and Obi-Wan on front, spaces for premium cards #16–25 on back
	AOTC	2002	17 × 24	Chio	•••	Jango and Clone Trooper on front, spaces for premium cards #26–30 on back
	AOTC	2002	17 × 24	Chio	•••	Anakin and Padmé on front, spaces for premium cards #31–40 on back
SWEDEN						
	SW	1977	27 × 39	Scandecor	•••••••	Cast against black with X-wing/TIE and logo above
	SW	1977	27 × 39	Scandecor	•••••••	Droids on Tatooine, pointy "W"
	ESB	1982	24 × 35	Scanlite	•••••••	*Millennium Falcon* and Star Destroyer; *Star Wars* logo
	ESB	1982	24 × 35	Scanlite	••••••••	"Imperial Star Destroyer" side view; *Star Wars* logo
	ESB	1982	24 × 34.5	Scanlite	•••••••	"Lord Darth Vader"; Vader in Bespin freeze with hands on belt
	ESB	1982	24 × 34.5	Scanlite	•••••••	"Lord Darth Vader"; Vader at top of Bespin freeze stairs with saber
	ESB	1982	24 × 34.5	Scanlite	••••••••	"Princess Leia Organa"; same as 1977 Factors poster
	ESB	1982	24 × 34.5	Scanlite	•••••••	Like US *Empire* Advance with Vader helmet
	ESB	1982	24 × 34.5	Scanlite	•••••••	"Luke Skywalker"; same as 1977 Factors poster
UNITED KINGDOM						
	ESB	1980	19 × 29	Express Dairies	•••••••	Premium touting *Empire* soundtrack; photo of AT-ATs on Hoth
	ESB	1980	27 × 39	Scandecor	•••••••	Darth Vader
	ESB	1980	27 × 39	Scandecor	•••••••	Luke in Dagobah cave
	ESB	1980	27 × 39	Scandecor	•••••••	Yoda
	ESB	1980	27 × 39	Scandecor	••••••••	*Empire* Style "A" artwork with added characters
	ESB	1980	24 × 34.5	Scanlite	•••••••	Vader and two stormtroopers against red; included with lamp-shade kit
	ESB	1981	17 × 24	Palitoy	•••••	Insert AT-AT toy poster with various other toys on back
	ROTJ	1982	16 × 23	Airfix	•••	Two-sided of Han/Leia and Jabba; included with model kits
	ROTJ	1983	24.5 × 35	Anabas Pdts.	••••	Luke and Leia on sail barge
	ROTJ	1983	24.5 × 35	Anabas Pdts.	••••	Photo of Wicket with *Jedi* logo in white
	SW	1992	23 × 33	Total Magazine	•••••	Artwork of X-wing in trench; magazine insert from Dec. '92 issue
	ESBSE	1997	25 × 36	GB Posters	•••	Drew Struzan artwork poster
	n/a	1997	25 × 36	GB Posters	•••	Yoda photomosaic by Robert Silvers
	n/a	1997	25 × 36	GB Posters	•••	Vader photomosaic by Robert Silvers
	ROTJSE	1997	25 × 36	GB Posters	•••	Drew Struzan artwork poster
	SWSE	1997	25 × 36	GB Posters	•••	Drew Struzan artwork poster
	TRILSE	1997	25 × 36	GB Posters	•••	Ingot art (copy of US version)
	ESB	1998	25 × 36	GB Posters	•••	Stormtrooper and AT-ATs (US video campaign artwork)
	n/a	1998	25 × 36	GB Posters	•••	Boba Fett portrait with text
	n/a	1998	25 × 36	GB Posters	•••	Vader with text; yellow border
	n/a	1998	25 × 36	GB Posters	•••	Luke with text; yellow border
	n/a	1998	25 × 36	GB Posters	•••	Leia with text; yellow border
	n/a	1998	25 × 36	GB Posters	•••	Yoda with text; yellow border
	n/a	1998	25 × 36	GB Posters	•••	Han with text; yellow border
	ROTJ	1998	25 × 36	GB Posters	•••	Yoda and duel (US video campaign artwork)
	SW	1998	25 × 36	GB Posters	•••	Vader and X-wing (US video campaign artwork)
	SW	1998	25 × 36	GB Posters	•••	Classic Style "C" artwork poster
	TPM	1999	25 × 36	GB Posters	•••	Advance poster art with Anakin and Vader shadow
	TPM	1999	25 × 36	GB Posters	•••	Drew Struzan art of release poster

COMMERCIAL POSTERS

Film	Year	Size	Publisher	Rating	Description
UNITED KINGDOM, CONT.					
TPM	1999	25 × 36	GB Posters	•••	Obi-Wan above, Qui-Gon, Obi-Wan, and Maul dueling below
TPM	1999	25 × 36	GB Posters	•••	Podrace with Anakin Skywalker
TPM	1999	25 × 36	GB Posters	•••	Trade Federation ship and Naboo fighters
TPM	1999	25 × 36	GB Posters	•••••••	Maul photomosaic (like Vader and Yoda versions); Fact Files premium
TPM	1999	25 × 36	GB Posters	•••	Heroes montage
TPM	1999	25 × 36	GB Posters	•••	Villains montage
TPM	1999	25 × 36	GB Posters	•••	Montage showing Maul in three poses
TPM	1999	25 × 36	GB Posters	•••	Maul above, duel below; *Star Wars* logo up the side
TPM	1999	25 × 36	GB Posters	•••	Obi-Wan above, duel below; *Star Wars* logo up the side
TPM	1999	25 × 36	GB Posters	•••	Amidala above, scene below; *Star Wars* logo up the side
TPM	1999	25 × 36	GB Posters	•••	Jar Jar, *Star Wars* logo up the side
TPM	1999	16 × 20	GB Posters	•	Advance poster art
TPM	1999	16 × 20	GB Posters	•	Drew Struzan art
TPM	1999	16 × 20	GB Posters	•	"Podrace"
TPM	1999	16 × 20	GB Posters	•	Podrace with Anakin Skywalker
TPM	1999	16 × 20	GB Posters	•	Podrace with Sebulba
TPM	1999	16 × 20	GB Posters	•	Heroes montage
TPM	1999	16 × 20	GB Posters	•	Villains montage
TPM	1999	16 × 20	GB Posters	•	Trade Federation ship and Naboo fighters
TPM	1999	16 × 20	GB Posters	•	Jedi vs. Sith
TPM	1999	16 × 20	GB Posters	•	Darth Maul
TPM	1999	39 × 54	GB Posters	••••••	Advance poster art with Anakin and Vader shadow
TPM	1999	39 × 54	GB Posters	•••••••	Drew Struzan art
TPM	1999	20 × 27	Pepsi	•	Esso premium poster: Anakin
TPM	1999	20 × 27	Pepsi	•	Esso premium poster: Maul
TPM	1999	20 × 27	Pepsi	•	Esso premium poster: Obi-Wan
TPM	1999	20 × 27	Pepsi	•	Esso premium poster: Jar Jar
AOTC	2002	25 × 35	GB Posters	•••	Anakin, Obi-Wan, and Vader; classic duel in background
AOTC	2002	25 × 35	GB Posters	•••	Jango and clone troopers
AOTC	2002	25 × 35	GB Posters	•••	Anakin and clone troopers
AOTC	2002	25 × 35	GB Posters	•••	Character photo montage; horizontal
AOTC	2002	25 × 35	GB Posters	•••	Anakin and Padmé back-to-back
AOTC	2002	25 × 35	GB Posters	•••	Dooku, Maul, Sidious, and Vader
AOTC	2002	16 × 20	GB Posters	•••	Dooku, Maul, Sidious, and Vader
n/a	2002	16 × 23	Hasbro	•••••	Figures for 2002; each figure image in white box
ESB	2004	23.5 × 31.5	GB Posters	••••	Embossed-style artwork of stormtrooper face and AT-ATs
ROTJ	2004	23.5 × 31.5	GB Posters	••••	Embossed-style artwork of Yoda and Luke/Vader duel
UNITED STATES					
SW	1977	17.5 × 22.5	20th Century Fox	••••••	Color photo of X-wing/TIE fighter battle; lobby sales
SW	1977	22 × 33	20th Century Records	•••••	Insert poster for soundtrack album; rolled version was store promo or in-house copy
SW	1977	18 × 24	Coca-Cola	•••	Burger Chef poster of Luke
SW	1977	18 × 24	Coca-Cola	•••	Burger Chef poster of R2 and C-3PO
SW	1977	18 × 24	Coca-Cola	•••	Burger Chef poster of Vader
SW	1977	18 × 24	Coca-Cola	•••	Burger Chef poster of Chewbacca
SW	1977	18 × 24	Coca-Cola	•••••	Burger Chef/King artwork, but Coke logo: Luke
SW	1977	18 × 24	Coca-Cola	•••••	Burger Chef/King artwork, but Coke logo: R2 and C-3PO
SW	1977	18 × 24	Coca-Cola	•••••	Burger Chef/King artwork, but Coke logo: Vader
SW	1977	18 × 24	Coca-Cola	•••••	Burger Chef/King artwork, but Coke logo: Chewbacca
SW	1977	18 × 23.5	Coca-Cola	••••	Burger King poster of Luke (with white border)
SW	1977	18 × 23.5	Coca-Cola	••••	Burger King poster of droids (with white border)
SW	1977	18 × 23.5	Coca-Cola	••••	Burger King poster of the Darth Vader (with white border)
SW	1977	18 × 23.5	Coca-Cola	••••	Burger King poster of Han and Chewbacca (with white border)
SW	1977	20 × 28	Factors	••••••	Stormtrooper firing into "tunnel of light"
SW	1977	20 × 28	Factors	•••••••	X-wing vs. TIE with three circular photos
SW	1977	20 × 28	Factors	•••••••	Luke photo on McQuarrie art background; "Jedi Knight"
SW	1977	20 × 28	Factors	••••	Hildebrandt art
SW	1977	20 × 28	Factors	••••	R2-D2 and C-3PO
SW	1977	20 × 28	Factors	••••	Darth Vader
SW	1977	20 × 28	Factors	•••••••••	Darth Vader with *Star Wars* logo
SW	1977	20 × 28	Factors	••••••	Luke in front of plain backdrop firing gun
SW	1977	20 × 28	Factors	••••••	Princess Leia
SW	1977	22 × 29	Topps	••••••	Premium poster of uncut sheet of blue border gum cards
SW	1978	20 × 28	Factors	•••••••••	Cantina art by Selby
SW	1978	20 × 28	Factors	•••••••	X-wing/TIEs in trench by McQuarrie; fan club exclusive
SW	1978	18 × 23	Proctor & Gamble	•••	Cheer/Dawn premium of Darth vs. Obi-Wan
SW	1978	18 × 23	Proctor & Gamble	•••	Cheer/Dawn premium of R2 and C-3PO
SW	1978	18 × 23	Proctor & Gamble	•••	Cheer/Dawn premium of Luke, Leia, Han, and Chewie
ESB	1980	22 × 28	American Can Co.	••••••	Dixie premium poster of Darth Vader
ESB	1980	22 × 28	American Can Co.	••••••	Dixie premium poster of Luke
ESB	1980	24 × 33	Coca-Cola	••••	Coke premium poster by Boris (theater sales)
ESB	1980	18 × 24	Coca-Cola	••••	Coke premium poster by Boris—Luke & Yoda
ESB	1980	18 × 24	Coca-Cola	••••	Coke premium poster by Boris—Luke on Tauntaun
ESB	1980	18 × 24	Coca-Cola	••••	Coke premium poster by Boris—Han in carbon freeze
ESB	1980	18.5 × 23	Crisco, etc.	•••	Premium from Crisco, Duncan Hines, Pringles—R2 and C-3PO
ESB	1980	18.5 × 23	Crisco, etc.	•••	Premium from Crisco, Duncan Hines, Pringles—Leia/Han
ESB	1980	18.5 × 23	Crisco, etc.	•••	Premium from Crisco, Duncan Hines, Pringles—Luke
ESB	1980	18.5 × 23	Crisco, etc.	•••	Premium from Crisco, Duncan Hines, Pringles—Vader
ESB	1980	20 × 28	Factors	••••	Style "A" artwork without logo; fan club exclusive
ESB	1980	20 × 28	Factors	••••••	Style "A" art with red *Empire* logo; includes Boba Fett and Lando
ESB	1980	20 × 28	Factors	••••••	Vader and stormtroopers
ESB	1980	20 × 28	Factors	•••••••	Boba Fett
ESB	1980	20 × 28	Factors	•••••	C-3PO and R2-D2
ESB	1980	20 × 28	Factors	••••••	Yoda
ESB	1980	20 × 31	National Geographic	•	*Geographic World* magazine insert poster of *Falcon* vs. Star Destroyer
ESB	1980	11 × 16	Noble	•••••••	Reproduction of early Noble graphite sketch for concept art; dated 2/14/80
ESB	1980	12 × 18	Preview	••••••	Preview magazine cover artwork print by Steranko; signed
ESB	1980	22 × 29	Topps	•••••	Premium poster of uncut sheet of silver-border cards (1st series)
ESB	1980	14 × 21	Weekly Reader	•••	Book Club photo poster (printed by Factors)
n/a	1980	18 × 22	Coca-Cola	••••	In-store giveaway for R2-D2 look-alike "Cobot"; photo of toy against stars
ESB	1981	12 × 20	Topps	••	*Empire* Style "A" reprint
SW	1981	12 × 20	Topps	••	*Star Wars* Style "A" reprint
ESB	1983	22 × 34	Sales Corp.	•••	*Empire* Advance with Vader helmet reprint

COMMERCIAL POSTERS

Film	Year	Size	Publisher	Rating	Description
UNITED STATES, CONT.					
n/a	1983	24 × 32	Edward Weston Graphics	••••	Melanie Taylor Kent "Hollywood Boulevard;" artwork includes Vader, droids leaving footprints at Chinese Theatre
ROTJ	1983	18 × 22	Coca-Cola	••••••••	Hi-C two-sided mail-in premium; Jabba and Ewoks blocked out
ROTJ	1983	18 × 22	Coca-Cola	••••	Hi-C two-sided mail-in premium artwork montage
ROTJ	1983	27 × 39	Film Freak	•••	Film Freak Shop reprint of Style "B" with small Lando; bleed border
ROTJ	1983	17 × 22.5	Oral B	••	Two-sided Luke and Vader duel art backed with sketch of figs, dental products, coupons
ROTJ	1983	22 × 33.5	Official SW Fan Club	••••••	ROTJ Poster Album; photos in "film frames" backed with text from fan club
ROTJ	1983	17 × 22	Proctor & Gamble	•••	Photo poster—Lando fighting
ROTJ	1983	17 × 22	Proctor & Gamble	•••	Photo poster—Luke at Jabba's Palace
ROTJ	1983	17 × 22	Proctor & Gamble	•••	Photo poster—R2-D2 and Ewoks
ROTJ	1983	17 × 22	Proctor & Gamble	•••	Photo poster—Leia and Jabba
ROTJ	1983	22 × 34	Sales Corp.	••••	*Revenge* artwork but "*Return*"
ROTJ	1983	22 × 34	Sales Corp.	•••	*Return* Style "A" reprint
ROTJ	1983	22 × 34	Sales Corp.	•••	*Return* Style "B" reprint
ROTJ	1983	22 × 34	Sales Corp.	•••	Vader and Royal Guards photo
ROTJ	1983	22 × 34	Sales Corp.	•••	Battle in front of Death Star with *Return* logo
ROTJ	1983	22 × 34	Sales Corp.	•••	Forest scene with cast photo
ROTJ	1983	22 × 34	Sales Corp.	•••	Ewok montage photos
SW	1983	22 × 34	Sales Corp.	•••	*Star Wars* Style "D" reprint
ROTJ	1983	24 × 25	Sales Corp.	••••••••	Mail-in premium of star-filled Vader helmet against blue
ROTJ	1983	26 × 70	Sales Corp.	•••••	Vader door poster (illustration)
ROTJ	1983	11 × 14	Sales Corp.	••	Mini-Poster: *Revenge* Advance
ROTJ	1983	11 × 14	Sales Corp.	••	Mini-Poster: *Return* Style "A"
ROTJ	1983	11 × 14	Sales Corp.	••	Mini-Poster: *Return* Style "B"
ROTJ	1983	11 × 14	Sales Corp.	••	Mini-Poster: Speeder bikes
ROTJ	1983	11 × 14	Sales Corp.	••	Mini-Poster: Battle near Death Star II
ROTJ	1983	11 × 14	Sales Corp.	••	Mini-Poster: Imperial Shuttle
ROTJ	1983	11 × 14	Sales Corp.	••	Mini-Poster: Jabba and "slave" Leia
ROTJ	1983	11 × 14	Sales Corp.	••	Mini-Poster: Max Rebo and the band
ROTJ	1983	11 × 14	Sales Corp.	••	Mini-Poster: Vader and Royal guards
ROTJ	1983	11 × 14	Sales Corp.	••	Mini-Poster: Emperor/Luke Jedi
ROTJ	1983	11 × 14	Sales Corp.	••	Mini-Poster: Ewoks
ROTJ	1983	11 × 14	Sales Corp.	••	Mini-Poster: Luke/Vader montage
ROTJ	1983	17 × 22	Scholastic	•	Ewoks photo from *Jedi* with blue border
ROTJ	1983	17 × 22	Scholastic	•	Darth Vader photo
ROTJ	1983	16 × 20	Weekly Reader	•	Photo montage
ROTJ	1983	16 × 20	Weekly Reader	•	Wicket the Ewok photo poster
ROTJ	1983	17 × 22	Weekly Reader	•	Ewok mother and child photo poster
ROTJ	1984	18 × 22	Kenner	••••••	"Star Wars Is Forever" two-sided mail-in premium; figures on reverse
ROTJ	1984	17 × 22	Kenner	•••••	Fifteen small photos against Falcon in space; mail-in premium from "To a Young Jedi" promotion
DROIDS	1985	17 × 20	Weekly Reader	••••••	Droids cartoon poster from TV series
EWOKS	1985	17 × 22	Sales Corp.	••••••	Ewoks "Friends come in all shapes and sizes"; art by Pat Paris
ROTJ	1985	17 × 18	Kenner	••••••	Planetary Map pack-in poster: The Death Stars
ROTJ	1985	17 × 18	Kenner	••••••	Planetary Map pack-in poster: The Planet Tatooine
ROTJ	1985	17 × 18	Kenner	••••••	Planetary Map pack-in poster: Endor: Sanctuary Moon
TRIL	1985	27 × 41	Kilian Enterprises	•••••••	Two-sided poster checklist: L'Affiche *Star Wars* Saga
n/a	1987	18 × 24	Star Tours (Disney)	•••••	Travel poster—"The Ultimate Adventure"
n/a	1987	18 × 24	Star Tours (Disney)	•••••	Travel poster—Bespin
n/a	1987	18 × 24	Star Tours (Disney)	•••••	Travel poster—Dagobah
n/a	1987	18 × 24	Star Tours (Disney)	•••••	Travel poster—Endor (moon)
n/a	1987	18 × 24	Star Tours (Disney)	•••••	Travel poster—Endor (Ewok village)
n/a	1987	18 × 24	Star Tours (Disney)	•••••	Travel poster—Hoth
n/a	1987	18 × 24	Star Tours (Disney)	•••••	Travel poster—Tatooine
n/a	1987	18 × 24	Star Tours (Disney)	•••••	Travel poster—Yavin
n/a	1987	18 × 24	Star Tours (Disney)	•••••••	Limited edition litho by Charles Boyer of Mickey, Goofy, & Donald looking up at X-wing and star speeders
ESB	1987	24 × 36	Portal Publications	•	*Empire* Advance reprint (inaccurately marked 1979)
SW	1987	24 × 36	Portal Publications	•	*Star Wars* Style "C" reprint (inaccurately marked 1977)
ROTJ	1987	24 × 36	Portal Publications	•	*Revenge* artwork but "*Return*" logo (inaccurately marked 1979)
ROTJ	1987	24 × 36	Portal Publications	•	*Return of the Jedi* Style "A" reprint (inaccurately marked 1983)
SW	1987	27 × 41	Kilian Enterprises	•••••••	Silver Mylar "A" teaser: The First 10 Years
SW	1987	27 × 41	Kilian Enterprises	•••••••••	Gold Mylar "A" teaser: The First 10 Years; Kilian mailing list exclusive
SW	1987	27 × 41	Kilian Enterprises	•••••••	Gold Mylar "A" teaser: The First 10 Years; British anniversary version dated November 28, 1977
SW	1987	27 × 41	Kilian Enterprises	•••••••	Style "B" sheet, 10th anniversary; edition size of 3000, signed by Drew
SW	1987	17 × 36	Minds Eye	••••••	John Alvin poster for *Star Wars* tenth anniversary; logo with characters and scenes inside letters
SW	1987	17 × 36	Minds Eye	••••••	John Alvin poster for *Star Wars* tenth anniversary; logo with characters and scenes inside letters; signed
SW	1987	22 × 25.5	Official SW Fan Club	••••	Bantha Tracks final issue fold-out poster with tenth anniversary highlights; also available at 1987 con rolled
n/a	1988	20 × 30	Star Tours (Disney)	••••••	Kriegler art for first anniversary; park giveaway
ESB	1990	27 × 41	Kilian Enterprises	•••••••	Tenth Anniversary; uses concept art by Noble from 1980; signed
ESB	1990	27 × 41	Kilian Enterprises	••••••	Tenth Anniversary; uses concept art by Noble from 1980
ESB	1990	27 × 41	Kilian Enterprises	••••••••	Style "A" gold Mylar with Vader helmet and *Empire* tenth logo
ESB	1990	27 × 41	Kilian Enterprises	••••••••	Style "B" silver Mylar with Luke on Tauntaun on the number ten
ESB	1990	27 × 41	Kilian Enterprises	••••••••••	Style "B" gold Mylar test, so marked
n/a	1990	18 × 24	Star Tours	•••••	Like "The Ultimate Adventure" poster but no park name
n/a	1991	22 × 28	Kilian/Bantam	•••••	Signed Tom Jung cover art for "Heir to the Empire"
n/a	1991	22 × 28	Kilian/Bantam	••••	Unsigned Tom Jung cover art for "Heir to the Empire"
n/a	1991	23 × 32	Nintendo	••••••	Premium poster of Vader with *Star Wars* logo in red
ROTJ	1991	24 × 36	Portal Publications	•••	Battle in front of second Death Star with *Star Wars* logo in red at upper right
ROTJ	1991	12 × 36	Portal Publications	•••	Ewoks montage of five photos against mint green background
ESB	1992	23.5 × 37	Lucasfilm Games	••••••	Enhanced photo of destroyed AT-AT with *Empire* logo; premium
n/a	1992	22 × 47	n/a	•••	Sci-fi Cafe; montage of sci-fi characters including *Star Wars*
n/a	1992	19.5 × 22	Mythical Realism Press	••••••••••	Litho of Yoda by Michael Whelan (cover art of "My Jedi Journal"); signed and numbered
SW	1992	24 × 36	M.T. Kent	••••	Melanie Taylor Kent 15th anniversary artwork
SW	1992	24 × 36	M.T. Kent	••••••	Melanie Taylor Kent 15th anniversary. artwork; signed
SW	1992	27 × 41	Kilian Enterprises	••••••	15th anniversary. reprint of style "D" poster; numbered
SW	1992	27 × 41	Kilian Enterprises	••••••	15th anniversary. Style "B" sheet using Hildebrandt artwork; numbered
SW	1992	27 × 41	Kilian Enterprises	•••••••	15th anniversary. Style "B" sheet using Hildebrandt artwork; numbered and signed by both brothers
SW	1992	27 × 41	Kilian Enterprises	•••••••	15th anniversary. Style "B" sheet using Hildebrandt artwork and "*A New Hope*" triangular logo in place of "*Star Wars*"; signed QVC exclusive
n/a	1993	11 × 17	Bantam Books	•••	Struzan cover art from "Truce at Bakura;" in-store giveaway from tear-off pad
n/a	1993	16 × 21	Official SW Fan Club	•••	Michael David Ward art; X-wings among nebulae
ROTJ	1993	27 × 41	Kilian Enterprises	•••••••	10th anniversary. Struzan "*Revenge*" art; test proof with no logo
ROTJ	1993	27 × 41	Kilian Enterprises	•••••••	10th anniversary Struzan "*Revenge*" art; "*Return*" logo in red foil

COMMERCIAL POSTERS

Film	Year	Size	Publisher	Rating	Description
UNITED STATES, CONT.					
ROTJ	1993	27 × 41	Kilian Enterprises	•••••••	10th anniversary Struzan "*Revenge*" art; "*Return*" logo in gold foil
ROTJ	1993	27 × 41	Kilian Enterprises	••••••••	10th anniversary Struzan "*Revenge*" art; "*Return*" logo in gold foil; signed "Drew" in silver
ROTJ	1993	27 × 41	Kilian Enterprises	••••••••	10th anniversary Struzan "*Revenge*" art; "*Return*" logo in gold foil and Lucasfilm Fan Club logo in gold foil
ROTJ	1993	28 × 41	Kilian Enterprises	••••••••••	10th anniversary Struzan "*Revenge*" art; "*Return*" logo in gold foil and Lucasfilm Fan Club logo also in gold foil; printers blocks at right
ESB	1994	21 × 32	Western Graphics	•••	*Empire* "Collectors Edition"; uses Boris Coca-Cola artwork
n/a	1994	10 × 19	Dark Horse	••••	Dark Empire II art by Dorman; folded
n/a	1994	23.5 × 30	Gifted Images	•••••••	Ken Steacy litho from Topps Galaxy poster; heavy rag paper and signed
n/a	1994	23.5 × 30	Gifted Images	••••••••	Gifted Images Ken Steacy litho from Topps Galaxy post.; heavy rag paper; printers proof edition size of 50
n/a	1994	25 × 37.5	New Frontier	•••••••	"Death Star Rising" by Michael David Ward; signed by Ward and Prowse; edition size of 500
n/a	1994	25 × 37.5	New Frontier	•••••••	"Death Star Rising" by Michael David Ward; artists proof
n/a	1994	18 × 25	Rolling Thunder	••••••	"Dark Empire" by Dorman; edition size of 1500
n/a	1994	18 × 25	Rolling Thunder	••••••	"Dark Empire II" by Dorman; edition size of 1500
n/a	1994	18 × 25	Rolling Thunder	••••••	Smuggler's Moon by Dorman; edition size of 1500
n/a	1994	19.5 × 23	Star Tours	••	Disneyland 40 Years of Adventure with Star Tours photo; Thrifty/Payless giveaway
ROTJ	1994	27 × 41	Kilian Enterprises	••••••	10th anniversary Kazu Sano Jedi concept art with gold credits; numbered
ROTJ	1994	27 × 41	Kilian Enterprises	•••••••	10th anniversary Kazu Sano Jedi concept art with gold credits; signed by Sano in white
ROTJ	1994	21 × 32	Western Graphics	•••	*Revenge* art; Return Collectors Edition
SW	1994	21 × 32	Western Graphics	•••	*Star Wars* "Collectors Edition"; Style "C" artwork poster
ESB	1995	27 × 41	Kilian Enterprises	•••••••	*Empire* 15th anniversary; Boba Fett on silver Mylar
ESB	1995	27 × 41	Kilian Enterprises	••••••••••	*Empire* 15th anniversary; Boba Fett—gold Mylar test proof; edition size of five
ESB	1995	24 × 36	Portal Publications	••••	Stormtrooper and AT-ATs; cover for 1995 video release with pearlescent logo
ESB	1995	23 × 35	Western Graphics	•••	*Empire* video cover art of Stormtrooper/AT-ATs
n/a	1995	20 × 34.5	New Frontier	•••••	"In a Faraway Galaxy" by Michael David Ward
n/a	1995	17 × 23	Pitarelli	••••••	Jeff Pitarelli print of art for '95 Atlanta SF con; signed edition of 500
n/a	1995	18 × 25	Rolling Thunder	••••••	Boba Fett: Bounty Hunter by Dorman; edition size of 1500
n/a	1995	16 × 22	Rolling Thunder	••••••	Heroes of the Alliance by Dorman
ROTJ	1995	24 × 36	Portal Publications	••••	Yoda and duel; cover for 1995 video release with pearlescent logo
ROTJ	1995	23 × 35	Western Graphics	•••	Return video cover art of Yoda/duel
ROTJ	1995	23 × 35	Western Graphics	•••	3-D Wars #1135; B-wings above Magic Eye art
SW	1995	24 × 36	Portal Publications	••••	X-wing/TIE and Vader; cover for 1995 video release with blue pearlescent *Star Wars* title above
SW	1995	23 × 35	Western Graphics	•••	*Star Wars* video cover art of Vader and X-wing/TIE
TRIL	1995	10.5 × 18	Blockbuster	•••	Three video covers against silver background
n/a	1996	19 × 21	Galoob	••••••••	McQuarrie Toy Fair exclusive print: Death Star
n/a	1996	19 × 21	Galoob	••••••••	McQuarrie Toy Fair exclusive print: Hoth Battle
n/a	1996	19 × 21	Galoob	••••••••	McQuarrie Toy Fair exclusive print: X-wing on fourth moon of Yavin
n/a	1996	19 × 21	Galoob	••••••••	McQuarrie Toy Fair exclusive print: Tatooine scenes
n/a	1996	24 × 36	Official SW Fan Club	••••••	*Slave I* by Sanda
n/a	1996	24 × 36	Official SW Fan Club	••••••	Vader by Sanda
n/a	1996	24 × 36	Portal	•••	"All I need to know I learned from *Star Wars*"
n/a	1996	16.5 × 24	Rolling Thunder	••••••	"Legacy of the Jedi" by Dorman
n/a	1996	16.5 × 24	Rolling Thunder	••••••••	"Legacy of the Jedi" by Dorman; artist proof
n/a	1996	16 × 22	Rolling Thunder	••••••	"Obi-Wan Kenobi—Jedi Knight" by Dorman
n/a	1996	16 × 22	Rolling Thunder	••••••	"Tales of the Jedi—Freedon Nadd Uprising" by Dorman
n/a	1996	16 × 22	Rolling Thunder	••••••	"Darth Vader—Dark Lord of the Sith" by Dorman
ROTJ	1996	25 × 36.5	Official SW Fan Club	••••••	*Falcon* over Death Star II artwork by Sanda
ROTJ	1996	24 × 36	Portal	•••	"There will be no bargain! Keep Out!" Rancor
SW	1996	24 × 36	Portal	•••	Art of Ralph McQuarrie; Luke/Vader duel from *Star Wars*
SW	1996	24 × 36	Portal	•••	Three X-wings
SW	1996	24 × 36	Portal	•••	Star Destroyer chasing Blockade Runner, prologue on right
SW	1996	23 × 35	Western Graphics	•••	Reprint of Selby cantina art; "You'll never find a more wretched hive..."
SW	1996	23 × 35	Western Graphics	•••	Reprint of McQuarrie Death Star trench fan club art
ESB	1997	24 × 36	Portal Publications	•••	Star Destroyer from *Empire*
ESB	1997	24 × 36	Portal Publications	•••	McQuarrie art of Cloud City
ESB	1997	20 × 36	Rolling Thunder	••••••	"Battle of Hoth" by Dave Dorman
ESBSE	1997	24 × 36	Pepsi	•••	Mail-in poster; *Empire* C-3PO
ESBSE	1997	20 × 35	Pizza Hut	••	Yoda with credits
ESBSE	1997	24 × 36	Portal Publications	•••	ESBSE Drew artwork
n/a	1997	23 × 35	Dismukes	••••	Dismukes—three panels of different ships
n/a	1997	23 × 35	Dismukes	••••	Dismukes—three panels of different ships; signed
n/a	1997	24 × 36	Official SW Fan Club	•••••••	Cantina group; Sanda art; large black area above
n/a	1997	17 × 36	Official SW Fan Club	••••••	Cantina group; Sanda art
n/a	1997	24 × 36	Official SW Fan Club	••••••	20th anniversary montage artwork by Sanda
n/a	1997	24 × 36	Official SW Fan Club	••••••	Yoda art by Sanda
n/a	1997	24 × 36	Official SW Fan Club	••••••	Drew cover art for Lucas biography
n/a	1997	24 × 36	Official SW Fan Club	••••••	Boba Fett with *Slave I* below; Sanda art
n/a	1997	24 × 36	Portal Publications	•••	"The Wisdom of Yoda"
n/a	1997	24 × 36	R. Silvers	•••••	Jedi Master Yoda photomosaic by Robert Silvers
n/a	1997	24 × 36	R. Silvers	•••••	Darth Vader photomosaic by Robert Silvers
n/a	1997	16 × 22	Rolling Thunder	••••••••	"Han Solo and Chewbacca" by Dorman; artist proof
n/a	1997	24 × 36	SciPubTech	•••••	X-wing and TIE Fighter technical poster
n/a	1997	24 × 36	SciPubTech	••••••	X-wing and TIE Fighter technical poster; signed edition size of 2500
n/a	1997	25 × 36	SciPubTech	•••••	*Falcon* cutaway
n/a	1997	25 × 36	SciPubTech	••••••	*Falcon* cutaway; signed edition size of 2500
n/a	1997	18 × 24	Spiderweb Gallery	•••••••	*Shadows of the Empire—Millennium Falcon* by Hildebrandts; signed by both with sketch of Chewbacca
n/a	1997	18 × 24	Spiderweb Gallery	••••••••	*Shadows of the Empire*—Droids in Endor forest by Hildebrandts; signed by both with sketch of stormtrooper
ROTJ	1997	24 × 36	Portal Publications	•••	McQuarrie art of droids in Jabba's palace
ROTJ	1997	24 × 36	Portal Publications	•••	McQuarrie art of B-wings in battle
ROTJ	1997	17 × 23	Rolling Thunder	••••••	"Princess Leia as Boushh" by Dorman; edition size of 1500
ROTJ	1997	17 × 23	Rolling Thunder	••••••••	"Princess Leia as Boushh" by Dorman; artist proof
ROTJ	1997	11 × 14	Rolling Thunder	••••••	"Knocking on Jabba's Door" by Dave Dorman
ROTJ	1997	23 × 35	Western Graphics	•••••	Max Rebo Band artwork; "Live at the Winterland"
ROTJSE	1997	24 × 36	Pepsi	•••	Mail-in poster; *Return of the Jedi* Yoda
ROTJSE	1997	20 × 35	Pizza Hut	••	Wicket with credits
ROTJSE	1997	24 × 36	Portal Publications	•••	ROTJSE Drew artwork
SOTE	1997	18 × 24	Spiderweb Gallery	••••••••	*Shadows of the Empire* Boba Fett artwork by Hildebrandts; edition size of 1500
SOTE	1997	18 × 24	Spiderweb Gallery	••••••••	*Shadows of the Empire* Vader artwork by Hildebrandts; edition size of 250
SW	1997	20 × 36	Rolling Thunder	••••••	"Dewback Patrol" by Dave Dorman; edition size of 1500
SW	1997	23 × 35	Western Graphics	••••••	Darth Vader black-light poster
SWSE	1997	11 × 14	Lays	••	Luke with saber artwork; Wal-Mart exclusive
SWSE	1997	24 × 36	Pepsi	•••	Mail-in poster; *Star Wars* Vader
SWSE	1997	20 × 35	Pizza Hut	••	Droids on Blockade Runner with credits

COMMERCIAL POSTERS

Film	Year	Size	Publisher	Rating	Description
UNITED STATES, CONT.					
SWSE	1997	24 × 36	Portal Publications	•••	SWSE Drew Struzan artwork
TRILSE	1997	11 × 17	Blockbuster	•••	Card stock premium of three Special Edition video covers
TRILSE	1997	24 × 36	Portal Publications	•••	Ingot art
ESB	1998	24 × 36	SciPubTech	••••••	AT-AT, AT-ST, and snowspeeder cutaway; signed by both artists; edition size of 2500
ESB	1998	24 × 36	SciPubTech	•••••	AT-AT, AT-ST, and snowspeeder cutaway; glossier than signed version
n/a	1998	22 × 28	Kenner	••••••	Power of the Force figures Ackbar to Zuckuss 1995–98; Wal-Mart exclusive
n/a	1998	10 × 13	Kenner	••	Kenner/Toy Fair "Heir to the Empire" figures
n/a	1998	16 × 22	Rolling Thunder	••••••	"Wedge" by Dave Dorman
n/a	1998	20 × 30	Rolling Thunder	••••••	"Boba Fett: Fall of a Bounty Hunter" by Dave Dorman
n/a	1998	20 × 36	Rolling Thunder	••••••	"In the Court of Jabba the Hutt" by Dave Dorman
n/a	1998	23 × 35	Western Graphics	•••	Han Solo: "I take orders from just one person. Me!"
ROTJ	1998	24 × 36	Official SW Fan Club	••••••	Palpatine and Vader by Hugh Fleming
TPM	1998	24 × 36	Official SW Fan Club	••••••	Luke and Biggs by Hugh Fleming
ESB	1999	24 × 36	At-A-Glance	•••	Luke and Yoda; scenes on right side
n/a	1999	24 × 36	Official SW Fan Club	••••••	Princess Leia montage
n/a	1999	24 × 36	Official SW Fan Club	••••••	"Star Wars Rocks" by Hugh Fleming; with signature card
ROTJ	1999	24 × 36	At-A-Glance	•••	Luke and Leia on barge; scenes on right side
SW	1999	24 × 36	At-A-Glance	•••	Luke on X-wing cockpit ladder; scenes on right side
TPM	1999	24 × 36	At-A-Glance	•••	Advance art (vertical)
TPM	1999	24 × 36	At-A-Glance	••••	Horizontal advance banner art
TPM	1999	24 × 36	At-A-Glance	•••	Drew Struzan art
TPM	1999	23 × 71	At-A-Glance	••••••	Darth Maul door poster
TPM	1999	22 × 33	At-A-Glance	••••••	Darth Maul black-light poster
TPM	1999	24 × 36	At-A-Glance	•••••	Boonta Eve Podrace with art and photos
TPM	1999	24 × 36	At-A-Glance	•••	Darth Maul—two poses and head shot
TPM	1999	24 × 36	At-A-Glance	•••	Obi-Wan with name along side and silhouettes of battle poses
TPM	1999	24 × 36	At-A-Glance	•••	Queen Amidala photo montage
TPM	1999	24 × 36	At-A-Glance	•••	Jedi vs. Sith horizontal art
TPM	1999	24 × 36	At-A-Glance	•••	Naboo fighters and Trade Federation ship
TPM	1999	24 × 36	At-A-Glance	•••	Jedi vs. Sith vertical art
TPM	1999	24 × 36	Official SW Fan Club	••••••	"Revenge of the Sith"; Obi-Wan, Qui-Gon and Maul dueling by Hugh Fleming
TPM	1999	11 × 17	Pepsi/Lays	••	Horizontal Anakin/Podrace
TPM	1999	11 × 17	Pepsi/Lays	••	Horizontal Amidala/Naboo
TPM	1999	11 × 17	Pepsi/Lays	••	Horizontal Maul/Duel
TPM	1999	11 × 17	Pepsi/Lays	••	Horizontal Jar Jar/Gungans
TPM	1999	7 × 14	Pepsi/Lays	•••	"Can You Resist?" premium poster—Obi-Wan
TPM	1999	7 × 14	Pepsi/Lays	•••	"Can You Resist?" premium poster—Darth Maul
TPM	1999	7 × 14	Pepsi/Lays	•••	"Can You Resist?" premium poster—Qui-Gon
TPM	1999	7 × 14	Pepsi/Lays	•••	"Can You Resist?" premium poster—Jar Jar
TPM	1999	7 × 14	Pepsi/Lays	•••	"Can You Resist?" premium poster—Darth Sidious
TPM	1999	7 × 14	Pepsi/Lays	•••	"Can You Resist?" premium poster—Nute and Rune
TPM	1999	7 × 14	Pepsi/Lays	•••	"Can You Resist?" premium poster—Sebulba
TPM	1999	7 × 14	Pepsi/Lays	•••	"Can You Resist?" premium poster—Anakin
TPM	1999	7 × 14	Pepsi/Lays	•••	"Can You Resist?" premium poster—R2-D2
TPM	1999	7 × 14	Pepsi/Lays	•••	"Can You Resist?" premium poster—Padmé
TPM	1999	7 × 14	Pepsi/Lays	•••	"Can You Resist?" premium poster—Watto
TPM	1999	7 × 14	Pepsi/Lays	•••	"Can You Resist?" premium poster—Queen Amidala
TPM	1999	24 × 36	Portal Publications	•••	Drew Struzan art of release poster
TPM	1999	24 × 36	Portal Publications	•••	Sith Lord
TPM	1999	24 × 36	Portal Publications	•••	Dogfight; horizontal
TPM	1999	24 × 36	Portal Publications	•••	"At Last We Will Have Revenge"; blue pearlescent with Maul
TPM	1999	24 × 36	Portal Publications	•••	Queen Amidala with gold ink
TPM	1999	24 × 36	Portal Publications	•••	Podrace
TPM	1999	24 × 36	Portal Publications	•••	Jar Jar
TPM	1999	24 × 36	Portal Publications	••••••	Heroes montage printed on silver Mylar
TPM	1999	24 × 36	Portal Publications	••••••	Villains montage printed on silver Mylar
TPM	1999	12 × 36	Portal Publications	•••••	Podrace
TPM	1999	12 × 36	Portal Publications	•••••	Battle droids
TPM	1999	22 × 24	Rolling Stone	••	Rolling Stone pullout poster of Jar Jar reading '77 RS; other trilogy issues on back
TPM	1999	17 × 22	Taco Bell	•	Anakin from set of four premium posters that combine to make horizontal mural (22 × 68)
TPM	1999	17 × 22	Taco Bell	•	Qui-Gon from set of four premium posters
TPM	1999	17 × 22	Taco Bell	•	Watto from set of four premium posters
TPM	1999	17 × 22	Taco Bell	•	Maul from set of four premium posters
ESB	1999	24 × 36	Official SW Fan Club	••••••	"Arrival of the Bounty Hunters" by James Cukr; edition of 3500
TRIL	2001	24 × 36	Official SW Fan Club	••••••	SW Insider magazine classic figure poster 1978–85
SW	2001	27 × 40	Trends International	••••	Star Wars Style "A" reprint
AOTC	2002	11 × 17	Celebration II	••	Skywalker family tree; Celebration II exclusive
AOTC	2002	22 × 28	Celebration II	•••••••	"George Lucas Selects" montage of photos; Celebration II exclusive
AOTC	2002	24 × 36	Trends International	•••	Drew Struzan art from release poster
AOTC	2002	22 × 34	Trends International	•••	Jedi starfighter and Slave I
AOTC	2002	22 × 34	Trends International	•••	Padmé Amidala
AOTC	2002	22 × 34	Trends International	•••	Duel of the Sith
AOTC	2002	22 × 34	Trends International	•••	Battle of Geonosis
AOTC	2002	22 × 34	Trends International	•••	Jango
ESB	2002	27 × 30	Billy Dee Williams	•••••••	The Empire Strikes Back art print by Billy Dee Williams; signed edition size of 1000
n/a	2002	18 × 23	Hasbro	••••	Figures for 2002; no borders around figs
n/a	2002	18 × 23	Hasbro	••••	"Jedi and Heroes" figures
n/a	2002	12 × 18	Topps	••	25 years of Topps Star Wars
n/a	2002	22 × 34	Trends International	••••••	25 years of Star Wars; Celebration II exclusive
AOTC	2003	20 × 30	Hasbro	•••	Clone Wars figures in scene; insert from Insider #71
AOTC	2003	24 × 30	Official SW Fan Club	•••••••	Print by Jerry Vander Stelt; edition size of 500
AOTC	2003	21 × 29	Official SW Fan Club	••••	Fold out poster of Hasbro figures in Geonosis battle scene
n/a	2004	11.5 × 16.5	Muscular Dystrophy	•••	Art collage by Paul Jordan; edition size of 1000
TRILSE	2004	19 × 28	20th C Fox Home Ent.	•••	Photocollage for classic trilogy release on DVD; premium with pre-order
TRILSE	2004	27 × 40	StarWarsShop.com	••••••	Embossed artwork of DVD sleeve graphics; StarWarsShop.com exclusive

INDEX

Alders, Troy, 207, 265
Alvin, John, 46, 167, 169, 180, 190, 230
American Library Association, 151
American Marketing Convention, 46
Anderson, Weldon, 24
Art of *Star Wars* show, 179, 182, *183–85*, *232–34*
Asamiya, Kia, 242
At-a-Glance, 250
Atari, 152, *153*, 156, *157*
Attack of the Clones (Episode II)
    advance posters, *229–30*, *254*
    advertising and promotional posters, *262–64*, 265, *277–79*
    Australian posters, *277*
    British posters, *261*
    Chinese posters, *259*
    commercial posters, *270, 271, 280*
    French posters, *278, 279*
    German posters, *259*
    Hungarian posters, *258–59*
    in IMAX theaters, 236, *256*, 257
    Italian posters, 234, *257*
    Japanese posters, 234, *260, 261, 262, 263, 279*
    Korean posters, 234
    opening of, 234
    Singaporean posters, *264*, 265
    theatrical posters, 236, *254–61*
    U.S. posters, *254–56*, 257, *262, 265–68, 269, 270, 271*
    on video, 262

B. Dalton, 106
Bantam Books, 179, *210*
Bart Wars, *252, 253*
Battle for Endor, 137–38, *149*
Berkey, John, 14, 16, *59*, 67
Bootlegs, 289
Bounty Hunter, *278, 279*
Boy's Photo News, 110, *111*
Bradley, Tom, 24
Brent, William, 216
Broderbund, *176*, 179
Burger Chef, 51–52, *63*
Burger King, 63, *112*

Canadian Association of Transplantation, 211
Caravan of Courage, 137, *148–49*
Cardy, Nick, 22
Carter, Bunny, 131
Cartoon Network, 277
Casaro, Renato, 138, *149*
Chantrell, Tom, 20, 22, 25, 27
Chantsev, Aleksandr, 43
Chapter III Productions, 123
Chaykin, Howard, 6, 11
Chiang, Doug, 228
Christensen, Hayden, 254
Christmas in the Stars album, 108, *109*
Cincinnati Pops, 118, *119*
Clone Wars, *276*, 277
Coca-Cola, 53, *60, 61*, 63, 112, 154, *155*, 156, *157*
Corporation of Public Broadcasting, 137
Crea magazine, 262, *263*

Daniels, Anthony, 108
Dark Horse, *192*
Decipher, *210*
Deko displays, *26–28*, 29, *86–87*, *134–35*
Dentsu, 175
Disney, 171, *172*, 175, *272*
Dixie Cups, *108*
Don Post Studios, *54, 55*
Doyle Dane Bernbach, 11, 12, 22

Drawing Board, 156, *157*
Droids television show, 161
Duel at Death Star Racing Set, *60*
Dybowski, Witold, 133, 138, 140

Echo Base Charity Con, 273
The Empire Strikes Back (Episode V)
    advance posters, *72, 73, 75, 88–92*
    advertising and promotional posters, *106, 108, 110–11, 112, 113, 115–16*, 117, *201, 203*
    Argentinean posters, *94–95*
    Australian posters, *92–93*
    British posters, *80–83, 85*
    charity premieres of, 76
    Chinese posters, *96–97*
    commercial posters, 112, *177–78*, 179, *191*
    difficulties with, 73
    fifteenth anniversary of, *191*
    French posters, *88–90*
    German posters, 84, *85, 86–87*, 89, *190*
    Indian posters, 98, *99*
    Italian posters, *98*
    Japanese posters, 89, *90, 91, 93*, 110, *111*
    logo for, 73
    New Zealand posters, *110*
    novelization of, 85
    Polish posters, 39, 89, *102, 103*
    radio series, 115
    rereleases of, *78–79*, 80, 89, *93*
    Romanian posters, 100, *101*
    soundtrack from, 85
    Spanish posters, 89, *101*
    Special Edition, 180, *201, 203*
    subway posters, 75
    tenth anniversary of, *168–69, 177–78*, 179
    theatrical posters, *72, 73, 74–103*
    Turkish posters, *102*
    U.S. posters, *72, 73, 74–79*, 80, *106, 108, 112–13, 115–16*, *177–78*, 179, *191, 201, 203*
    on video, 180, *190*
    video game, 116, *117*
Erol, Jakub, 33, 39, 102
Erwert, Scott, 257
Estes, *58*, 59
The Ewok Adventure, 137
Ewoks and the Marauders of Endor, 138, *149*

Factors Etc., 20, 65, 68
Ferracci, René, 33
Ferrero, 270
Filmoteka 16, 179
Fisher, Carrie, 16
Fleming, Hugh, 244
Force Commander, 246
Ford, Harrison, 89
Fox Home Video, *188–90*, 204, *238–40*, 246, *247, 252, 253*, 262
Frazetta, Frank, 14, 20
Friedkin, Johnny, 11
Frito Lay, 210, *211*
Fuji Film, *50*

Ganis, Sid, 76, 80, 85, 88, 123, 128, 130, 131, 169
General Electric, *118*
George Lucas Exhibition, 179, 182
The George Lucas Super Live Adventure, 175, *180*
Gore Graphics, 124, 171

Hamill, Mark, 11, 16
Heir to the Empire, 179
Hildebrandt, Tim and Greg, 14, 16, 20, 22, 24, 33, 37, 41, 65
Hollywood Bowl, 46
Hungry Jacks, 277

Immunization posters, 62, *150*
Industrial Light & Magic (ILM), 59, 130, 252, 281

Jedi-Con, 234, *235*
Jedi Starfighter, *269*
Johnson, Bob, 49
Johnston, Joe, 12
Jones, Jeff, 14
Jouin, Michel, 133
Jung, Tom, 7, 14, 16, 20, 22, 25, 27, 29, 33, 37, 40, 55, 65, 75, 76, 80, 81, 85, 88–89, 95, 101, 102, 127, 128, 131, 133, *152*, *179*, *194*

Kalter, Ronald, 21
Kastel, Roger, 75, 76, 80, 85, 89, 101
Kazanjian, Howard, 123, 130
Kenner Products, 24, 52, 60, 118, *154*, *155*
Kidney Foundation, 211
Kilian, Jeff, 167–69
Kilian Enterprises, 167, 177, 191, 289
King Records, 55
Kirby, Josh, 130, 137
Kriegler, Richard, 172
Kulov, Aleksandr, 45
Kunzel, Erich, 118, 283
Kurtz, Gary, 11, 12, 14, 16, 22, 73, 85
Kwan, Johnny, 250

Ladd, Alan, Jr., 11
Lee, Ellen, 220, 222, 226, 228
Lee, Stan, 11
LEGO, 246, *247*
Lionel, 60
Lippincott, Charles, 11, 14, 20
Lucas, George, 7, 11–12, 14, 16, 25, 34, 45, 68, 76, 123, 130, 167, 175, 179, *180*, 182, 184, 226, 267, 275
Lucasfilm magazine, *284*, 285

Majstrovsky, Igor, 43
Marvel Comics, 11
Max Rebo Band, 216, *217*
McCaig, Ian, 234
McMacken, David, 236, *257*
McQuarrie, Ralph, 11, 14, 49, 68, 108, 115, 171, 172, 176, *179*, 185
Mehta, Zubin, 46
Mr. Pibb, 53
Mitsubishi Motors, *194*
Morinaga, 60
Moss, Bill, 124
My Jedi Journal, *181*

National Public Radio, 114–15
National Screen Service, 76
New Wave Entertainment, 285
New York Subway posters, *75*
Nichols, Del, 63
Nintendo, 209, 210
Noble, Lawrence, 168–69, *179*

Official Mexican Fan Club, 283
Official *Star Wars* Fan Club, 68, 128, 137, 168–69, 214–16, 226, 244–45, 277, *280*
Ohrai, Noriyoshi, 34, 89, 93, 98, 133, 162, 197
Oldsmobile, 172

Panasonic, *174–75*
Papuzza, 30, 33
Paris, Pat, 161
Paykos, Melanie, 128, 130
Peak, Bob, Jr., 73
Pepperidge Farm, *154*, *155*
Peters Ice Pops, *159*
Pevers, Marc, 46
The Phantom Menace (Episode I)
    advance posters, 220–21, 222, 226
    advertising and promotional posters, 230, 236, 242, 243, 246–47, 250–51
    Australian posters, 250, *251*
    Brazilian posters, 222, *225*
    British posters, 230, 250, *251*
    Canadian posters, 250, *251*
    Chinese posters, 222, *224*
    Danish posters, 222, *225*
    Finnish posters, 222, *224*
    French posters, 222, *224*, 230
    German posters, 222, *225*, 236
    Greek posters, 222, *225*
    Hebrew posters, 222, *225*
    Italian posters, 222, *225*
    Japanese posters, 222, *224*, 229, 242, 243, 246, *247*
    Korean posters, 222, *224*, 226–28
    Norwegian posters, 222, *225*
    opening of, 229
    pinball game, *250*
    Spanish posters, 222, *225*
    Swedish posters, 222, *225*
    Thai posters, 222, *224*
    theatrical posters, 220–21, 222–29
    on TV, 236, 250, *251*
    U.S. posters, 220–21, 222–23, 230, *231*, 246–47, 250–51
    on video, 246, *247*
    video game, 246, *247*
Phior, Rio, 128, 130
Phipps, Ken, 246
PlayStation, *242*, 246, *247*
Portal Publications, 194
Portman, Natalie, 254
Power of Myth tour, 230
Prowse, David, 179

Radio series posters, 114–15
RCA, *117*
Reagan, Ronald, 147
Reamer, Tim, 124, 128, 130
Rebel Assault, *179*
Rebel Assault II, *187*
Reneric, David, 73
Reprints, 289
Return of the Jedi (Episode VI)
    advance posters, 122, 123, 124, 128–29, 136, 137
    advertising and promotional posters, 150, 153–61, 202, 203
    Australian posters, 150, *159*
    British posters, 128–31, 137
    Canadian posters, 156, *157*
    Chinese posters, 132, *133*
    commercial posters, 162–63, 186, 187
    Croatian posters, *179*
    French posters, 133
    German posters, 133–35, *154*, *155*, *190*
    Hungarian posters, 140, *141*
    Japanese posters, 133, 136–38, 162, 163
    New Zealand posters, 158, *159*
    Polish posters, 133, 138, 139–40
    rerelease of, *127*, 131, 169
    Special Edition, 180, 202, 203
    tenth anniversary of, 169, *186*, 187
    theatrical posters, 124, *125–41*
    title changes of, 123, 124, 128, 137
    U.S. posters, 122, 123, 124–27, 150, 153–57, 162, 186, 187, 202, 203
    on video, 180, *190*
    video game, 156, *157*
Revenge of the Jedi
    advance posters, 122, 123, 124, 128, 136, 137
    bootleg posters, 289
    trailer for, 22
Revenge of the Sith (Episode III)
    advance posters, 236, 240, 285
    commercial posters, 284, 285
    French posters, 284, 285
    theatrical posters, 236, 285–88

U.S. posters, *285–88*
Rice, Suzy, 11–12, 46
Rinaldi, Hugo, 49
Rivkin, Sandy, 124, 128
Rolling Stone magazine, 252
Roman, Greg, 180, *189*
RSO, 108

Sales Corp. of America, 156, 162
Sanda, Tsuneo, 215, *216*, 234
Sano, Kazuhiko (Kazu), 127, 130–31, 137, *138*, 149, 169
Sansweet, Steve, 194
Scandecor, 67
Sega, 240, *241*
Seidemann, Bob, 24, 65
Seiniger, Tony, 11, 24, 73
Seito, 34
Selby, Bill, 68
Sezon Museum of Art, 179, 182
Shadows of Empire, 209, *210*
Shioya, Hiroaki (Hiro), 175, 180
Showtime, 236
Siggraph convention, 281
The Simpsons, 252, *253*
SingTel Mobile, 265
Smithsonian Institution, 179, 182, 205, 207
Smolen, Smith, and Connolly, 16, 20
Sony, 242, 246
Sounds of Space concert, *48–49*
Soundtracks, *55–57,* 66, 67, 85
Space World, *208,* 210
Spielberg, Steven, 130
Star Tours, *171–73,* 175
Star Wars (Episode IV)
    action figures, 21, 24
    advance posters, *10,* 11, *12–14,* 32, 33, *42, 43*
    advertising and promotional posters, *50–62,* 114, *117, 118,* *152–54, 155,* 176, *187, 192–93,* 200, *203,* 211, *236, 237*
    Australian posters, *118*
    books, 59, *193,* 210
    bootleg posters, 289
    British posters, 22, *23–25,* 59, *192, 193, 232–33*
    Canadian posters, *198,* 211
    Chinese posters, *36, 37*
    commercial posters, *63–69,* 166, 167, *168–70, 196–98,* 215
    dubbed version of, 34
    Finnish posters, 234
    first anniversary of, 21, 24
    French posters, *29,* 33
    German posters, *26–28,* 29, *190, 196–97*
    Hebrew posters, *37*
    Italian posters, 29, *30–31,* 33
    Japanese posters, *30–35,* 50, 55, *56, 60–61, 192, 208,* 210
    logo for, 11–12
    opening of, 7, 14
    Polish posters, 33, *38, 39*
    Poster 1, 6, 7, *10,* 11
    radio series, 114
    release date of, 14
    rereleases of, 22, 123
    Romanian posters, *39*
    Russian posters, 33, *42–45*
    soundtrack from, *55–57,* 66, 67
    Spanish posters, 29, *40, 41*
    Special Edition, 180, 200, 203, *236, 237*
    Swedish posters, *40,* 67
    tenth anniversary of, 166, 167, *168–70,* 171
    Thai posters, *39*
    theatrical posters, 14, *15–19,* 20, *21–45,* 65
    trailers for, 11
    Turkish posters, *41*
    on TV, *118,* 236, *237*
    twentieth anniversary of, 215
    U.S. posters, *10,* 11, *12–19,* 20, *21–22,* 46–49, *51, 53–55, 57–58, 59,* 60, *62–66,* 67, *68–69, 152–54, 155,* 166, 167, *168–70,* 171, *176, 187,* 200, 203, *205–7,* 215, *236, 237*
    on video, 180, *190*
    video games, 152, *153,* 176, 179, *187,* 242
Star Wars: Science and Art exhibit, *274–75*
Star Wars: The Magic of Myth exhibit, 179, 182, *205–7*
Star Wars Celebration, 230, *231*
Star Wars Celebration II, *265–68, 269*
Star Wars Concert, 46, *47*
Star Wars/Empire double-bill posters, *104–5,* 106, *107*
Star Wars/Empire/Jedi trilogy
    advertising and promotional posters, *188–90,* 198, *199, 203–4,* 210, *211,* 283
    arcade game, 240, *241*
    Australian posters, 137, 144, *145, 189*
    bootleg posters, 144, 289
    British posters, 137, *142–43*
    on DVD, 283
    French posters, *147*
    German posters, 137, *146, 147, 190,* 240
    Italian posters, 137
    Japanese posters, 239, 240, *241*
    Special Edition, 180, 198, *199, 203–4, 211,* 228
    Swedish posters, *160,* 161
    theatrical posters, 137, *142–47*
    U.S. posters, 137, 144, *188, 189,* 198, *199, 203–4,* 210, *211, 238, 239,* 283
    on video, 180, *184–85, 188–90, 203–4, 238–40*
Star Wars en Concierto, *282,* 283
Star Wars Fact Files, 250, *251*
Star Wars Insider, 244, 252
Star Wars Roleplaying Game, *248–49*
Star Wars Trading Card Game, 279
Star Wars Weekends, 272
Stedry, Dayna, 177
Strain, Celia, 114, *115*
Stride-Rite, 152
Struzan, Drew, 20, 25, 29, 123, 128, 137, 149, *167–68,* 171, 180, *184–85,* 189, 198, 203, 222, 228, 229, 230, 249, 254, 257, 288

Taidemuseo Tennispalatsi, 234
Tamaki, Hisao, 192
Terpning, Howard, 76
Thermos Lunch Kit, *155*
Thomas, Roy, 11
Tip-Top, 110, *158, 159*
Trends International, 269, *270*
20th Century Fox, 11, 12, 14, 16, 20, 22, 85, 124, 171

Unisource Papers, 250, *251*
U.S. Department of Health, 62

Vallejo, Boris, 112
Vander Stelt, Jerry, 280
Van Hamersveld, John, 52
Venables, Bell & Partners, 229, 254

Walks, Russell, 269
Ward, Jim, 220, *221–22,* 226, 229
Warren, Adam, 192
Watts, Bob, 46
Weekly Reader, 161
Weitzner, David, 12, *13,* 14, 16, 20, *24–25,* 65
Werner, Christopher, 130, *131*
Western Graphics, 216
Whelan, Michael, 181
White, Charles, III, 20, 25, 29
Williams, Billy Dee, 80, 85
Williams, John, 49
Williams Episode I pinball game, 250
Winters, Greg, 179
Wizards of the Coast, 249, 279
Wonder Bread, 52

Yamakatsu, 162

Zahn, Timothy, 179
Zig Zag, 197

Acknowledgments

The authors would like to thank the following people who helped to make this book possible by sharing ideas, giving interviews, and providing photos: John Alvin, Matthew Azeveda, John Berkey, Scott Carter, Howard Chaykin, Jon Connolly, Johnny Friedkin, Sidney Ganis, Jacob T. Gardner, Amy Gary, Greg Hildebrandt, Jan Hughes, Duncan Jenkins, Michelle Jouan, Tom Jung, Ronald Kalter, Roger Kastel, Howard Kazanjian, Linda Kelly, Jeff Kilian, Tera Killip, Gary Kurtz, Neal Lemlein, Charles Lippincott, Sarah Malarkey, Ralph McQuarrie, Phil Meyers, Tina Mills, Iain Morris, Bill Moss, Del Nichols, Lawrence Noble, Doug Ogan, Melanie Paykos, Marc Pevers, Rio Phior, Bill Plumb, Ed Poole, Ben Price, Tim Reamer, David Reneric, Suzy Rice, Dan Rickard, Jonathan Rinzler, Sandy Rivkin, Matt Robinson, Kazuhiko Sano, John Scoleri, Benjamin Shaykin, Drew Struzan, Eimei Takeda, Hideyuki Takizawa, Carol Titelman, Jim Ward, David Weitzner, Charles White III, and Paul Wilson. Not to mention the countless wonderful people we've met buying and trading *Star Wars* posters.

Credits

The vast majority of the posters reproduced in this book are from the collection of Stephen J. Sansweet. Photography by Joe McDonald and from the Lucasfilm archives.

Posters on pages 23 (lower left) and 46 are from the collection of Hideyuki Takizawa. Posters on pages 13, 54, 56, 60 (left), 76, 115 (bottom), 141, 205, 237, 248–9, and 251 (upper right) are from the collection of Peter Vilmur. Centerpiece poster on page 87 is from the collection of Paul Wilson.